El Alamein 1942

By the same author

Wall of Steel: The History of 9th (Londonderry) HAA Regiment, RA (SR) (North-West Books, Limavady, 1988)

The Sons of Ulster: Ulstermen at war from the Somme to Korea (The Appletree Press, Belfast, 1992)

Clear The Way! A History of the 38th (Irish) Brigade, 1941–47 (Irish Academic Press, Dublin, 1993)

Irish Generals: Irish Generals in the British Army in the Second World War (The Appletree Press, Belfast, 1993)

Only the Enemy in Front: The Recce Corps at War, 1940–46 (Tom Donovan Publishing, London, 1994)

Key to Victory: The Maiden City in the Second World War (Greystone Books, Antrim, 1995)

The Williamite War in Ireland, 1688–1691 (Four Courts Press, Dublin, 1998)

A Noble Crusade: The History of Eighth Army, 1941 to 1945 (Spellmount Publishers, Staplehurst, 1999)

Irish Men and Women in the Second World War (Four Courts Press, Dublin, 1999)

Irish Winners of the Victoria Cross (with David Truesdale) (Four Courts Press, Dublin, 2000)

Irish Volunteers in the Second World War (Four Courts Press, Dublin, 2001)

The North Irish Horse (Spellmount Publishers, Staplehurst, 2002)

The Sound of History: El Alamein 1942 (Spellmount, Staplehurst, 2002)

Normandy 1944: The Road to Victory (Spellmount, Staplehurst, 2004)

Ireland's Generals in the Second World War (Four Courts Press, Dublin, 2004)

The Thin Green Line: A History of the Royal Ulster Constabulary GC, 1922–2001 (Pen & Sword, Barnsley, 2004)

None Bolder: A History of 51st (Highland) Division, 1939–1945 (Spellmount, Staplehurst, 2006)

The British Reconnaissance Corps in World War II (Osprey, Oxford, 2007)

Eighth Army in Italy: The Long Hard Slog (Pen & Sword, Barnsley, 2007)

The Siege of Derry 1689: The Military History (Spellmount, Stroud, 2008)

Only the Enemy in Front: The Recce Corps at War, 1940–46 (revised p/bk edn) (Spellmount, Stroud, 2008)

Ubique: The Royal Artillery in the Second World (Spellmount, Stroud, 2008)

Helmand Mission: With the Royal Irish Battlegroup in Afghanistan, 2008 (Pen & Sword, Barnsley, 2009)

In the Ranks of Death: The Irish in the Second World War (Pen & Sword, Barnsley, 2010)

The Humber Light Reconnaissance Car 1941–45 (Osprey, Oxford, 2011)

Hobart's 79th Armoured Division at War: Invention, Innovation and Inspiration (Pen & Sword, Barnsley, 2011)

British Armoured Divisions and Their Commanders 1939–1945 (Pen & Sword, Barnsley, 2013)

Victory in Italy: 15th Army Group's Final Campaign (Pen & Sword, Barnsley, 2014)

Churchill's Greatest Fear: The Battle of the Atlantic 3 September 1939 to 7 May 1945 (Pen & Sword, Barnsley, 2015)

The Somme: 24 June to 19 November 1916 (Northern Ireland War Memorial, Belfast, 2016)

El Alamein 1942

Turning Point in the Desert

Richard Doherty

Pen & Sword
MILITARY

First published in Great Britain as *The Sound of History:*
El Alamein 1942 by Spellmount Ltd, Staplehurst.
This revised edition published by
Pen & Sword Military
an imprint of
Pen & Sword Books Ltd
47 Church Street
Barnsley
South Yorkshire
S70 2AS

ISBN 978 1 52670 079 7

A CIP catalogue record for this book is available from the British
Library

Typeset in Ehrhardt by
Mac Style Ltd, Bridlington, East Yorkshire
Printed and bound in England by
TJ International, Padstow, PL28 8RW.

Pen & Sword Books Limited incorporates the imprints of Atlas,
Archaeology, Aviation, Discovery, Family History, Fiction, History,
Maritime, Military, Military Classics, Politics, Select, Transport,
True Crime, Air World, Frontline Publishing, Leo Cooper,
Remember When, Seaforth Publishing, The Praetorian Press,
Wharncliffe Local History, Wharncliffe Transport,
Wharncliffe True Crime and White Owl.

For a complete list of Pen & Sword titles please contact
PEN & SWORD BOOKS LIMITED
47 Church Street, Barnsley, South Yorkshire, S70 2AS, England
E-mail: enquiries@pen-and-sword.co.uk
Website: www.pen-and-sword.co.uk

Contents

El Alamein

There are flowers now, they say, at Alamein;
Yes, flowers in the minefields now.
So those that come to view that vacant scene
Where death remains and agony has been
Will find the lilies grow –
Flowers, and nothing that we know.

So they rang the bells for us and Alamein,
Bells which we could not hear:
And to those who heard the bells what could it mean,
That name of loss and pride, El Alamein?
Not the murk and harm of war,
But their hope, their own warm prayer.

It will become a staid historic name,
That crazy sea of sand!
Like Troy or Agincourt its single fame
Will be the garland for our brow, our claim,
On us a fleck of glory to the end:
And there our dead will keep their holy ground.

But this is not the place that we recall,
The crowded desert crossed with foaming tracks,
The one blotched building, lacking half a wall,
The grey-faced men, sand powdered over all;
The tanks, the guns, the trucks,
The black, dark-smoking wrecks.
So be it: none but us has known that land:
El Alamein will still be only ours
And those ten days of chaos in the sand.
Others will come who cannot understand,
Will halt beside the rusty minefield wires
And find there – flowers.

John Jarmain
(Killed in action, Normandy, 1944)

Dedication

With love to the memory of a dear aunt,
Sister Mary Richard Coyle OSF
Missionary Franciscan Sisters
1919–2000
We knew that we were listening to the sound of history.

and

with admiration and respect for
George France Morrison,
Lieutenant, 7th Battalion The Black Watch (Royal Highland
Regiment)
Killed in action at El Alamein, 23 October 1942
Aged 21 years.
This war is being fought to protect people like you from horrible things, and it's only right that some should have the privilege – yes, the privilege – to give themselves for the cause of the good and the right.

and

in memory of
Peter Willett
Lieutenant, and Troop Leader, The Queen's Bays (2nd Dragoons)
My troop was the leading troop of the leading squadron of the leading regiment of 1st Armoured Division.

Maps

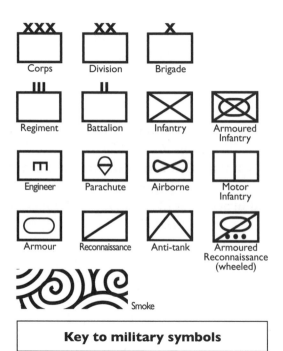

Key to military symbols

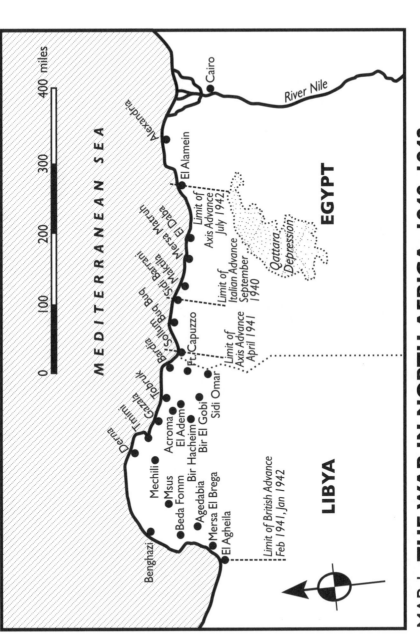

MAP 1 **THE WAR IN NORTH AFRICA, 1940-1942**

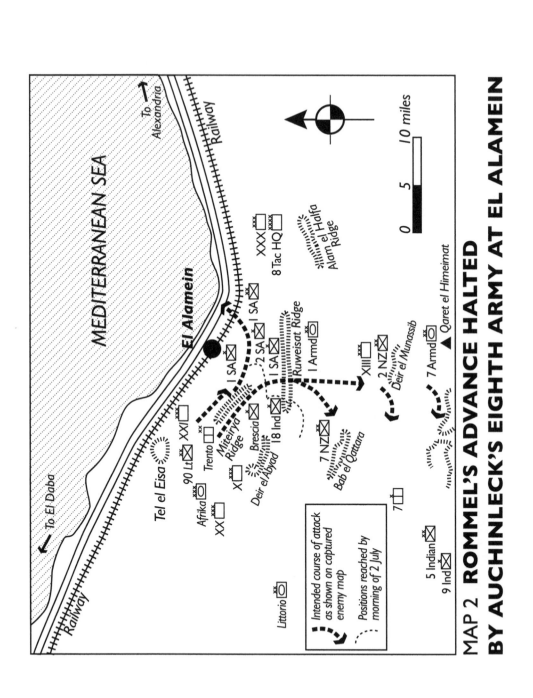

MAP 2 **ROMMEL'S ADVANCE HALTED**
BY AUCHINLECK'S EIGHTH ARMY AT EL ALAMEIN

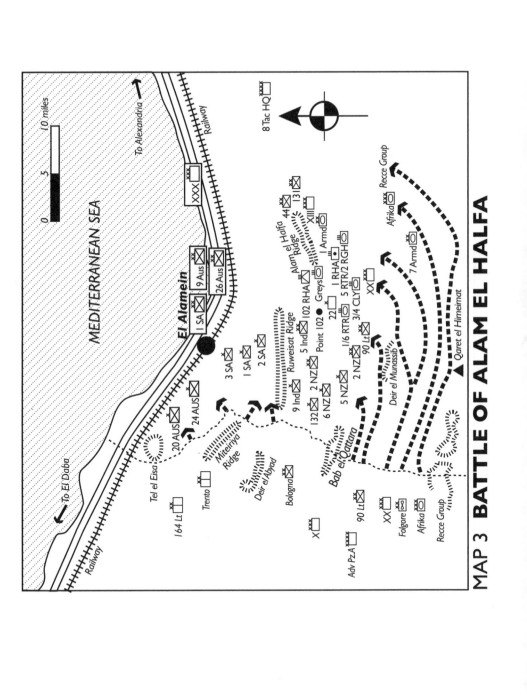

MAP 3 **BATTLE OF ALAM EL HALFA**

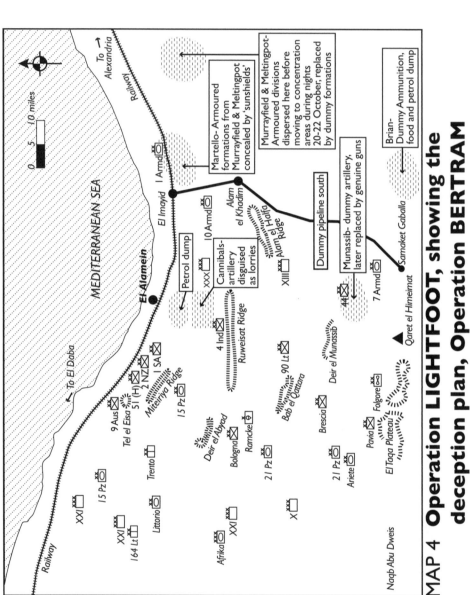

MAP 4 **Operation LIGHTFOOT, showing the deception plan, Operation BERTRAM**

Within the map image:

MEDITERRANEAN SEA

To Alexandria
Railway
El Imayid

To El Daba
El Alamein
To El Daba

Railway

0 5 10 miles

Martello- Armoured formations from Murrayfield & Meltingpot concealed by 'sunshields'

Murrayfield & Meltingpot- Armoured divisions dispersed here before moving to concentration areas during nights 20-22 October; replaced by dummy formations

Brian- Dummy Ammunition, food and petrol dump

Dummy pipeline south

Munassib- dummy artillery, later replaced by genuine guns

Cannibals- artillery disguised as lorries

Petrol dump

I Armd
10 Armd
Alam el Khadim
Alam el Halfa
XIII Alam el Ridge
XXX

44
7 Armd
Samaket Gaballa
Qaret el Himeimat

I SA
2 NZ
51 (H)
Miteiriya Ridge
9 Aus
Tel el Eisa
15 Pz
4 Ind
Ruweisat Ridge
90 Lt
Bab el Qattara
Deir el Munassib

15 Pz
Trento
Deir el Abyad
Bologna
Ramcke
21 Pz
Brescia
21 Pz
Ariete
Pavia
Folgore
El Taqa Plateau

XXI
15 Pz
XXI
164 Lt
Littorio
Afrika
XXI
X

Naqb Abu Dweis

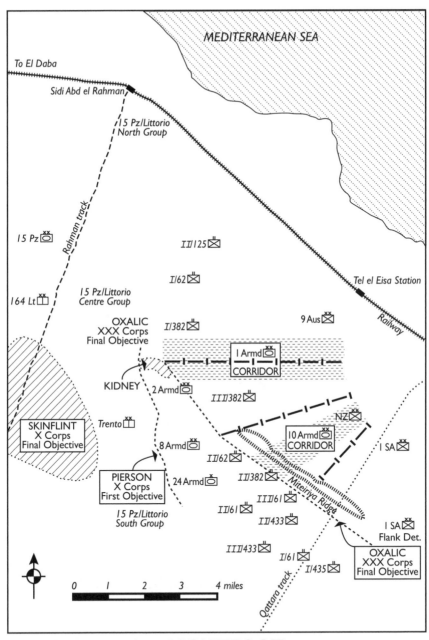

MEDITERRANEAN SEA

To El Daba

Sidi Abd el Rahman

15 Pz/Littorio
North Group

15 Pz

II/125

Tel el Eisa Station

I/62

164 Lt

15 Pz/Littorio
Centre Group

OXALIC
XXX Corps
Final Objective

I/382

9 Aus

Railway

1 Armd
CORRIDOR

KIDNEY

2 Armd

III/382

NZ

SKINFLINT
X Corps
Final Objective

Trento

10 Armd
CORRIDOR

1 SA

8 Armd

II/62

Miteiriya Ridge

PIERSON
X Corps
First Objective

24 Armd

III/382

15 Pz/Littorio
South Group

III/61

1 SA
Flank Det.

II/61

II/433

III/433

I/61

OXALIC
XXX Corps
Final Objective

I/435

Qattara track

0   1   2   3   4 miles

MAP 5 **Operation LIGHTFOOT
X and XXX Corps, 23-24 October**

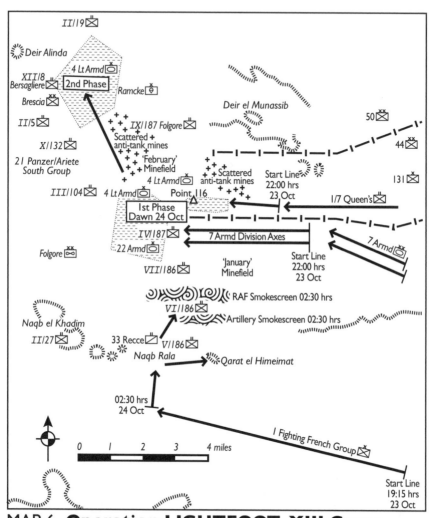

II/19

Deir Alinda

4 Lt Armd
XII/8
Bersagliere   2nd Phase   Ramcke

Brescia

II/5

X/132   IX/187 Folgore

21 Panzer/Ariete   Scattered
South Group   anti-tank mines   Deir el Munassib   50

                     'February'
                     Minefield   44

III/104   4 Lt Armd   Scattered   Start Line
          4 Lt Armd   Point 116   anti-tank mines   22:00 hrs   131
                                                            23 Oct
          1st Phase   1/7 Queen's
          Dawn 24 Oct

          IV/187   7 Armd Division Axes
Folgore   22 Armd   7 Armd

          VII/186   'January'   Start Line
                           Minefield   22:00 hrs
                                            23 Oct

                        RAF Smokescreen 02:30 hrs
              VI/186
                        Artillery Smokescreen 02:30 hrs
Naqb el Khadim
II/27   33 Recce V/186
              Naqb Rala   Qarat el Himeimat

          02:30 hrs
          24 Oct

                                I Fighting French Group
0   1   2   3   4 miles

                                            Start Line
                                            19:15 hrs
                                            23 Oct

MAP 6 **Operation LIGHTFOOT, XIII Corps**
23-24 October

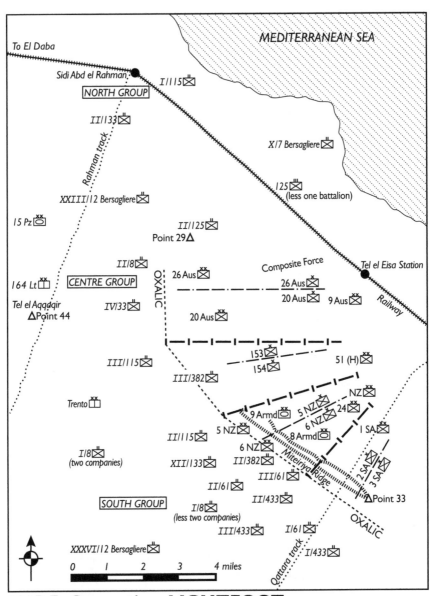

MAP 7 **Operation LIGHTFOOT
Situation Early on 24 October**

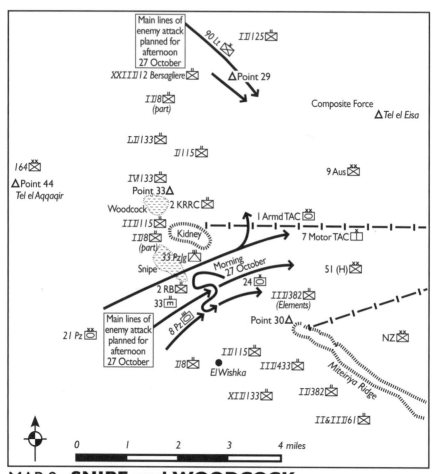

MAP 8 **SNIPE and WOODCOCK**
Attack by 1st Armoured Division
26-27 October

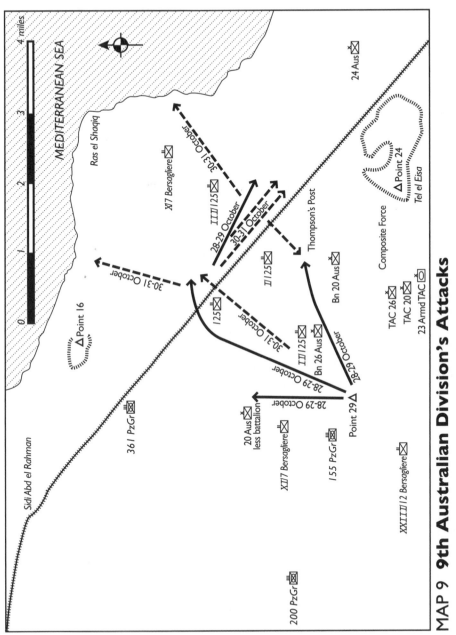

MAP 9 **9th Australian Division's Attacks
28-29 October and 30-31 October**

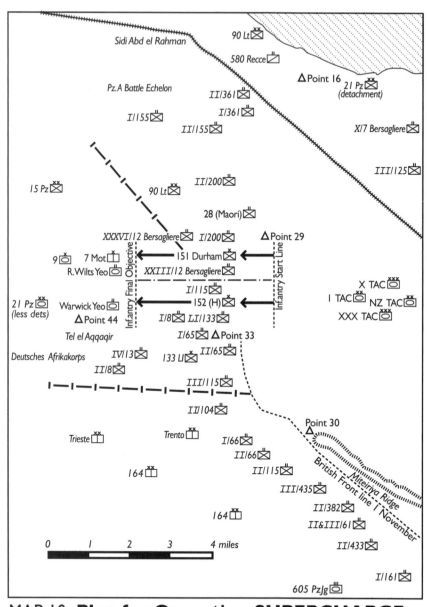

Sidi Abd el Rahman

90 Lt

580 Recce

△ Point 16

21 Pz
(detachment)

Pz.A Battle Echelon

II/361

I/361

X/7 Bersagliere

I/155

II/155

III/125

15 Pz

90 Lt

II/200

28 (Maori)

XXXVI/12 Bersagliere   I/200

△ Point 29

9   7 Mot

151 Durham

R.Wilts Yeo

XXIII/12 Bersagliere

X TAC

I TAC

I/115

NZ TAC

21 Pz
(less dets)

Warwick Yeo

152 (H)

XXX TAC

△ Point 44

I/8   LI/133

Tel el Aqqaqir

I/65   △ Point 33

Deutsches Afrikakorps

IV/13

133 LI   II/65

II/8

III/115

II/104

Trieste

Trento

I/66

Point 30

△

II/66

164

II/115

III/435

164

II/382

II&III/61

II/433

I/161

605 PzJg

Infantry Final Objective

Infantry Start Line

Miteriya Ridge

British Front line 1 November

0   1   2   3   4 miles

MAP 10 **Plan for Operation SUPERCHARGE**
1-2 November

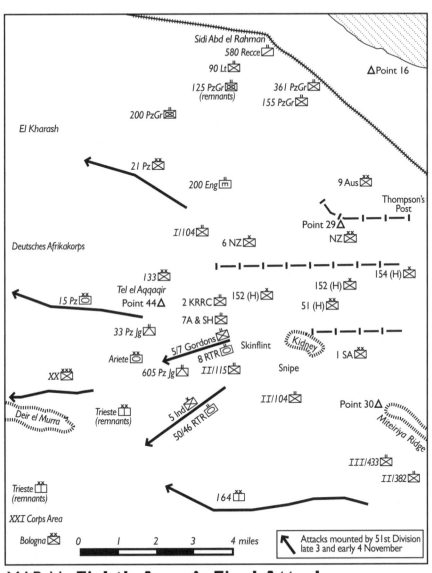

Sidi Abd el Rahman
580 Recce
90 Lt
△ Point 16
125 PzGr
(remnants)
361 PzGr
155 PzGr
200 PzGr

El Kharash

21 Pz
200 Eng
9 Aus
Thompson's Post
Point 29 △
NZ
I/104
6 NZ
Deutsches Afrikakorps
154 (H)
133
152 (H)
Tel el Aqqaqir
15 Pz
Point 44 △
2 KRRC
152 (H)
51 (H)
7A & SH
33 Pz Jg
5/7 Gordons
Skinflint
Kidney
Ariete
8 RTR
605 Pz Jg
II/115
Snipe
I SA
II/104
XX
Point 30 △
Deir el Murra
Trieste
(remnants)
5 Ind
50/46 RTR
Miteiriya Ridge
III/433
II/382
Trieste
(remnants)
164
XXI Corps Area
Bologna
0   1   2   3   4 miles

Attacks mounted by 51st Division
late 3 and early 4 November

MAP 11   Eighth Army's Final Attacks
3-4 November

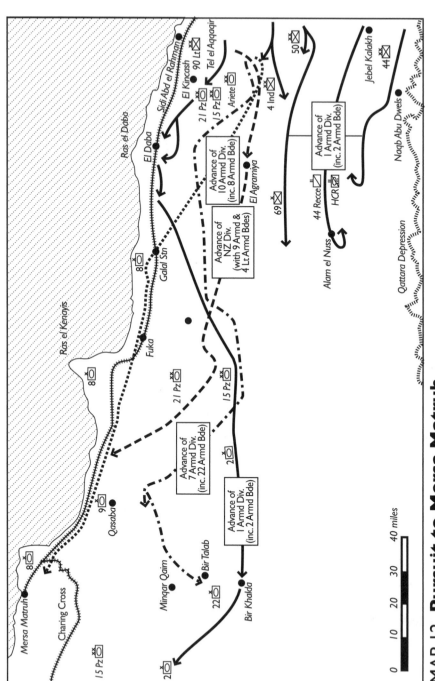

MAP 12 **Pursuit to Mersa Matruh
4-7 November**

Acknowledgements

When I researched and wrote the original version of this book almost two decades ago I had the support and assistance of a wide range of individuals and institutions. Without them the book could not have been produced and I owe them now, as I did then, a debt of thanks. I gladly acknowledge that debt and wish to thank:

The National Archives, Kew, Richmond, Surrey. I have been using the National Archives for more than three decades and have always found the staff of the Reading and Search Rooms to be courteous, knowledgeable and ever helpful.

The Imperial War Museum (IWM), London. The Department of Documents, the Department of Printed Books and the Photographic Archive have also been very helpful. The new surroundings of the first two mentioned may no longer be the interior of the grand cupola that is the trademark of the IWM as much as the two naval guns that stand on guard outside but the staff are still willing to help and to share their knowledge of the material housed in the Museum. I must pay a special tribute to the late Roderick Suddaby of the Department of Documents who was especially helpful in my research for this book.

The National Army Museum (NAM), Chelsea, London. The staff of the Reading Room were ever courteous and ready with advice. Some of my research there involved the Lummis Files, to which I refer below.

The Military Historical Society. When I researched this book the Lummis Files, chronicling the deeds of those who have earned the Victoria Cross, were the property of the Society although held in NAM. The late Dennis Pillinger was the custodian of the files, which have since been handed over to NAM, and he was very helpful in responding to my enquiries. A gentleman of the 'old school', he was professional and courteous in his dealings with everyone.

Derry Central Library, Foyle Street, Londonderry. The library staff, now under Libraries Northern Ireland, have always been helpful and were especially so in searching for secondary source material for this book.

The British Library Newspaper Library, Colindale, London. In its previous site at Colindale the Library (now in Boston Spa, Lincolnshire with digital access in St Pancras) provided much information for this work.

D.C. Thomson Newspapers, Dundee. The group were kind enough to publish a request from me for information about Lieutenant George France Morrison, Black Watch, who was killed at El Alamein. I am also grateful to Mr Roy Stewart of Perthshire who knew the Morrison family and who responded to my appeal with relevant information for which I am very grateful.

Mrs Audrey Harris gave permission to use quotations from her late husband's account lodged in the Department of Documents of the IWM and Mr Jack Merewood kindly allowed the use of an extract from his book *To War With The Bays: A Tank Gunner Remembers*.

In some cases, and in spite of best endeavours, it has not proved possible to trace current copyright holders but the author and publisher are prepared to make the necessary arrangements to rectify this at the earliest opportunity.

Material from war diaries, official narratives of the campaign and other contemporary documents held in the UK National Archives at Kew are reproduced under the Open Government Licence.

My thanks to my publishers, Pen & Sword Books Ltd, and to all the team – Brigadier Henry Wilson, for agreeing to undertake this new edition, Matt Jones for his diligence and patience and Jon Wilkinson for his excellent jacket design.

A special debt of thanks is due to my late aunt, Sister Mary Richard Coyle OSF, whose vivid description of the sound of Eighth Army's bombardment opening Operation LIGHTFOOT on 23 October 1942 inspired the title of the original edition, *The Sound of History*. When I visited her in Our Lady of the Angels Convent in Tenafly, New Jersey, in October 1997, she and her fellow Missionary Franciscan Sisters could not have been kinder and gave me a day that will live long in my memory.

As ever, I thank my wife, Carol, my children, Joanne, James and Catríona, son in law Steven and grandchildren Ciaran, Katrina, Joshua and Sophie for their patience and support.

Richard Doherty
Co. Londonderry
July 2017

Prologue

Silence pervaded Sacred Heart Convent on Alexandria's Rue de Tanis. The Missionary Franciscan Sisters had long since finished the last meal of the day, evening prayers had been said in the chapel and the 'great silence', which would last until morning prayers, had begun. On that October Friday night, however, the silence in the convent was broken by the drone of aero-engines. The nuns waited for the air raid alarm but none came. Since the sound was dying to the west and the engines had the steady rhythm associated with British aircraft, Alexandria would be safe that night. Bombs would fall elsewhere, probably on the German and Italian soldiers dug in some sixty miles away along the Mediterranean coast.

The drone from the aircraft died away. Silence reigned once more, but only for a brief spell. To the rooms of Sacred Heart Convent came an almighty wave of sound. The building's windows shook and rattled; the walls quivered as if in fear. It seemed as if the convent would fall down around the Sisters. Prayers were offered urgently and silently. The sound persisted. But it was not the sound of bombs dropping nearby, not the old familiar sound that prompted the dash to the air raid shelters in the convent grounds. This sound was different. A deep, grumbling, angry sound, akin to thunder – but to no thunder that any of the Sisters had ever heard before – filled their consciousness. And then they knew. It was 'the sound of history' as Sister Mary Richard described it to me as we discussed her memories of that night in Our Lady of the Angels Convent in New Jersey in October 1997. Sixty miles away the guns of General Bernard Law Montgomery's Eighth Army were putting down the greatest artillery bombardment since the First World War.

In the artillery lines of Eighth Army the sound was deafening. It was deafening, too, to the soldiers of Eighth Army who waited for the signal to join battle: infantrymen crouched waiting, checking their weapons for the hundredth time; tankmen sat nervously in their armoured engines of war; Gunners sweated in their emplacements in spite of the cool of the night; Sappers moved out on their mine-clearing tasks; military policemen were busy ensuring that all traffic due to move forward could do so without hindrance; doctors and medics awaited the call to deal with casualties; chaplains prayed with and for the soldiers under their care. On the receiving end German and Italian soldiers sheltered as best they could from the storm of white-hot steel that cascaded around them; gunners died at their guns as British shells found their targets and turned German and Italian artillery into so much scrap metal; doctors did their best for the injured and chaplains ministered to the dying. And those German and Italian soldiers knew, as did their British counterparts, that the long-awaited hour of reckoning had come. The final Battle of El Alamein had begun.

The battle had opened with an aerial bombardment of *Panzerarmee Afrika*'s rear areas by RAF bombers; over 100 tons of bombs were unleashed by Wellingtons, the aircraft that had first disturbed the silence of Sacred Heart Convent, with Fleet Air Arm Albacores dropping flares to mark the target areas. For fifteen minutes the Wellingtons dropped their deadly loads. Then, as the sounds of bombing and bombers faded away into a beautiful moonlit night, the guns added their contribution to the shattering of the peace of that night. Over 800 field and medium guns poured their shells into the enemy positions; the first targets were the Axis artillery lines where the British rounds exacted a heavy toll in a fifteen-minute bombardment. Then the guns shortened their range to provide a curtain of fire for the advancing infantry of Eighth Army.

As the guns switched their attention from the Axis artillery they fell silent for a few moments, during which the savage skirl of bagpipes could be heard in the lines of 51st (Highland) Division as the Jocks prepared to do battle. Soon the guns were firing again, this time in a more intense bombardment as they began laying down their creeping curtain of fire for the infantry.

The battle that opened that October Friday night would rage and roar from El Alamein on the Mediterranean coast to the rim of the Qattara Depression, some forty miles to the south, for almost two weeks. It would be 4 November before Eighth Army achieved the breakthrough that Montgomery had planned. By then the Italo-German *Panzerarmee Afrika* was in full retreat. The third and final Battle of El Alamein was over and Eighth Army had achieved one of the significant victories of the war, one of those on which the course of the war hinged. It was also the last victory won by a British army in a major battle and was soon to enter popular consciousness at home while the general who oversaw it, Bernard Montgomery, was to achieve legendary status and become Field Marshal the Viscount Montgomery of Alamein.

This story of the Battle of El Alamein does not pretend to be a definitive history of the battle, nor does it claim to bring new thinking to its history. It does, however, examine the three battles in their full context, showing how

Eighth Army prepared for each, and especially how the beginning of the preparation for the final battle and the defeat of *Panzerarmee Afrika* had begun before Montgomery's arrival in Egypt. In writing this book I have tried to show how the roles of all the arms and support services from the United Kingdom, the Commonwealth and the Empire came together to play their part and how those parts were interdependent.

Since this book was first published, as *The Sound of History: El Alamein 1942* in 2002, at least three other books on El Alamein have been released. Of these, by far the best is Niall Barr's *The Pendulum of War: The Three Battles of El Alamein*. Jonathan Dimbleby's *Destiny in the Desert: The Road to El Alamein – the Battle that Turned the Tide*, although good on the political ramifications of the campaign but weak on the British Army of the day, argues for the historical importance of the battle. The most recent, Simon Ball's *Alamein* in the OUP's *Great Battles* series, deals only briefly with the battle and the campaign in North Africa but much more with El Alamein as a British cultural phenomenon; it is a well-argued and interesting work.

It is now seventy-five years since the final battle was fought and won and there are very few surviving veterans. Peter Willett, the third dedicatee of this edition, died in November 2015 at the age of 96. He had been the last surviving officer of The Queen's Bays (2nd Dragoon Guards) to have served at El Alamein and, at one point of the battle, his was probably the foremost of Eighth Army's tanks. Only months before his death his memoir *Armoured Horseman* was published, providing another important part of the overall story of El Alamein. With Peter's passing, we are reminded of the constant thinning of the ranks of El Alamein veterans and of the inevitability that before long there will be no one alive who was there. I hope, therefore, that this book will stand as tribute, however small, to those who fought at El Alamein, all who served in the Desert Campaign and all those who lost their lives there.

Richard Doherty
July 2017

Chapter One

War Comes to North Africa

Then let the trumpets sound

Of the battle of El Alamein Winston Churchill wrote that it might almost be said that before Alamein Britain had never had a victory but that after Alamein there had never been a defeat. That word 'almost' is important: there had been British victories *before* Alamein and there were defeats thereafter. But there was something almost spiritual about Alamein in the British psyche that was probably summed up much more accurately by Churchill in his Mansion House speech on 9 November 1942 when he said: 'This is not the end. It is not even the beginning of the end. But it is, perhaps, the end of the beginning.'

Nor did that comment relate entirely to Eighth Army's victory. Churchill was thinking also of the Operation TORCH landing, on 8 November, the relief of Malta and the Red Army's resilience on the Eastern Front. But, to many, it seemed as if Churchill spoke primarily about Alamein and succeeding generations have tended to link his words with the British achievement there. That is understandable, especially with hindsight, since Alamein was one of three pivotal battles of the Second World War: the United States Navy stopped the Japanese advance in the Pacific at Midway in June 1942; Eighth Army defeated the Italo-German army at Alamein in November and the Red Army was destroying the German Sixth Army at Stalingrad. Between June 1942 and February 1943 the Allies were opening the door to success and Midway, Alamein and Stalingrad may be seen as that door's hinges. They also represent each of the major Allies: the United States, the United Kingdom and the Union of Soviet Socialist Republics.

There is an obvious politico-strategic logic in the USA fighting Japan in the Pacific and in Germans and Russians battling at Stalingrad. The logic of Britain fighting Germany and Italy in Egypt is less obvious, especially since Egypt was neutral. So why was this major battle fought on Egyptian soil? Why were rival armies fighting in North Africa at all? British troops had been stationed in Egypt for sixty years at the time of the battle of El Alamein, although they had fought in that country – against France – at the beginning of the nineteenth century. In 1882 troops commanded by Sir Garnet Wolseley arrived in Egypt, one element landing at Ismailia from Britain and a second, from India, disembarking at Suez. Wolseley's force then defeated Khedive Ismail's army at Tel el Kebir and the Royal Navy bombarded Alexandria.

British interest in Egypt intensified with the opening of the Suez Canal in 1869. Since the canal shortened the sea journey to India its security became a priority. Egypt, part of the Ottoman Empire, was ruled by a dynasty created by the Turkish viceroy Mehmet Ali (1769–1849) but Khedive Ismail bankrupted Egypt and repudiated his foreign debts. As one of Ismail's principal creditors, Britain took military action to protect its investment: Egypt was occupied and a protectorate established, although there was no final break with Turkey. That came when Turkey allied with Germany in the Great War and Britain declared Egypt's independence from its former masters. The country became a battleground of the war and a major logistical base for campaigns in Gallipoli, the Balkans and Palestine. In 1936 Egypt became independent but a small British presence remained; the Anglo-Egyptian Treaty gave Britain control of the Suez Canal for another twenty years with British bases in Egypt to defend the canal, the route to India and the Persian Gulf oilfields.

Developments in military technology also helped make Egypt even more important to Britain in the inter-war years. The Army said goodbye to the horse and became mechanized; the Royal Navy changed to oil-burning ships and the young Royal Air Force came of age and burgeoned in strength, all of which meant that those Gulf oilfields assumed great strategic value for Britain. In turn, Egypt's strategic value increased as part of the protection of the oilfields.

On its west Egypt was bordered by Libya, another former Ottoman possession that had become part of the Italian empire. Italy also had colonies in east Africa, Eritrea and Italian Somaliland, to which was added Ethiopia following the Italian invasion in 1935. Modern Italy, which came into being in the late-nineteenth century, strove to regain some of the glory that was Rome by seeking overseas colonies. That was possible only in Africa but, since other nations, including the new German nation-state, had similar ideas, and more muscle, Italy gained only Eritrea and Italian Somaliland (the southern part of modern Somalia). An attempt to annex Abyssinia (Ethiopia) was rebuffed at the battle of Adowa in 1896. However, the crumbling of the Ottoman Empire allowed Italy a foothold in Mediterranean Africa and Italian forces invaded Tripolitania and Cyrenaica. Following the Great War, with the collapse of the Ottoman Empire, those Italian gains were ratified. When the Fascist Benito Mussolini became Italy's prime minister in 1922 he introduced an aggressive and expansionist foreign policy in parallel with a programme of domestic modernization. Communications were improved in North Africa with a new coastal road from Tripoli to the Egyptian frontier assisting speedier movement of troops in the region. Punitive action was taken against any opponents of Italian rule and in 1935 Tripolitania, Cyrenaica and Fezzan were united as Libya, with Tripoli as the capital, while Eritrea and Italian Somaliland were renamed Italian East Africa. Britain and Egypt saw a threat to Egypt and the Anglo-Egyptian Sudan and the British garrison in Egypt was strengthened and its equipment modernized. The Munich crisis of 1938 brought the realization that the threat to Egypt had increased since Italy was a partner of Germany in the Berlin-Rome Axis. Thus it was that a British official was sent to tell King Farouk that 'British control of Egypt would now have to be both retained and increased until the Axis had been defeated'. Farouk's response was to accept this reality grudgingly but to exhort: 'when it's all over, for God's sake lay down the white man's burden, and Go!'[1]

As a result of the Italian threat a Mobile Force was deployed to Mersa Matruh, some 170 miles from Alexandria, to meet any Italian incursion. The Mobile Force included the Cairo Cavalry Brigade of three cavalry regiments – 7th, 8th and 11th Hussars – as well as 1st Battalion Royal Tank Corps,[*] 3rd Regiment Royal Horse Artillery, a company of RASC and an RAMC field ambulance. Before long the Mobile Force would become 7th Armoured Division, perhaps the best-known British armoured formation of the Second World War, and adopt a divisional sign, designed by its commander's wife, of a jerboa or desert rat, from which was born the divisional soubriquet of the *Desert Rats*.[2]

This situation came to a head in June 1940 as France collapsed under the German invasion. Mussolini, keen to gain some of France's possessions in North Africa, declared war on France and Britain on 10 June but failed in his aim of expanding Italy's African empire to the west as demilitarized zones were created in France, Tunisia, Algeria and Morocco. *Il Duce*'s only chance of increasing his empire was by taking territory from Britain: both Egypt and the Sudan came into his sights. That Egypt was now independent, and neutral, did not concern him: the land of the pharaohs and neighbouring Sudan represented an irresistible prize for Italy which could control all of north-east Africa and, perhaps, strike even deeper into the continent.

---

[*] The Royal Tank Corps became the Royal Tank Regiment in 1939 when the Royal Armoured Corps was formed as the parent body for all armoured regiments in the Army.

And so it was that Marshal Italo Balbo, governor of Libya, was ordered to invade Egypt, a plan of which he did not approve – he was one of many senior Italian officers who were convinced that Italy could not win an easy victory over British arms in North Africa – and which he was fated not to put into action. On 28 June 1940 Balbo, Italy's most famous airman, died when Italian anti-aircraft gunners shot down his aircraft as it approached Tobruk. Marshal Rodolfo Graziani succeeded Balbo and inherited the invasion order. Although also reluctant to implement Mussolini's plan, Graziani eventually did so, but waited until 13 September before deploying his army into Egypt. Even then, it halted at Sidi Barrani after three days, having advanced only fifty miles, and began preparing defences.

As it pushed into Egypt the Italian Tenth Army was harried by elements of 7th Armoured Division, which had been raiding into Libya ever since 11 June 1940, when armoured cars of the Light Armoured Brigade[3]* crossed the frontier. Although the Italians outnumbered British forces in Egypt much of their equipment was inferior and their training in desert warfare no match for that of 7th Armoured Division. In support of 7th Armoured was the nucleus of what would become the Desert Air Force, including No.208 Squadron, which would play a vital role at El Alamein in 1942. The Italians had used the one good all-weather road, the *Via Balbia*, along the coast and were reluctant to move far from it, thus bestowing an immediate advantage to their foes. Before the war British commanders in Egypt had trained their soldiers in desert warfare and Royal Engineers had explored the vast southern sand seas of Egypt and Libya, producing excellent maps showing where 'good going' for vehicles might be found.[4] Alien though it was to Europeans, the desert held no fears for British forces.

It is worth considering the terrain over which the opposing forces would fight for more than two years, and especially to find why the El Alamein position was of such significance. The desert war of 1940–43 was fought chiefly between El Alamein and El Agheila, on the gulf of Sirte, a distance of some 600 miles, an empty land with no water, little food and no roads. (The El Agheila position was known as Mersa Brega, or Mersa el Brega, to Axis forces.) To the south the area over which fighting took place had its southern limits at Jarabub and Siwa

---

* The Light Armoured Brigade included 7th, 8th and 11th Hussars, the former two equipped with light tanks and the latter with armoured cars. Alongside them was the Heavy Armoured Brigade, which included 1st and 6th Royal Tanks. There was also a Pivot Group of 3 RHA, F Battery 4 RHA and 1st King's Royal Rifle Corps.

oases, some 150 miles from the sea; farther south is the vast scorching waste of the Sand Sea where only Bedouin Arabs or British could live or move. The few settlements in the area are along the Mediterranean littoral on a narrow strip of fertile land; otherwise few civilians suffered the intrusions of battling armies.

Although the desert appears featureless at first sight, those who soldiered there soon realized otherwise. There are features such as the low rocky ridges that were so important at the Alamein position – Ruweisat and Miteiriya ridges – and small hills such as Tel el Eisa, the hill of Jesus, which saw some of the fiercest and bloodiest fighting of the battle. Such features are obvious on a map, although they do not appear so obvious to the untrained eye on the ground; but possession of them offers dominating views of the surrounding area. But there are also depressions, or *deirs*, such as Deir el Shein, which is quite shallow and akin to a saucer or the deeper, steep, almost cliff-sided Munassib Depression. Most forbidding of all, the Qattara Depression, covers several thousand square miles with its floor some 400 feet below sea level; the salt marsh that is the Qattara Depression is impassable by heavy vehicles, although jeeps or even light armoured cars might, and did, with care, find a way through.

The ridges and *tels*, the *deirs* or depressions are all noticeable to the naked eye. Not quite so noticeable, except to the trained eye of a soldier or hunter, are the many folds in the desert. Such undulations may only be three- or four-feet deep but offered welcome cover to the soldier and could hide anti-tank guns, such as the German Pak 38 or the British 6-pounder, both low-profile weapons, from an approaching tank until too late; the tops of the shields of either weapon come only to about waist height on a man of about six feet. War added further features to the desert: the detritus of battle could be used as landmarks whenever the need arose.

Most of the desert is a region of gritty dust, rock and stone-littered wasteland rather than the rolling sand dunes beloved of filmmakers. It is of a dusty colour with a pink hue but, closer to the coast, limestone predominates and the colour changes, becoming much paler with whitish stones; the sands of the Mediterranean shore are blindingly white, contrasting vividly with the waters. But between the coastal areas and the deep desert is the feature dominating everything, the 500-foot escarpment that faces north to the coast and runs down from the limestone plateau where most of the fighting occurred. That escarpment has been compared to a terrace, broken only in a few places and

everywhere a barrier to wheeled vehicles and in most places even to tanks. The gaps that are passable by all vehicles became therefore immensely important – Fuka, Halfaya and Sidi Rezegh.[5]

However, those chokepoints may be outflanked by mobile forces sweeping southwards. Almost everywhere it was impossible to create a defensive line that could not be outflanked. Not so on the El Alamein line. In the north the line was anchored on the coast close to the little railway halt of El Alamein and Tel el Alamein, the hill of the twin cairns, or two flags, while in the south the Qattara Depression presented a flank that could only be turned by force. There was no opportunity for Axis forces to drive deep into the desert and threaten the British rear, as was done elsewhere. Thus the El Alamein line became Egypt's final defence.

This then was the battleground, the vastness of which almost defies imagination – the Western Desert covers some two million square miles. For three years North Africa was Britain's principal theatre of land war with, for most of that time, fighting raging between El Agheila and El Alamein. The first shots were fired in June 1940; by the end of the year Britain's first land victory of the war had been won in the desert. That victory was gained by Western Desert Force, under General Richard O'Connor, an Irishman, as were so many desert generals, which attacked Tenth Italian Army at Sidi Barrani in Operation COMPASS on 8 December 1940 before pursuing it across the chord of the Cyrenaican bulge to defeat it in detail at Beda Fomm in early-February 1941. However, O'Connor was forced to stop at El Agheila, not because of Italian opposition, for Tenth Army had been destroyed, but because prime minister Winston Churchill had decided to send an expeditionary force to assist Greece against Italian invasion and O'Connor's command, now XIII Corps, was to provide much of that force.

As Britain went to the aid of the Greeks so, too, did Germany move to assist Italy in the campaign. German forces were also sent to North Africa: a small expeditionary force, under Major General Erwin Rommel, landed in Tripoli to bolster the Italian army in Libya. Rommel did not have orders for an immediate offensive by his command, the *Deutsches Afrikakorps*, but he was prepared to take risks and, following an aerial reconnaissance soon after his arrival, decided to use speed and surprise against the weakened British force in Cyrenaica, commanded by Lieutenant General Sir Philip Neame VC. This was a gamble, but it paid off, since much of Neame's Cyrenaica Command was fresh to the desert and his main armoured formation, 2nd Armoured Division, was weak in tanks and dispersed. Soon Rommel had reached the Egyptian frontier. Only the port of Tobruk, garrisoned by Australian soldiers, held out against Rommel. British offensives, Operations BREVITY and BATTLEAXE, were defeated by superior German tactical deployments of tanks and anti-tank guns. In June 1941 General Wavell was relieved by General Sir Claude Auchinleck, who immediately came under pressure from Churchill to launch an offensive. Auchinleck wanted time to build up his forces before any major offensive and it was late-November before he launched Operation CRUSADER. By then there were two British corps, XIII and XXX, and a new army – Eighth – had been created as their parent formation,[6] under Lieutenant General Sir Alan Cunningham, who had defeated the Italians in East Africa. (In August 1941 German forces in Africa became *Panzergruppe Afrika.* This new formation included *Afrikakorps* – 15th and 21st Panzer Divisions – 90th Light Division, the Italian XX and XXI Corps and *Savona* Division. On 30 January 1942 *Panzerarmee Afrika* was created.)

The CRUSADER battles were some of the most complicated of the Second World War but, after several weeks' fighting, Eighth Army forced Rommel to withdraw, Tobruk was relieved and isolated Axis garrisons surrendered to Eighth Army. In the course of these battles Auchinleck was forced to relieve Cunningham as Eighth Army commander, assuming command himself and turning the battle. Major General Neill Ritchie was later appointed as acting commander but the announcement of this as a permanent appointment in the House of Commons led to the appointment being confirmed. It had been a Pyrrhic victory for Eighth Army's armour which had heavy losses: the Germans had shown superior skills in handling armour and anti-tank weapons; the British 2-pounder anti-tank gun was no longer capable of destroying German tanks and British tanks, armed with 2-pounders, were under-gunned. With British tank development having fallen behind that of Germany there was a marked superiority in German armour. This was not entirely technical: much of it, as we have seen, was due to better handling and a more scientific tactical doctrine. For example, the Germans had no parallel to the British concepts of infantry support, or I-tanks, and cruisers; that one specific tank type should be dedicated to supporting infantry and another to cavalry-style operations, and tank-to-tank combat, was alien to the Germans.

Axis forces withdrew once more to El Agheila but Rommel was not quiescent for long and a new counter-offensive in late-January 1942 pushed Eighth Army back to the Gazala line. As the situation stabilized, Churchill again pressed for an offensive. Aware that his foe was planning further operations, Auchinleck informed the prime minister that Eighth Army would attack, but that the enemy might pre-empt that move. And so it happened that Rommel did attack before Eighth Army could launch its offensive. In a series of bloody battles in late-May and June, Eighth Army's armour, badly dispersed, was almost destroyed, Tobruk fell, and Ritchie began a retreat to the frontier, which became a retreat to Mersa Matruh where he intended to stand and give battle. Once again Auchinleck took command of Eighth Army, relieving Ritchie, and brought order to the situation, taking the army back to the El Alamein line where the southern flank could not be turned by Rommel's armour.

When Tobruk surrendered Rommel's credit was high in Germany: the port seemed to have had the same mesmeric effect on Hitler as it did on Winston Churchill and the Führer promoted Rommel to the rank of field marshal, the youngest in the German army. Rommel was also authorized to continue his advance on Egypt in pursuit of Eighth Army. Always prepared to take risks, Rommel saw an opportunity to destroy Eighth Army and push through to the Nile Delta. Mussolini was so impressed by Rommel's plan that he flew to Libya with a white charger on which to make a triumphal entry into Alexandria and Cairo while a medal to mark the conquest of Egypt was struck for issue to Axis forces. On previous occasions Rommel had overcome his supply problems by using captured British material – he included Stuart tanks in his own headquarters – and he continued to do so: much of *Panzerarmee*'s transport was captured, built either in Britain or Detroit, and his artillery included captured British weapons, for which there were adequate stocks of ammunition.

Field Marshal Albert Kesselring favoured an attack on Malta as he believed the island's capture would secure the North African theatre. Rommel had earlier agreed with Kesselring and with the decision to halt after the fall of Tobruk until Malta had been conquered. Plans had been made for the assault on Malta and additional forces brought in for it, including the Italian *Folgore* Parachute Division. While Malta remained unconquered Axis supply routes from Europe would not be safe from interdiction by British forces based there. However, Rommel's will prevailed when he appealed over the heads of his superiors, including Kesselring, to Hitler and Mussolini. Kesselring later noted that, when he visited 'the new Field Marshal at his HQ in Tobruk' on 22 June, he found him briefing his officers for an advance on Sidi Barrani that would begin that very morning. However, Kesselring wrote that such an advance coincided with his own 'view of things without prejudicing the attack on Malta'.[7]

The Axis advance went well initially, appearing to justify Rommel's decision. His forces swept south of the frontier defences and then towards the coast east of Sidi Barrani, which was reached at dusk on 24 June. In just twenty-four hours Rommel's forces had covered 100 miles. By nightfall on the 25th Axis troops were facing the Mersa Matruh defences. Eighth Army appeared to be in a 'state of rout and dissolution' with one observer claiming that he had not seen 'a formed unit of any kind'.[8] Since the opening of Rommel's offensive at Gazala Eighth Army had suffered some 80,000 casualties, mostly in prisoners. Before long, however, British resistance stiffened. Rommel was confident of reaching the Nile Delta by the end of the month: on 26 June he assured Kesselring, Cavallero and senior Italian commanders that such would be the result of a breakthrough on the frontier.

Part, at least, of the reason for Rommel being allowed to strike towards the Nile was that both Hitler and Mussolini baulked at the idea of an assault on Malta. The former recalled the losses suffered in the conquest of Crete while Mussolini had never been enthusiastic about the plan and the prospect of achieving his goal of Italian hegemony over Egypt seems to have woven an enchantment about him. Rommel's plan for an invasion of Egypt – something he had always wanted to do – fitted in with Hitler's dream of Plan ORIENT, in which German forces, having conquered the Middle East and taken control of its oil, could then provide the southern arm of a massive nutcracker movement in conjunction with a German southward drive through the Caucasus. Indeed, Rommel was a believer in Plan ORIENT. Hitler referred to the strategic possibilities in a letter to Mussolini written the day after Tobruk fell, an event that seems to have buoyed the Führer as much as it depressed Churchill. With the benefit of hindsight it is easy to dismiss such thinking as fanciful. It did not appear so in June and July 1942 and Ninth British Army in the Levant stood ready to meet a German attack from the north. On 28 June the German southern offensive opened in Russia and, by late August, German forces had passed through some of the mountain passes of the Caucasus to reach the Black Sea's east coast.

And so the *Panzerarmee* menaced Mersa Matruh on 25 June. But Eighth Army was no longer in Ritchie's hands. Auchinleck, who noted that, in armoured warfare, Eighth Army was still 'an amateur army fighting professionals',[9] had taken over as he had during CRUSADER. A new sense of purpose began to permeate Eighth Army. There would be no last stand at Mersa Matruh. The Auk had signalled General Sir Alan Brooke, Chief of the Imperial General Staff, that he was reasonably confident of defeating Rommel in time, although he did suggest that Brooke might wish to relieve him (Auchinleck) of his command. At 4.15am on the 26th Auchinleck issued the order for Eighth Army to withdraw to the Alamein positions that were being prepared by XXX Corps. He proposed to

keep all troops fluid and mobile, and strike at enemy from all sides. Armour not to be committed unless very favourable opportunity presents itself. At all costs and even if ground has to be given up [I]intend to keep 8th Army in being and to give no hostage to fortune in shape of immobile troops holding localities which can be easily isolated.[10]

Ritchie had deployed X Corps, brought in from Syria, in Matruh; the corps included 10th Indian and 50th (Northumbrian) Divisions. Lieutenant General Sir Bernard Freyberg's 2nd New Zealand Division was at Minqar Qaim, their commander having refused to be locked up in Matruh, and 29 Indian Brigade held the Sidi Hamza box while two battlegroups, Gleecol and Leathercol, held Eighth Army's centre. XIII Corps had become the army's mobile element and included 1st Armoured Division with 159 tanks, deployed in open desert south of Minqar Qaim. Sixty of the division's tanks were the American Grants with their 75mm main armament, capable of taking on the German tanks. (However, the Grant had a serious flaw: its main gun was in a side sponson on the tank's hull which not only meant limited traverse but also required the high-profile tank to expose itself before it could fire; Grants could not fire their main guns from true hulldown positions.) This armoured force had been created as a result of Auchinleck's scouring his Middle East command for tanks.

In a signal to Brooke Auchinleck noted that his plan of defence was based on employing the maximum amount of artillery, kept fully mobile, with the minimum number of infantry needed for local protection.

Armour in reserve only to be used if circumstances are favourable as to make success reasonably certain. Matruh ... is not essential and will not be allowed to become a trap .... Intention is to keep Army in being at all costs and this entails fullscale mobility and readiness to fight fluid battle unimpaired by necessity for defending fortified positions .... .[11]

Rommel moved against the Mersa Matruh positions on the morning of the 26th, attacking before dawn. Anxious to make best speed he sent his forces forward without full reconnaissance, expecting to meet a continuously held front line, into the centre of which he sent 90th Light and 21st Panzer Divisions. Both pushed through the gap between the Indians and New Zealanders and, in the evening, elements of 90th Light were wheeling left for the coast east of Matruh. Throughout the 27th there was confused fighting with Strafer Gott's XIII Corps attempting to conduct the mobile defence ordered by Auchinleck. The Axis advance began losing momentum as it met increasingly stubborn resistance. Kesselring commented: 'But soon the resistance stiffened to such an extent that we had to envisage throwing in fresh troops or speeding up the refreshment of old formations. The fighting became tougher ....'[12]

It has often been said that the British soldier is at his most courageous in circumstances such as those he now faced. There were many individual acts of courage and of stubborn determination not to be beaten. This was true not only of the infantry but also of the gunners and, perhaps especially, of those manning anti-tank guns in Royal Artillery regiments and infantry battalions. A number of artillery units from 12 Anti-Aircraft Brigade, with other gunner units and some infantry under command, were falling back in a series of rearguard actions on desert landing grounds and fighting in good order. Eighth Army headquarters assigned two infantry brigades to this body, known as Calforce; it held defensive positions at ten landing grounds with all its artillery support coming from anti-aircraft guns sited for ground tasks. So successful was Calforce that it was retained throughout the July battles at El Alamein and not withdrawn until September after the battle of Alam el Halfa.

As the panzers advanced they met frequent stubborn resistance as anti-tank gunners strove to slow their progress. South of Mersa Matruh, on the morning of 27 June, 9th Durham Light Infantry was attacked by enemy armour. One DLI company position was covered by a single 2-pounder anti-tank gun on a forward slope in front of the position and the gunners did their utmost to prevent the enemy engaging the company boarding vehicles to quit the position. An enemy tracked vehicle, towing a light gun, approached the position and opened fire. The men on the 2-pounder responded and damaged the tractor. Then another enemy light gun was brought forward to bombard the Durhams' 2-pounder and their fire killed or wounded all the gunners. But one man, Private Adam Wakenshaw from Newcastle, continued to fire the 2-pounder although his left arm had been torn off above the elbow by enemy fire. From a family of thirteen, Wakenshaw had tried to enlist in 1930, when he was sixteen, but his mother brought him home; he finally joined up on 11 November 1940. Less than two years later his Army career would end in an act of outstanding gallantry in the Egyptian desert.

In spite of his horrific wound Wakenshaw crawled back to his gun and, with his good arm, loaded and fired it no fewer than five times. He damaged one of the two enemy guns but was then knocked over by a shellburst and badly wounded again. Not to be deterred, he dragged himself back to the 2-pounder and managed to place a round in the breech but, before he could fire, the gun received a direct hit and was destroyed. Adam Wakenshaw was killed outright but his courage had allowed his company to escape. On 8 September 1942 Adam

Wakenshaw's courage and self-sacrifice were recognized when the *London Gazette* carried the announcement that he had been awarded a posthumous Victoria Cross. He is buried in El Alamein war cemetery.[13]

Nor was Wakenshaw the sole Durham showing great courage that day. Two other battalions of the regiment were also engaged with Axis armour, the first being the 8th which was attacked from the south-west by captured Stuart tanks; these were driven off after five of them had been knocked out. An hour later, at 6.30am, HQ and B Companies of 6th Durhams were attacked by two enemy self-propelled guns and several armoured cars. In a two-hour battle the Durhams fought off the enemy, destroying an SPG, an armoured car and two other vehicles but with the loss of fourteen men killed, another fourteen wounded and fifty-three missing. The three Durham battalions formed 151 Brigade of 50th Division in X Corps.

Freyberg's New Zealanders were cut off for over a day and suffered some 800 casualties in fierce fighting – Freyberg himself was wounded – and 4 New Zealand Brigade fought its way out at bayonet-point during the night of the 27th/28th. X Corps HQ lost contact with Eighth Army HQ for nine hours and only when communications had been restored between Army and X Corps – at 4.30am on the 28th – did the latter discover that XIII Corps had already withdrawn. Gott had ordered his corps to move eastwards during that night, which it did, against strong opposition. Communications breakdowns continued: X Corps slipped out of its positions that night to make for high ground from where it would turn east and rally at El Daba. The corps commander, Holmes, was told by Auchinleck that XIII Corps would cover his withdrawal but that cover did not materialize due to another breakdown in communications. In its withdrawal X Corps became scattered and there was

a spirited rough and tumble. Nearly every column ran across an enemy leaguer at one point or another and the confusion on both sides was indescribable. To break clear was made still more difficult by the presence of the enemy at Fuka, and the 10th Indian Division suffered particularly heavy losses in men and vehicles. General Holmes's Corps Headquarters barged its way through, like the rest, and was sent back to take over the 'Delta Force', which was being hastily formed, while the two divisions set about re-forming in rear of the El Alamein positions.[14]

X Corps was scattered to such an extent that Auchinleck had to adjust his plans for occupying the Alamein positions. On 29 June he ordered XXX Corps, now including 1st South African, 10th Indian and 50th Divisions, to take over the right sector of the line, pinned on the coast around El Alamein, while XIII Corps, with 2nd New Zealand and 5th Indian Divisions, took the left sector, pinned on the Qattara Depression. Both armoured divisions, 1st and 7th, were to be held in Army Reserve; 7th was an armoured formation on paper only, most of its tanks having been lost in the battles since Gazala; the division's history notes that at one stage in the retreat 3rd/5th Royal Tanks had only wheeled vehicles.[15]

Eighth Army's soldiers were exhausted. Stuart Hamilton, a troop commander in 8th Royal Tanks, who had fought through all those battles, described that exhaustion.

> You know that marvellous feeling you have, just before you wake up in the morning, when you are semi-conscious, and you sort of stretch luxuriously – well, I remember doing that and feeling the heat of the sun on my face and I could hear someone whistling and there was the marvellous smell of bacon being cooked when I suddenly sat bolt upright and thought, 'God Almighty! I never went on sentry duty! That bloody man Simpkins fell asleep and he never woke me up!'

Hamilton woke Sergeant Simpkins and berated him for his failure.

> He was an awful looking sight, he was unshaven, dirty with red-rimmed eyes and both his hands were bandaged with desert sores. He looked up at me blearily and then rather angrily said, 'I bloody well woke you Sir.' 'No you didn't' I said. 'Yes I did!' he said, 'I woke you up twice.' I said. 'What!'

Sergeant Simpkins had indeed woken his troop commander twice. On the first occasion Hamilton had sworn at him angrily and then said irritably, 'Oh! Alright!' but as Simpkins walked away he looked back and saw that Hamilton had fallen asleep again. He woke him once more and this time, just before he got into his own blankets, looked across and saw Hamilton putting on one of his desert boots. It was on hearing this that Stuart Hamilton remembered that when he woke up he had found one leg out of his blankets with a desert boot on the foot. He realized that he had fallen asleep yet again and had not gone on guard duty. Had there been a German breakthrough, and had he survived, Hamilton would have been court-martialled and 'wouldn't have had a leg to stand on'.

How on earth could I have possibly expected, several weeks later, for anyone on the court who was fresh from a good night's sleep, bathed, shaved, in clean clothes, to understand that I was completely at the end of my tether, that I was not compos mentis and that I was simply and utterly exhausted both physically and mentally – as indeed we all were. Most certainly I would have been for the high jump.[16]

And the strain that led to such exhaustion was to continue in the weeks ahead. Field Marshal Lord Carver, then a major in XXX Corps headquarters, noted that, when he arrived at Alamein, he calculated that he had averaged only two-and-a-half hours' sleep per day in the month since the attack at Gazala.[17]

As formations and units arrived at El Alamein, order was being restored from the chaos of retreat. Auchinleck was determined to stop Rommel on the Alamein line, fighting *Panzerarmee* with balanced forces, and then moving to the offensive. In Eighth Army's Operations Order No.83 the Auk made clear his intention to 'stop the enemy's Eastward advance and defeat him in the area El Alamein-Naqb Dweiss-Ras El Qattara'.[18] Auchinleck's leadership of Eighth Army was invigorating. Air Chief Marshal Tedder, commanding the Royal Air Force in the Middle East, noted the change in atmosphere as soon as Auchinleck relieved Ritchie.

I was much impressed by the contrast between his calm authority and Ritchie's fumbling. Auchinleck had grasped the essentials of a most confused situation in about two hours .... I felt that passive bewilderment was being replaced by active command.[19]

Early in the morning of Wednesday 1 July *Afrikakorps* tanks reached the front before El Alamein and Axis artillery opened fire on Eighth Army's forward positions. They were met with British fire in response. Rommel's former aide, Heinz Werner Schmidt, summarized the clash.

Our own artillerymen found an observation post on a ridge named Tel el Eisa. An armoured reconnaissance vehicle came rushing up. In it was Rommel himself. He gave orders for the troops to attack the northern sector of what appeared to be the new enemy line, taking advantage of the sinking sun. Infantry of the 90th Light, supported by a few pieces of artillery, went forward. They were met by machine-gun fire, detrucked and dug in under cover of their own vehicles.[20]

What had become known as the first battle of El Alamein had begun although, as Schmidt noted, those present 'did not know it'. As the guns roared at Alamein there was every appearance of panic in Cairo where both GHQ and the British Embassy were burning confidential documents. Smoke rose from chimneys in 'an amazing sight' and the pieces of charred or burnt paper floating through the hot Cairene air ensured that the day would become known as 'Ash Wednesday'. Personnel at GHQ and RAF HQ were told to prepare for evacuation to Palestine. The Mediterranean Fleet abandoned Alexandria harbour and British civilians were evacuated, including the Missionary Franciscan Sisters of the Sacred Heart Convent on Alexandria's Rue Tanis, who were removed to Palestine.[21]

Sir Claude Auchinleck remained calm and unflustered. Rommel, on the other hand, knew that time was running out for his gamble. However, he was aware, from intelligence sources, of the panic in Cairo and must have believed that there was still the opportunity to best the British and conquer Egypt. It was then that he made one of his most serious mistakes. It is an old but, nonetheless, true military maxim that 'time spent in reconnaissance is seldom wasted' although, from his experience on 1 July, Rommel might well have suggested substituting the word 'never' for 'seldom'. Many times before he had sacrificed adequate reconnaissance to momentum and exploitation and he tried to do so again at Alamein. His plan was straightforward and, on paper, sound. *Afrikakorps* and 90th Light would drive south of the defensive perimeter around El Alamein and north of Deir el Abyad and Deir el Shein, after which *Afrikakorps* and XX Italian Corps, would wheel right to cut off XIII Corps by advancing twenty-two miles in the dark to Alam Nayil in the south. At the same time, 90th Light, supported by Italian infantry, would wheel left – northwards – and race for the coast to cut off the El Alamein box from the east. A repeat of his plan at Matruh, Rommel intended to get his troops in the rear of the British which, he was convinced, would cause their defence to collapse.

> In view of our experiences at Matruh I think that this plan offered a real hope of victory. The German forces were too weak for any heavy fighting, but they were still capable of manoeuvre. It is quite possible that if Rommel had got his divisions across the British rear, they would have been stampeded once more into a headlong flight.[22]

However, the plan made no allowances for the presence of 1st South African Division's brigades in the very area where 90th Light would begin its wheel to the sea – and the South Africans had a mission to avenge the loss of 2nd

South African Division in Tobruk. Rommel's failure to make time for adequate reconnaissance was to have dire consequences for 90th Light as the Germans were unaware of the positions of the South African brigades. The division, its soldiers as exhausted as those of Eighth Army, arrived in its assembly area in good time but soon lost direction – a sandstorm caused problems for 90th Light and *Afrikakorps* – and blundered into the defences around El Alamein instead of skirting them. Not until early afternoon did 90th Light resume its advance, using the cover of dust to extricate itself from the Alamein defences. But it was a case of frying pans and fires as it then ran into intense South African artillery fire, which seems to have been too much for its soldiers. General Frido von Mellenthin described it as

A crescent of fire from the 1st, 2nd and 3rd SA Brigades and their supporting artillery, and [90th Light] was thrown into confusion not far removed from panic. Rommel himself went to 90th Light to try and urge the division forward but the volume of fire was so heavy that even he was pinned down.[23]

When 90th Light informed Rommel's headquarters of their plight, exacerbated by the fact that their divisional artillery was not battleworthy, Rommel sent in *Kampfstaffel* Kiel south of the division. Driving up in an armoured car to see the situation for himself, he was left in no doubt that the South Africans were masters of the field.

Nor did *Afrikakorps* fare any better. Its day had not started well: at 1.30am on the 1st its headquarters reported that it would not be ready at the time ordered, 3.00am. A heavy sandstorm then frustrated matters and 15th and 21st Panzer Divisions became mixed up while elements of 1st Armoured Division were still moving back to the Alamein line on the same axis. By 6.00am confusion prevailed in *Afrikakorps'* ranks. When it seemed as if matters could get no worse for them the RAF ensured that they did: at 6.15am British aircraft struck heavily at the German armour. When the panzers finally moved forward they skirted Deir el Abyad but then discovered that Deir el Shein was in British hands. It was daylight and General Walter Nehring, *Afrikakorps'* commander, decided to attack the position, held by 18 Indian Brigade. This brigade, temporarily commanded by Lieutenant Colonel E.C. Gray of 2/3rd Gurkha Rifles, had recently arrived from Iraq and was under command of 1st South African Division whose engineers had helped the brigade in three days of digging and building defences that included a partial minefield. Two of the three battalions had never been in action and the brigade had no artillery although, on 30 June and into the early hours of 1 July, it received twenty-three 25-pounders, drawn from three field regiments, and the anti-tank company of the Buffs, plus sixteen of the new 6-pounder guns. There were also nine Matilda tanks, with scratch crews. Although there was a shortage of small-arms ammunition there was no shortage of courage, of which much would be demonstrated in the hours ahead.

Nehring's attack began with artillery firing at the Deir el Shein position and registering targets within it. A demand to surrender was rebuffed and a heavy bombardment began falling on 18 Brigade's positions. This was followed by infantry attacks. Under cover of clouds of dust German infantry gapped the minefield's north-east corner. Some dozen tanks passed through but met stern resistance and could make little headway until joined by a further eight at 4.00pm when the battle began to turn in the Germans' favour. Several anti-tank guns were disabled and, by 5.00pm, all the Matildas were knocked out. Much of 18 Brigade's position had also been overrun with the greatest weight of the *Afrikakorps*' attack falling on 2/5th Essex and 4/11th Sikhs; the third battalion of the brigade, 2/3rd Gurkhas, suffered little since the attack did not strike against their defensive locations.

> The casualties of 18 Indian Infantry Brigade during this hard fought action were severe. The whole of Brigade HQ was lost as was 2/5 Essex, save for a dozen men. 4/11 Sikh Regt lost 7 British officers and 509 men, 2/3 GR 1 officer and 228 men. 21 25-pdr guns, 21 6-pdr and 14 2-pdr were lost, three, five and seven of these natures respectively managing to get clear. It later became apparent that the Brigade had in fact delayed for a day almost the whole of the remaining German armoured forces, amounting to some 55 tanks.[24]

During the battle at Deir el Shein 1st Armoured Division was ordered to intervene. It was hardly in a fit state to do so, having arrived at Alamein almost side-by-side with *Afrikakorps*, and was in need of replenishment of both fuel and ammunition. One of its brigades was in serious trouble: 4 Armoured Brigade had been moving south of the El Alamein box when it sank into soft sand. At 1.30pm XXX Corps learned, through 1st South African Division, that Deir el Shein was under attack and ordered 1st Armoured to assist. However, an hour later, armoured cars reported that all appeared quiet but, another two hours on, came an urgent order to intervene and 22 Armoured Brigade moved out – 4 Armoured was still stuck in the sand south-east of the Alamein box –

and met part of 15th Panzer with which it clashed south of Deir el Shein. The Germans were driven off.

The tenacity of 18 Indian Brigade was crucial. Both prongs of Rommel's pincer movement had been fought to a halt. Rommel himself had travelled by armoured car between 90th Light and *Afrikakorps* and felt the full vigour of the defence that faced his men; he believed Deir el Shein to be held by a division, such was the ferocity of that defence.[25] The torrents of fire falling on the Axis soldiers were such that, at one stage, Rommel and Colonel Bayerlein, his chief of staff, had to lie in the open for two hours.[26] He must have regretted bitterly his failure to make a proper reconnaissance. Rommel's gamble had failed. The stubborn courage of 18 Indian Brigade meant that the *Panzerarmee* would not be sweeping up Eighth Army. On the rocks and dust of Deir el Shein, and in the blood shed by Indian and British soldiers, Rommel's vision of breaking through to Alexandria and Cairo had perished.

Next day the fighting continued.

Chapter Two

Race for the Nile

Perish the man whose mind is backward now

T
he Desert Air Force had supported the ground forces effectively on the retreat to Alamein, leapfrogging from landing ground to landing ground as Axis troops drew closer. They had also played their part in the actions of 1 July, although restricted by confusion on the ground. Nonetheless, the effects of air action had been significant: *Afrikakorps* complained of having been bombed many times during the 1st and were bitter about the Luftwaffe's absence. During the night Axis supply columns were hit hard by bombing. Rommel's logistical situation was worsening with fuel and ammunition supplies running low.[1]

In such a situation most generals would have considered waiting until the supply situation had improved. Few would have chosen to continue the offensive, with all its risks. However, that is exactly what Rommel did. While he may have been influenced by news from Kesselring that the Royal Navy had left Alexandria, when 90th Light was again sent to ground by sustained artillery and machine-gun fire Rommel realized a change of plan was necessary and withdrew *Afrikakorps* from its effort to sweep round Eighth Army's rear. Instead it would participate in the attempt to break through to the coast road east of El Alamein in a fresh attack that afternoon.[2]

Eighth Army was also preparing to attack *Panzerarmee*. Auchinleck had ordered XIII Corps to attack towards Deir el Abyad with 1st Armoured Division striking westwards from south of Ruweisat Ridge while the remainder of the corps struck northwards. Both attacks were launched almost simultaneously and virtually cancelled each other out. Rommel's attack was blunted by 1 South African Brigade and Robcol, an ad-hoc column from 10th Indian Division; Ackcol, from 50th Division, later replaced the South Africans.[3] British bombers hit 90th Light, the formations of aircraft being dubbed 'party-rally raids' by the Germans, who were reminded of formation flypasts at pre-war Nazi Party rallies.[4] Although the bombers struck at regular intervals, as little as twenty minutes, there were few casualties since 90th Light was well dispersed.

However, morale suffered badly and there were further complaints about the Luftwaffe's absence.[5]

Afrikakorps' armour clashed with two British armoured brigades: 15th Panzer met 4 Armoured south of Ruweisat Ridge; 21st Panzer met 22 Armoured. The panzer divisions were but shadows of their former selves, their tank state being down to only twenty-six runners. (There were many more Italian tanks but these were thinly armoured and lightly armed.) The armoured battle lasted until dark when *Afrikakorps* withdrew south of Deir el Shein, leaving the British tanks holding the field; they had been supported well by artillery and by columns from 2nd New Zealand Division and 7 Motor Brigade. The bloody nose given to *Panzerarmee* on the 1st was being pummelled even more. But Rommel was not yet ready to admit defeat.

Among the anti-tank assets deployed by Eighth Army at this stage was a troop of 3.7-inch heavy anti-aircraft guns. One member of that troop, H.G. Harris, has left an account of the troop's actions. Harris, an operator fire control (OFC), was responsible for the gun-laying (GL) radar used to track aircraft which, on the Alamein line, was used to terrible effect against ground targets.

> We ... set up in front of a small hill. Put radar set up with guns deployed either side of us and no attempt ... to construct gunpits or any sort of defence. The only concession we made was to put out camouflage nets. Two days later we were ordered to stand to and start the [GL] set up, concentrating on ground targets and ignoring any air targets. With this set we had the outside telescope. ... We quickly found targets and the man on the telescope reported them as gun-towing 'Quads'. In fact they were Germans towing 88s. The 3.7 fires a shell weighing 52 lbs, has a muzzle velocity exceeding that of most anti-tank guns, and outranges the 88 by several thousand yards. Using the GL set we were able to ascertain the exact range within a yard or two and opened fire immediately. The initial targets were the vehicles. Then the guns; ... [we] wiped out the entire unit without coming under fire.[6]

The 3.7s then engaged two German tanks, believed to have been Mark IVs, which were hit by shells set to 'safe' to produce 'solid' shot. Both tanks were disabled. The troop continued in action against tanks and infantry for several days, using solid shot with some success. A system of 'skipping' rounds was also developed by the gunners, firing at the ground in front of a target so that the shell rose above the target to explode in the air, creating an airburst, which was devastating to soldiers in the open. The degree to which the 3.7s were used is indicated by the fact that all four weapons had barrel changes, the replacement barrels being fitted one at a time so that the troop would not have to go out of action.[7]

Aware that Rommel had a feeling for weakness in defensive dispositions, Auchinleck had begun improving the Alamein line. The term 'line' is a misnomer: Eighth Army held a series of defended localities rather than a continuous line but those to the south, in the area of Bab el Qattara and Naqb Abu Dweiss, were not ideal. Since these could be cut off the Auk decided to make his defences more compact by abandoning them: 6 NZ Brigade was withdrawn from Bab el Qattara, leaving only a column there, to prepare for a mobile role; 5th Indian Division was also to ready itself for mobile work at Qaret el Himeimat.

On the morning of the 3rd Rommel made a probing attack to detect weak spots in Eighth Army's defences: his general plan was for *Afrikakorps* to renew its eastward move, with XX Italian Corps on its right flank; X Italian Corps would hold El Mreir. But, as we have seen, *Afrikakorps'* two armoured divisions could muster only twenty-six tanks while 4 Armoured Brigade deployed sixty-three and 22 Armoured had fifty-six; the heavy Grants accounted for thirty-eight of the British tanks. Not only was Rommel weak in tanks but his fuel stocks had suffered from night bombing by the RAF whose aircraft had concentrated on Axis fuel and ammunition dumps near the coast: one Wellington bomber was destroyed in the explosion caused by its own bombs at Ras Gibeisa.[8]

Auchinleck had made some changes in his dispositions: 1st Armoured Division came under XXX Corps' command while XIII Corps was ordered to advance north-west of Deir el Shein to threaten Rommel's rear. As the Axis forces attacked, however, the British armour stood its ground south of Ruweisat, drawing the Germans on to their lines; Eighth Army was repaying Rommel in his own tactical coin. For ninety minutes the armour fought until *Afrikakorps'* soldiers could take no more; Rommel's assault had been held. That day RAF aircraft flew some 900 sorties – 770 by machines of the Desert Air Force – and although the Luftwaffe carried out operations these were less than one in four of those performed by their foes, who had been bombing at the rate of ten tons per hour.[9] To the south, in XIII Corps' area, New Zealand columns opened fire on Italian infantry and *Ariete* Division's artillery, which was advancing on *Afrikakorps'* flank. An exchange of fire began soon after 7.00am in which the Italians came off worse: 19th NZ Battalion put in an attack that overran part of *Ariete* and took 350 prisoners, forty-four guns and much other equipment and vehicles. Then followed an operation by 5 NZ Brigade which deployed to cut off *Ariete*'s retreat and attacked El Mreir, held by *Brescia* Division; the brigade seized a position near the western extremity of the depression.[10]

That night Rommel signalled to OKH (*Oberkommando des Heeres* – German army supreme command) his intention to go on to the defensive and remain so 'for at least a fortnight' since his divisions were reduced to 1,200 to 1,500 men each, while his artillery ammunition was almost exhausted. His supply problem was also emphasized because RAF interdiction had closed almost completely the road and tracks that his vehicles would use.[11] Nor was the Western Desert Railway of much use to him: the British had destroyed all the locomotives and, although some diesel locomotives were shipped across later, the rolling stock – about 300 wagons abandoned at El Daba during Eighth Army's retreat – had suffered considerably from the attentions of Allied aircraft with few serviceable wagons surviving.[12]

Rommel wrote that Auchinleck was 'handling his forces with very considerable skill and tactically better than Ritchie had done'[13] and was not allowing himself to be pushed into an undesirable situation. That evening Rommel decided to withdraw his mobile forces for regrouping, replacing them with Italian infantry. Kesselring commented:

> The battles at El Alamein brought the offensive to a standstill and threw us back on the defensive. … Our army and air force were both winded; they stood in need of an immediate flow of reinforcements and material. In addition, Rommel was clamouring for new formations … .[14]

It can be argued that this was the moment when Rommel accepted defeat, although he may not have realized it at the time. His decision to maintain the defensive for at least two weeks was, in practice, an admission of defeat. As Ronald Lewin commented, 'the essence of mobile operations is motion, and the most difficult problem is to get on the move again after a decisive halt.'[15] Rommel had always been prepared to take risks with his supplies, to the extent that some of his critics suggest that he did not appreciate the science of logistics, in contrast to other commanders who wanted to be assured that they were well supplied before moving. Most British commanders of the war come into the second category and General Montgomery, whom we shall meet shortly, suffered, in Lewin's words, from 'an obsessive preoccupation with his supply-train' that made him hesitate to advance even when advantage favoured him.[16] Within the next few days, Auchinleck would convince Rommel that, for *Panzerarmee Afrika*, the time for taking risks had passed.

Throughout most of July the two armies tussled along the El Alamein-Qattara line. However, both were tired and the battles in the heat of that summer can be compared to two exhausted heavyweights slugging at each other in the hope of landing a telling blow. There were to be no telling blows in this bout.

Realizing that Rommel's forces were tired, at the end of a very long supply line and lacking armour and fuel, Auchinleck continued pressing hard. On 4 July he thought that Rommel might be considering retreat but the Desert Fox was regrouping: the Italian X and XXI Corps replaced *Afrikakorps*, 90th Light Division and XX Corps over a period of some days, in spite of receiving almost constant pounding from Allied aircraft. However, all but the western tip of Ruweisat Ridge, that much fought-over feature, was in Eighth Army's hands by evening on the 4th. That night Auchinleck stressed to his commanders the importance of allowing the enemy no rest; but his formations moved too slowly. The Auk had hoped that XIII Corps might outflank the enemy and strike northwards against Rommel's lines of communication. That did not happen; although formations moved into forming-up positions for a renewed British offensive their deployment was too slow. Auchinleck, aware that his commanders were worn out, replaced Norrie with Ramsden at the head of XXX Corps, although he left Gott in command of XIII Corps. (In his book *El Alamein: Ultra and the Three Battles*, Alexander McKee recounts how Auchinleck was seen talking to soldiers on the ground and encouraging them to give their best. McKee comments that the Auk was prepared to take command even at battalion level to keep a grip on the situation.) Such slow reaction from Eighth Army gave Rommel some respite which he used to advantage; on 6 July he increased his tank strength to forty-four, laid down more minefields and received fresh supplies of artillery ammunition.[17]

Appreciating that Eighth Army lacked the strength to sweep around the Axis south-west flank, Auchinleck determined on a less ambitious offensive for which he drew up plans during the 6th and 7th. During the night of 8/9 July the New Zealanders were withdrawn from the Bab el Qattara box, leading Rommel to assume that another British retreat had begun. He ordered *Littorio* Division to occupy the area vacated by the New Zealanders, ready for a general advance to begin on the 10th. Rommel was now spreading his forces over too great an area while his rival was concentrating his to the north: reinforcements were arriving for Eighth Army, including 8th Indian and 9th Australian Divisions; the latter moved into XIII Corps' area.[18] New formations were arriving in the Middle East, or were en route from Britain, including 8th Armoured Division, which had already arrived (while at sea, 8th Armoured Division, less 24 Armoured

Brigade, was diverted to Australia to meet the threat of a Japanese invasion but the US Navy victory at Midway led to those orders being cancelled and the division was brought back to Aden), and 10th Armoured Division, which had moved from Palestine.[19] En route from the United Kingdom were two fresh British infantry divisions, 44th (Home Counties) and 51st (Highland), the latter due in August. However, Auchinleck could not forget his overall responsibility as Commander-in-Chief Middle East: he had also to consider his northern flank and the possibility of a German attack on the Gulf oilfields through the Caucasus. It seemed as if only Russian resistance at Stalingrad was preventing the German armies from striking south, and there was doubt about the capacity of the Soviet forces to sustain that resistance.

On 8 July, with his eye fixed firmly on the Eighth Army front, Auchinleck ordered General Ramsden to plan the capture of two Italian-held features west of El Alamein itself: Tel el Eisa and Tel el Makh Khad. The attacks would be carried out by 9th Australian and 1st South African Divisions, with mobile groups preventing the Italians being reinforced from the south. The operation would begin with an artillery bombardment at 3.30am on 10 July. At much the same time as Auchinleck and Ramsden were preparing this attack, Rommel, his readiness to take risks seemingly undiminished, was planning a further advance. After visiting Bab el Qattara on 9 July to supervise preparations for an armoured attack from the southern end of the line, he told General von Bismarck, commanding 21st Panzer Division, that his tanks would soon be driving into the Nile Delta. Thus it was that the British bombardment in the early morning of the 10th, and the attacks on the Italians, surprised him.[20]

Rommel's reaction was fast: he rushed northwards to help the Italians with a battlegroup from 15th Panzer Division but, by 7.30am, Australian troops had cleared positions east of the railway and their South African comrades were on their first objective near Tel el Makh Khad. Some three hours later the position was in South African hands and Italian troops of *Sabratha* Division were fleeing in panic in a rout that almost led to the capture of *Panzerarmee* headquarters,

on the coast, only a few miles behind the front, and early that morning I was startled to see hundreds of Italians rushing past the headquarters in the final stages of panic and rout. Rommel had spent the night in the Qaret el Abd box, far to the south, and it was for me [von Mellenthin] to decide what to do. When a headquarters is threatened the first instinct is to move and safeguard its irreplaceable equipment and documents. It was clear to me, however, that *Sabratha* was finished – their artillery was already 'in the bag' – and something must be done immediately to close the road to the west. I called on the staff and personnel of headquarters to form a rough battle line, which I strengthened with our anti-aircraft guns and some infantry reinforcements which happened to arrive; we succeeded in holding the Australians, who had captured the mounds of Tel el Eisa, and were seeking to thrust up the coast road.[21]

Although the worst was averted this clash had serious consequences for *Panzerarmee*. Lieutenant Seebohm, the 'brilliant head' of Rommel's Wireless Intercept Section, was killed in the fighting and most of his unit suffered a similar fate.[22] This loss meant that Rommel's intelligence from wireless intercepts, hitherto a most valuable asset, was never to be of the same standard again. In spite of the gallant defence by *Panzerarmee*'s headquarters, and a counter-attack by 15th Panzer's battlegroup, Tel el Eisa fell to the Australians in the early hours of 11 July.

Rommel was also losing the air battle to the Desert Air Force. The Luftwaffe's chief in North Africa, General Hoffmann von Waldau, complained on 3 July about lack of co-operation between *Panzerarmee* and the Luftwaffe.[23] He would have more cause for complaint throughout July as the advantage in the air moved to the British, even though 113 British aircraft were lost against ninety-eight Axis, of which eighty were German. Although, on the British side, the long trek back from Gazala had allowed the arrangements for army/air co-operation to degrade, these began stabilizing during July; it would, however, be some time before full efficiency would be attained. The retreat to El Alamein also meant that the Desert Air Force had lost its forward landing grounds and thus its wings and squadrons had to 'squat' on bases behind the line where there were not enough airfields to accommodate all the aircraft in Egypt. To remedy this problem, medium and heavy bombers were relocated to Palestine; light bombers and fighters took over the airfields around Amiriya with their main bases at Cairo and in the Canal Zone.[24]

In spite of such disadvantages the airmen achieved remarkable results during July; aircraft in Egypt and the Levant flew almost 15,400 sorties between 1 and 27 July, not including attacks on enemy shipping.[25] That represented an average of 570 sorties each day in support of Eighth Army. Small wonder that, in his *Despatch*, Auchinleck wrote:

Our air forces could not have done more than they did to support and sustain the Eighth Army in its struggle. Their effort was continuous by day and night, and the effect on the enemy was tremendous. I am certain that, had it not been for their devoted and exceptional efforts, we should not have been able to stop the enemy on the El Alamein position, and I wish to record my gratitude and that of the whole of the Eighth Army to Air Chief Marshal Tedder,* Air Marshal Coningham, and the air forces under their command.[26]

Air operations fell into three general categories: interdiction of enemy supply lines; operations against Axis air forces, in the air and on the ground; and ground support. These last operations were especially important whenever Eighth Army was attacking or being attacked. In addition, there were bombing raids on Benghazi, Tobruk and Mersa Matruh while Heraklion and Suda Bay in Crete were occasional targets and there were many reconnaissance flights of varying natures – strategic, tactical, meteorological, photographic and survey.[27]

Good army/air co-operation was achieved in spite of the fact that Auchinleck was controlling operations from an advanced HQ near El Imayid, about fifteen miles east of El Alamein, whereas Coningham's air HQ was some forty miles away, close to Eighth Army's Main HQ at Amiriya. The tactical situation improved as the month wore on and information from ground units played an increasingly important part in allowing aircraft to operate much closer to British positions. In turn, the soldiers on the ground appreciated this.[28] It was not appreciated by Axis troops, however, who took to dispersing their vehicles more widely during daylight hours. Since British air operations had become round-the-clock affairs, concentrations of vehicles in leaguer, or undergoing maintenance, found themselves lit up by flares dropped by Fleet Air Arm Albacores and pounded by Wellington bombers. Although the RAF suffered a shortage of fighter aircraft, the Axis noted no diminution of 'flying ability or combat performance'.[29] The arrival of Spitfires in Egypt increased the effectiveness of the Desert Air Force and improved morale amongst its airmen.

XXX Corps' attack at Tel el Eisa was followed by further offensives. Noting that Italian morale was shaky, Auchinleck decided to hit at the Italian formations. He told Roger Parkinson that he was ascertaining the locations of Italian troops and then hitting them as hard as possible, thereby further lowering their morale and reducing overall Axis strength.[30] Rommel's reaction, on 11 and 12 July, of sending German troops to bolster the Italians was noted as a validation of the

---

* Tedder was promoted to Air Chief Marshal on 1 July 1942.

tactic and plans were made for further attacks on Italian formations. The next targets, chosen by Auchinleck and his Deputy Chief of General Staff, Major General Eric Dorman-Smith, were *Pavia* and *Brescia* Divisions. This attack could also break through the Axis centre and destroy their forces east of the El Alamein-Abu Dweiss track and north of Ruweisat. As the New Zealanders and 5 Indian Brigade prepared for this operation, Rommel made another two unsuccessful attacks on the South Africans in the El Alamein box.[31]

The New Zealanders and Indians attacked at 4.30am on 15 July, making good initial progress. *Brescia* broke under the weight of the onslaught but the attack lost momentum through lack of artillery support and armoured back-up. The British armour had still to absorb fully the lessons of infantry/armour co-operation in spite of Auchinleck's efforts to cure that problem[*32] and, although Eighth Army took temporary possession of Ruweisat Ridge, 4 and 5 New Zealand Brigades were overrun. The commander of 5 NZ Brigade, Brigadier Howard Kippenberger, was scathing of the armour's role in this action:

[a]t this time there was throughout Eighth Army, not only in New Zealand Division, a most intense distrust, almost hatred, of our armour. Everywhere one heard tales of the other arms being let down; it was regarded as axiomatic that the tanks would not be where they were wanted in time.[33]

From the commander of 4 NZ Brigade, Kippenberger learned later that British tanks had sat 1,200 yards away and allowed a smaller number of German tanks to overrun 4 Brigade in spite of promises that the armour would assist the New Zealanders who held prisoner four Italian generals and what was believed to be a corps headquarters, all of whom were rescued by the panzers.[34] The New Zealanders and Indians had inflicted heavy casualties in the Italian ranks before coming under attack by battlegroups from 15th and 21st Panzer Divisions.

---

* These efforts had included the establishment of a higher-war course at Sarafand to train officers who were likely to become divisional commanders. Additional initiatives by Auchinleck to improve the effectiveness of leadership and training and bring about closer battlefield co-operation led to the expansion of the Staff College at Haifa where an RAF element was introduced to ensure closer inter-service co-operation. Throughout Middle East Command, all tactical and weapon training schools were ordered to 'ensure that a uniform doctrine, which took account of the characteristics of all three arms [artillery, armour and infantry] and was attuned to modern conditions, was taught under a single direction'.

Over four days of fighting the New Zealanders suffered over 1,400 casualties; 4 Brigade was not to see action again in North Africa, so serious were its losses. The British official historian notes that the New Zealand losses were 'aggravated by a bitter feeling that the Division had been let down by the Armour', although he goes on to comment that most things that went wrong were those that might be expected to go wrong in 'a complicated night action for which there has not been the time to prepare thoroughly'.[35]

The western end of Ruweisat had been retaken by the Axis but, on 17 July, a company from 4/6th Rajputana Rifles of 5 Indian Brigade moved into a position less than a mile west of Point 64. Next day they were followed by 2nd West Yorkshires, the remnants of 9 Indian Brigade, who, with support from a troop of 1st Light AA Regiment, a battery from 149th Anti-Tank Regiment and a 6th Rajput machine-gun company, recaptured the feature and drove off a determined counter-attack that included ten tanks.[36]

During the fighting of these mid-July days two New Zealanders earned the Victoria Cross. For one, Captain Charles Hazlitt Upham of the 20th Battalion (The Canterbury Regiment), it was his second VC, a Bar to the decoration gained in Crete a year before. Upham was the only man awarded a double VC during the Second World War. The citation for his Bar notes that, on 14/15 July

at El Ruweisat Ridge ... Captain Upham, in spite of being twice wounded, insisted on remaining with his men. Just before dawn he led his company in a determined attack, capturing the objective after fierce fighting; he himself destroyed a German tank and several guns and vehicles with hand grenades. Although his arm had been broken by a machine-gun bullet, he continued to dominate the situation and when at last, weak from loss of blood, he had his wounds dressed, he immediately returned to his men, remaining with them until he was again severely wounded and unable to move.[37]

Upham was later captured. New Zealand's second Victoria Cross of this battle went to Sergeant Keith Elliott of the 22nd Battalion* who gained his Cross on 15 July, leading his platoon in an attack in the face of sustained machine-gun and mortar fire. Although wounded in the chest

---

* After the war Keith Elliott chose to enter the Church and was ordained as a clergyman. The Revd Keith Elliott VC died in 1989, aged 73 years. Charles Upham VC and Bar died in 1994, aged 86 years.

he carried on and led seven men in a bayonet charge which resulted in the capture of four enemy machine-gun posts and an anti-tank gun, killing a number of the enemy and taking fifty prisoners. Although badly wounded in four places, Sergeant Elliott refused to leave his platoon until he had reformed them and handed over his prisoners, who by then amounted to 130.[38]

The Australians had renewed their offensive from Tel el Eisa on the 16th, completing the destruction of *Sabratha*. Although checked by a German counter-attack and heavy artillery fire, they moved forward again on the 17th and, with strong armour support, penetrated the front held by *Trieste* and *Trento* Divisions. Their advance might have gone farther but for the arrival of German reinforcements that launched counter-attacks that afternoon with Luftwaffe support. Eventually the Australians were pushed back, losing several hundred men as prisoners.

By now the battle had become one of attrition and, although Eighth Army was suffering heavy losses, von Mellenthin noted that *Panzerarmee* was undergoing a dangerous crisis.

> We were forced to introduce German units into the Italian divisional sectors to give them the required stiffening, and we sought by every means to improve our minefields and defences. British authorities have criticized Auchinleck for his persistent attacks in July 1942, but he was several times on the verge of a decisive success.[39]

Not only was *Panzerarmee* suffering from British attacks on the ground but pressure from the air continued taking its toll, both on Rommel's forces at the front and on their lines of communication. RAF and USAAF bombers carried out a daylight raid on Tobruk – the first such – on 17 July while over the three days of heavy ground fighting the Desert Air Force made almost 2,000 sorties.[40]

Auchinleck was now convinced that his foe was in very bad shape and especially did he believe that the Italians were about to collapse. Thus he considered that a strong attack in the centre could bring about a major defeat of Rommel's command. Much Axis artillery had been destroyed; about half their anti-tank guns were lost; manpower was reduced to about a third, with the Italians having lost the equivalent of four divisions in the days since 10 July; and by 21 July there were fewer than 100 Axis tanks.[41] Between 18 and 21 July Rommel was allowed something of a breather with Eighth Army's activities restricted to patrols and harassing fire. This gave the Axis an opportunity to strengthen their front for the inevitable assault, which Auchinleck planned for the evening of the 21st.

The main weight of the attack was to be borne by XIII Corps with 1st South African and 9th Australian Divisions playing major roles. By now both the New Zealand and 5th Indian Divisions were each reduced to two brigades. Also taking part were 1st and 7th Armoured Divisions and two fresh formations – 23 Armoured Brigade Group and 161 Indian Motor Brigade. XIII Corps was to break through at Deir el Shein and Deir el Abyad and exploit westwards while XXX Corps was 'to contain the enemy on its front by vigorous local action'.[42]

On the night of 21/22 July, Eighth Army attacked with 200 guns supporting the advancing troops; this considerable concentration of artillery presaged the bombardment that would open Operation LIGHTFOOT in October. Both 23 Armoured and 161 Indian Motor Brigades failed to gain lodgements in the Italian sector but 6 New Zealand Brigade reached the El Mreir depression to the south, only to come under determined German counter-attack in daylight. The panzers caught the New Zealanders in an exposed position at El Mreir and knocked out their anti-tank guns and the armoured vehicles of the armoured's liaison officers, destroying communication with the artillery. The brigade suffered badly.[43]

Minefields also helped blunt the offensive, nocturnal clearance operations having failed to secure lanes through them. British tanks were trapped and picked off by enemy anti-tank gunners and 21st Panzer Division. Ninety-three British tanks were lost, plus 2,000 infantrymen, almost 700 from 6 NZ Brigade.[44] At Tel el Eisa Private Arthur Stanley Gurney of 2/48th (South Australia) Battalion, Australian Imperial Force, earned a posthumous Victoria Cross – Australia's first of the desert war – when his company was held up by intense machine-gun fire that caused severe casualties, including all the company's officers. Undeterred, the 33-year-old Gurney,

> realizing the seriousness of the situation, charged the nearest machine-gun post, silencing the guns and bayoneting three of the crew. He bayoneted two more at a second post, and was then knocked down by a grenade but picked himself up and charged a third post. Nothing more was seen of him until later, when his body was found by his comrades, whose advance he had made possible.[45]

Although this phase of the July battles also failed to achieve a breakthrough, and continued showing up deficiencies in armour/infantry co-operation,

Auchinleck still believed that Eighth Army could break through and planned yet another attack in the northern sector, Operation MANHOOD, which opened on 26 July. The previous day, in a Special Order of the Day to Eighth Army, he told his soldiers:

> You have done well. You have turned a retreat into a firm stand and stopped the enemy on the threshold of Egypt. You have done more. You have wrenched the initiative from him by sheer guts and hard fighting and put HIM on the defensive in these last weeks. You have borne much but I ask you for more. We must not slacken. If we can stick it we will break him. STICK TO IT.[46]

Auchinleck might almost have been reading Rommel's letters home to his wife, Lu, (he was certainly privy, through ULTRA, to much of what the enemy commander was reporting to *OKH* in Germany) as the latter's correspondence was very pessimistic at this time. On 17 July he had written to Lu:

> Things are going downright badly for me at the moment, at any rate in the military sense. The enemy is using his superiority, especially in infantry, to destroy the Italian formations one by one, and the German formations are too weak to stand alone. It's enough to make one weep.[47]

On the 18th his letter was even gloomier.

> Yesterday was a particularly hard and critical day. We pulled through again, but it can't go on like this for long, otherwise the front will crack.[48]

In spite of Auchinleck's hopes, Operation MANHOOD floundered. Eighth Army's soldiers were extremely tired and, once again, lack of armoured support told. The infantry trudged forward with grim determination but suffered heavy losses and the day's fighting drew to an inconclusive close. As Philip Warner notes, the 300 Sherman tanks promised to Churchill by Roosevelt after the fall of Tobruk would have been a most valuable asset for the Auk.[49]

On 27 July Eighth Army went over to the defensive. The first battle of El Alamein was at an end and Auchinleck considered that he needed at least four additional divisions – two infantry and two armour – before renewing his offensive. He may not have broken Rommel but he had stopped him. He had saved Egypt. More importantly, he had saved Eighth Army. Perhaps the best summary comes from Rommel's despatch after the fighting of the 26th.

> Although the British losses in this Alamein fighting had been higher than ours, yet the price to Auchinleck had not been excessive, for the one thing that had mattered to him was to halt our advance, and that, unfortunately, he had done.[50]

Auchinleck had sown the seeds of victory but the harvest was to be reaped by another general whose name would forever be linked with that of El Alamein.

Chapter Three

Rommel's Last Try

The sun doth gild our armour

While Rommel had no doubt that Auchinleck had halted *Panzerarmee Afrika*'s advance, Winston Churchill did not share that view. Instead Churchill saw the July battles from a perspective that owed much to his political position. He had returned from the United States where he had learned, from Roosevelt, of the fall of Tobruk, to face a 'no confidence' vote in the Commons. Although that vote was defeated, Churchill believed that military failures had been responsible for its having been tabled and considered that he needed a victory. That Auchinleck gave him such a victory, albeit of a defensive nature but of strategic significance, during July did not impress the prime minister. The stubborn Irish general had lost the confidence of his prime minister for his 'refusal to accept … prodding' and had 'received a form of ultimatum' on 12 July, warning that, unless Rommel was defeated, Auchinleck's northern front, now under threat from the German advance in the Soviet Union, would not be strengthened.[1] Yet, on 17 July, Rommel told the Italian High Command: 'Any more blows like today and I do not anticipate being able to hold the situation.'

One of Auchinleck's biographers commented that:

> Churchill remained unable to see the fight for Egypt being won almost under his nose, and even Brooke [the CIGS] held fears for the desert battle and his friend's grip upon it. When, on 27 July, Auchinleck put the Eighth Army on the defensive once more, Churchill considered his signal announcing the decision to be 'very depressing'.[2]

By contrast Auchinleck was not depressed but planned an offensive to evict Rommel from Egypt. He was making plans for training and reinforcing Eighth Army for that operation, in which he was supported by his fellow-Irishman and acting chief of staff, Major General Eric Dorman-Smith, known as 'Chink'. Chink had been at the Auk's side during the retreat to Alamein, providing him with much advice and a seemingly-endless fund of optimism. (Dorman-Smith is usually criticized by writers of this period, often taking their cue from some of his contemporaries who had axes to grind. On the other side, Auchinleck's supporters do not always acknowledge Chink's work. Fortunately, an excellent and balanced biography of Chink, by Lavinia Greacen, *Chink*, does much to set the record straight.) Sir Francis de Guingand, whose abilities as a staff officer were identified first by Auchinleck, although his name is more closely connected with Montgomery, wrote of this period:

> to put the record straight – for there has been much controversy over this point – a great deal of the Staff's time was taken up in carrying out the studies necessary for producing plans for a future offensive against Rommel.[3]

On 27 July Dorman-Smith produced an 'Appreciation of the Situation in the Western Desert', presenting a remarkably accurate picture of forthcoming events. This appreciation, which noted Eighth Army's object as being 'The defence of Egypt by the defeat of the enemy forces in the Western Desert', included a summary of the existing situation, factors affecting operations – including comparative manpower and armour strengths, as well as morale and ground, political considerations and the linkage to the Russian front – summaries of courses open to both armies and of tactical techniques and future organization. He concluded that Eighth Army was committed temporarily to a defensive battle: it lacked the strength to dislodge the enemy and required re-equipment and training before being fit for offensive operations. Since neither side was likely to be reinforced strongly on land during August, he argued that no immediate offensive by either was likely, but an Axis offensive was possible towards the end of August. Provided there was no change in the land and air situation, Eighth Army would receive reinforcements of two armoured and two infantry divisions about mid-September, which might allow a new Allied offensive in late-September.[4]

One factor omitted by Dorman-Smith was the supply of Sherman tanks from the United States. Dorman-Smith quotes Eighth Army's heavy tank strength as 'some 60 Grant tanks' with another sixty due in early-August, but with no further tanks coming until September. However, Roosevelt had already promised 300 Shermans to Churchill and these, with a hundred M-7 105mm self-propelled howitzers (known as 'Priests' in British service, the soubriquet deriving from the mounting for an anti-aircraft machine gun which resembled a pulpit. A British-designed and built self-propelled 25-pounder, on a Valentine tank chassis, was already known as Bishop, 'for no accountable reason'[5] while the clerical theme continued with a Canadian variant, Sexton, a 25-pounder on a Ram chassis, and a self-propelled 6-pounder anti-tank gun, known as Deacon.) were en route from the USA, travelling in seven fast ships, one of which was sunk, to Egypt. Dorman-Smith seems to have been unaware of the promised Shermans which began arriving in Egypt at the beginning of September. They were not ready for battle until October; some units received new tanks on the opening day of the final battle.

Dorman-Smith's Appreciation has been criticized by a number of writers, most of whom choose to quote in isolation to advance arguments that ignore the document's main message. They also choose to ignore other factors that do not suit their own arguments, including the efforts made by Auchinleck and Dorman-Smith to improve training and, especially, co-operation between arms. Auchinleck has often been pilloried for allowing Eighth Army's formations to fight in small packets. Chief among his critics was Montgomery, who claimed that it was he who ordained that divisions should fight as divisions and not be broken up. Apart from the fact that divisions were broken up under Montgomery, it was Auchinleck and Dorman-Smith who espoused the principle that 'battles are best fought by divisions fighting as divisions or, better still, corps fighting as corps; but *mobile* divisions and corps'.[6]

Pitt points out that battlegroups were created at this time, giving the erroneous impression to some that the Jock Columns of 1941 had returned. However, the purpose of these battlegroups was to create mobility and ensure, as far as possible, that immobile infantry would not be retained at the front.

To promote better co-operation between arms, Auchinleck had already established a higher war course at Sarafand for officers likely to become divisional commanders, had expanded the Staff College at Haifa (adding an RAF wing to it) and had grouped in one area in Palestine all the tactical and weapon-training schools in Middle East Command 'to ensure that a uniform doctrine, which took account of the characteristics of all three arms and was attuned to modern conditions, was taught under a single direction'.[7]

Such changes take time and although there were improvements on the ground – artillery being used to much greater effect through concentration – these were not always noticeable to the average soldier. Animosity continued between infantryman and tankman, between tankman and gunner and between gunner and infantryman.

Air co-operation, however, was good. The airmen had provided excellent support in the withdrawal and, once the battle had become clearer on the ground, became an invaluable part of Eighth Army's fighting strength. Although Luftwaffe elements had been transferred to support Rommel, the RAF dominated the skies over the battlefield and was also providing first-class intelligence through tactical reconnaissance missions flown over enemy lines, much of them by the Hurricanes of No.208 Squadron RAF. Farther afield, RAF bombers continued pounding Axis supply ports while torpedo-bombers harassed convoys carrying supplies for Rommel.

In theory the Axis logistical situation should have been much better than that of the Allies: for the German and Italian armies, supplies had only to be ferried across the Mediterranean from Italy to North Africa whereas British supplies had to be shipped from the United Kingdom, North America, India or the southern hemisphere Dominions via South Africa to the Suez canal. However, the theoretical smoothness of the Axis logistical machine was abraded by the presence of a very hard piece of grit in its workings: Malta. We have seen how, after the fall of Tobruk, the Axis strategic imperative should have been the conquest of Malta but that Rommel persuaded the Führer otherwise and had been permitted to carry out Operation AIDA, which Auchinleck had stopped at El Alamein. Now Rommel's panzers thirsted for fuel that was being despatched to the bottom of the Mediterranean by the RAF and by British submarines operating from Malta, while his soldiers were short of food, clothing and ammunition for the same reasons. Captured British stores could only provide so much. Malta was strangling the Axis endeavours in North Africa. Hitler and his generals would have done well to recall Napoleon's axiom that 'I would rather see the English on the heights of Montmartre than in possession of Malta'.

Those endeavours had also suffered from errors made by German planners. Taking Italian advice, they had not sent diesel-engined vehicles to Africa, although such engines were better suited to desert conditions than petrol engines. Nor, initially, had they adapted their vehicles, including tanks, for desert conditions while their soldiers never achieved the same level of familiarity with desert conditions as did their British counterparts. Among the worst examples of bad German planning was the failure to supply fuel oil for cooking or workshop furnaces, relying instead on wood shipped from Italy in space that could have better used.[8] Even though many of these problems had been overcome by the summer of 1942, they reveal a logistical weakness that cannot be laid entirely at Rommel's door.

Having read and accepted Dorman-Smith's Appreciation, although he initially refused to agree it because '*it did not contain a sufficient offensive spirit*',[9] [author's italics] Auchinleck then sent off his own, regular, report to London in which he noted that 'We must now stand on the defensive and recruit our strength for a new and decisive effort', which was not likely before mid-September. Winston Churchill, far from pleased with this prediction, decided to fly out to Egypt and assess the situation himself. Brooke, already planning such a trip, had suspected that Churchill was 'very intent on following along close behind me if possible' and learned on 30 July that 'Winston had decided to follow me at once to the Middle East'.[10] Churchill had wanted Auchinleck to come to London but the latter had refused to do so while fighting raged along the El Alamein line. Now the two would meet in Egypt.

Brooke arrived in Egypt a scant thirty minutes before Churchill and began a round of visits and meetings, including one with Auchinleck. He also met General Corbett, Chief of the General Staff in Cairo, with whom he was unimpressed, deciding that he was not fit for his job. Since Corbett had been suggested as a possible Eighth Army commander by Auchinleck, this, in Brooke's view, was an unfavourable indication of Auchinleck's ability to select men, which confirmed Brooke's 'fears in that respect'.[11] However, the suggestion had been that Corbett should take over on a temporary basis until a new army commander was appointed; Auchinleck proposed that the man to fill this post should be Lieutenant General Bernard Montgomery. Although he had not enjoyed good relations with Monty in Britain, the Auk considered Montgomery to be the best man for the field command in the Western Desert.

Churchill's visits to Eighth Army's tactical HQ behind Ruweisat Ridge and the RAF HQ at Burg el Arab left him with the impression that the RAF was much better organized than Eighth Army. At Ruweisat the prime minister breakfasted with Auchinleck in the latter's spartan surroundings, a wire cage surrounded by flies, whereas luncheon in the RAF mess at Burg el Arab had been brought specially from Shepheard's Hotel and there was 'white napery, gleaming silver, brandy in goblets' and a cooling breeze from the nearby Mediterranean. Such contrasting meals helped shape Churchill's attitude to the commanders in the Middle East.[12]

Of one thing Churchill was already convinced: Auchinleck's place was in Cairo, not at the front with Eighth Army which needed a new commander. Auchinleck agreed with him, having already suggested Montgomery for the role. Churchill, however, was advocating that command should go to Lieutenant General 'Strafer' Gott, who had been on active service in the Middle East since the beginning of the campaign. Brooke interviewed Gott, who he felt needed a rest and was too tired to assume command of Eighth Army, but Churchill's view prevailed. Gott was appointed.

At one stage Churchill had even suggested that Brooke should take over Eighth Army but, although tempted, the CIGS considered that his duty lay in remaining in his existing post. In his discussions with Brooke, the prime minister suggested that Auchinleck should be removed as C-in-C Middle East. Since he felt that Auchinleck might keep Montgomery, his favoured candidate for Eighth Army, on too tight a rein, Brooke was inclined to agree. Their choice of replacement was General Sir Harold Alexander, another Irishman and Churchill's favourite general. Unwilling to dismiss Auchinleck outright, the decision was made to divide Middle East Command with a new Near East Command, headed by Alexander, under which Eighth Army would serve, and a redrawn Middle East Command, encompassing Persia and Iraq, under Auchinleck. However, the war cabinet, while agreeing to divide Middle East Command, insisted that that title should be retained by Alexander's command, to avoid confusion in the eyes of the public, and that the title 'Persia-Iraq Command' be adopted for Auchinleck's area of responsibility.

News of the changes was delivered to Auchinleck by a staff officer. In a subsequent meeting with Churchill the Auk declined the Persia-Iraq Command, believing that the division of the original Middle East Command would prove impracticable in the event of crisis and that his appointment to a command with much reduced responsibilities

> would look to the public too much like the appointment of an unsuccessful general to an operational sinecure – a policy of which he would thoroughly disapprove had it happened to anyone else ... [13]

By the time Auchinleck learned of the planned changes, Gott was dead, killed when the aircraft in which he was flying was shot down by a German fighter. Brooke's first choice, Bernard Montgomery, was to command Eighth Army. Auchinleck would retire to India, although he would be appointed C-in-C India less than a year later. His chief of staff, Eric Dorman-Smith, was to go also: Brooke disliked him intensely, as did many others, and a subsequent episode in the Anzio beachhead would destroy Chink's career. Thus did the men who had stopped Rommel, saved Egypt and the Middle East, bow out physically of the history of the desert war; but their ghosts continue to haunt discussion of that war.

Although Churchill, who had left Egypt for Moscow, had suggested to the war cabinet that the handover of responsibilities should take place on 12 August, both Auchinleck and Alexander, who had arrived in Cairo on 8 August, agreed to delay this until the 15th to allow time for Auchinleck to brief both Alexander and Montgomery. The latter arrived in Egypt on 12 August and reached Middle East HQ in Cairo at about 10 o'clock that morning. Already enjoying 'a reputation for taking over commands and making them his own',[14] Montgomery 'decided at once to take action'.[15] Thus it was that Montgomery began issuing orders as Eighth Army commander two days before he was due to take command and sent a signal to GHQ from Eighth Army HQ stating that he had assumed command from 2.00pm on 13 August. That he knew he was wrong to do so is shown by his admission that 'this was disobedience'.[16] He then made himself scarce by going off to visit Freyberg, acting-commander of XIII Corps.[17]

Montgomery was later to describe the prevailing situation as 'quite unreal and, in fact, dangerous' and claimed that there was 'an air of uncertainty about everything in the operational line'. That this is inaccurate and designed to promote the image of Montgomery as the saviour of Eighth Army is indicated by his further suggestion that Eighth Army and its air force partners appeared to be fighting separate battles and lacked the close relationship that was essential. Rommel's men would hardly have agreed.

On arriving in Egypt Montgomery had a meeting with Auchinleck from which

> he formed the extraordinary belief, which he was soon disseminating, that the present C-in-C was planning a retreat up the Nile, and possibly into Palestine, by the entire Eighth Army should Rommel attack heavily. The most charitable view of this belief is that Montgomery failed to understand Auchinleck correctly, in which case he was guilty, as Roger Parkinson put it, of 'an acute and unprofessional loss of concentration'.[18]

Montgomery's account, when published in his *Memoirs* in 1958, led to controversy and to an agreement by Montgomery and his publishers that a footnote of withdrawal should be included in future editions in which Montgomery acknowledged that Auchinleck had stopped Rommel's advance at El Alamein in July 1942 and that it was the Auk's intention to launch an offensive from that line when Eighth Army had been rested and re-organized. One who did not accept Montgomery's original version was his brother, Brian, who wrote:

But the evidence which I have seen and quoted confirms in me the view I have always held that Bernard's condemnation of Auchinleck on this particular point (his allegation that the latter was planning for nothing except a future withdrawal) was most unfair and wholly unjustified.[19]

There was no doubt that Auchinleck planned to fight Rommel, either when the German attacked again, or when Eighth Army was strong and fit enough to renew the offensive. Pulling Eighth Army back from engaging the enemy was not an option for Auchinleck but he had contingency plans to deal with a possible Axis breakthrough. Any good general would have drawn up such plans. Montgomery claimed that he had all such plans scrapped. Interestingly, in the light of this comment, similar plans were still in place under Montgomery, including the deployment of 51st (Highland) Division as South Delta Force to protect Cairo should *Panzerarmee* attack around Eighth Army's right flank.[20] Nor was the Highland Division alone in being so employed. HQ Middle East realized that a danger

remained of penetration or airborne attack to sabotage and cause panic. GOC, BTE (Lt Gen R.G.W.H. Stone) arranged to strengthen BARFORCE about Faiyum and to carry out daily aircraft and air recce of approaches to Delta from SW. From 25 Aug onwards the defences of the Delta were fully manned and when the Egyptian Government decided that Egyptian Army units would not oppose enemy raiders, a number of guards on VPs [vulnerable, or vital, points] in the Delta were taken over by British troops, who relieved Egyptian personnel of their duties.[21]

It is noteworthy that these plans relate to a period when British Intelligence was aware, through ULTRA, of an impending Axis attack, the offensive subsequently known as the battle of Alam el Halfa, predicted by Dorman-Smith at the end of July. What is clear is that the military maxim of always having a plan to deal with any contingency, in this case a possible Axis breakthrough, existed under Alexander and Montgomery as much as it had done under Auchinleck. Brigadier C.E. Lucas-Phillips states that all these plans were Alexander's work and did not suggest any possibility of Eighth Army, under Montgomery, retreating.[22] As with Auchinleck, Alexander drew up these plans as C-in-C Middle East as contingency measures should Rommel break through Eighth Army. If Montgomery had no fall-back plan then he stands guilty of dereliction of duty.

Montgomery also decided that Eighth Army's morale needed improving.

> From what I had learned the troops had their tails down and there was no confidence in the higher command. This would have to be put right at once, but until I had actually got the feel of things myself I could not decide how to set about it.[23]

This statement should be taken with a sizeable pinch of salt. While soldiers lacked the degree of confidence that they should have had in their higher command, morale was nowhere near as poor as Montgomery asserted in his *Memoirs*. His comment contradicts what Alexander wrote during the war and included in his *Despatch* as C-in-C Middle East.

> I visited many of the troops in the field during the last two weeks of August and found that they were fit and that their morale was good. They appeared, however, to have a feeling of frustration and bewilderment at finding themselves on the defensive so close to their base after two highly successful campaigns. They seemed at a loss to account for their failures. To restore confidence by a clear policy of action is the first essential.[24]

After all, these were soldiers who had just bloodied Rommel's nose and knew that they could do so again. The problems of lack of confidence in their commanders and lack of trust between the fighting arms had been identified clearly by Auchinleck who had initiated corrective measures. Montgomery would reap the benefit of Auchinleck's efforts in this respect, as well as of his own attempts to create an image of himself as the army commander.

Those attempts were based on the appreciation that Rommel was better known to the average British soldier than any British general. This situation Montgomery set out to rectify. His method of doing so was simple: he visited as many units as possible and spoke to their soldiers. On such visits he would stand on a platform, or a vehicle's bonnet, and tell the men to gather around, often urging them to remove their headgear, to emphasize the impression of informality. Having done so, he would outline his plans, stressing the importance of their part in them. This endeared him to many soldiers and he soon acquired the soubriquet 'Monty'.

Even when Monty met soldiers in the more formal setting of a parade, his attitude was noticeably different from that of most senior officers, being less concerned with the attention given to 'spit and polish' than with an individual's bearing. He would look into men's eyes with such intensity that soldiers gained the impression that this little general meant business, knew what he was doing and could be trusted. It was a difficult state to achieve: after all, he was only another in a line of army commanders, all of whom, bar Auchinleck, had let the fighting man down; and he had the disadvantage of being small, sharp-featured and still white-kneed – hardly the image of a great commander.

Possibly aware of this, Monty's image-building took another turn. He set out to make himself distinctive by adopting a headdress very different from the red-banded cap of a general. His first choice, an Australian bush hat, decorated liberally with cap badges from various units under his command, was worn at the time of the Alam el Halfa battle. However, this proved awkward to wear and was, perhaps, just a little too theatrical, leading Monty to opt for a much simpler headdress that became his hallmark – the black beret of the Royal Tank Regiment. He retained the Royal Tanks' badge, to which he added his own general's badge in one of the outstanding public relations exercises of the war: Monty with his black beret and two badges was among the most popular images of the conflict for the British public. Montgomery later told King George VI that his headgear was worth at least a corps in terms of morale.

One wonders what Montgomery would have done had he realized the origin of the black beret as the official headgear of Britain's tankmen. It was chosen as the Royal Tank Corps' headgear on the recommendation of Alec Gatehouse who was involved in the task of designing a practical uniform for the new corps. At the time – 1925–26 – Gatehouse, on the staff at Sandhurst, consulted a fellow staff member about aspects of the uniform and especially a practical hat for the confines of a tank: this had 'to protect men's hair from the oil in a tank but not take up space in the cramped interior'. Gatehouse's colleague took him to his room where, hanging on the wall, was a Basque beret from Pamplona which Gatehouse tried on and decided to recommend as the Corps' headdress. His fellow officer at Sandhurst was none other than Eric Dorman-Smith – Chink – who 'after Alamein was to speculate about Montgomery's reaction if told that his famous beret had links with the unorthodox Hemingway set'.[25]

Montgomery also claimed credit for another Dorman-Smith idea, the creation of a *corps de chasse*, a British equivalent of *Afrikakorps* within Eighth Army. Lucas-Phillips describes its creation.

Soon after Montgomery's arrival in the desert, 10th Corps, a defunct formation headquarters, was resuscitated. It was initially an all-armour corps and was intended by Montgomery to act, in his own phrase, as a *corps de chasse.* Lumsden, previously commander of 1st Armoured Division, was appointed to command it.[26]

The use of the adjective 'defunct' to describe X Corps is strange, implying that the corps had been dead, whereas it had fought at the first battle of El Alamein as an infantry formation. Later, Lucas-Phillips describes X Corps as being re-formed but that first mention of it as 'defunct' seems to be intended to colour the reader's view of the re-formation as an armoured formation. Headquarters X Corps had been used as a formation headquarters for Delta Force and thus there had simply been a change in nomenclature. In Dorman-Smith's Appreciation both XIII and XXX Corps are shown, with the former commanding a mobile wing that was to include 7th Armoured Division. In that mobile wing can be seen the genesis of an armoured corps; the two fresh armoured divisions expected to arrive in Egypt were to be trained for a breakthrough battle 'about El Alamein' and a subsequent pursuit. Two fresh infantry divisions were to be trained likewise. Dorman-Smith also noted that Eighth Army should have a reserve of corps strength. X Corps' time out of the order of battle was hardly long enough to justify describing it as 'defunct' in August.

X Corps was to include 1st Armoured Division, already desert veterans, plus both new armoured divisions, 8th and 10th, and 2nd New Zealand Division. Each armoured division was to include two brigades, one armoured and one infantry, as well as divisional troops, while the New Zealand Division had two infantry brigades and an armoured brigade; 4 New Zealand Brigade had been so badly mauled in the July battles that it had been withdrawn from the divisional order of battle and would not return until the North African campaign was over, by which time it had been converted into an armoured brigade. In the meantime 9 Armoured Brigade would become an integral part of 2nd New Zealand Division. However, 8th Armoured Division lacked an infantry brigade and its part in the forthcoming battle would be restricted to its headquarters, divisional signals and other troops taking part in the overall Eighth Army deception plan while its armour fought under other commands.

As these preparations were underway, intelligence was being amassed on the Axis offensive expected at the end of August. Rommel's German divisions had been reinforced to full strength, a further division, 164th Light, had arrived from Crete and entered the front line but 'without transport of its own';[27] 288 Parachute Brigade, the Ramcke Brigade, had also arrived as had the Italian *Folgore* Division, another airborne formation with first-class fighting troops. Rommel, therefore, had seven infantry divisions, two German and five Italian, plus an independent German brigade, against Montgomery's infantry strength of four divisions. Two new infantry divisions were to join Eighth Army, 44th (Home Counties) and 51st (Highland); the former would endure its baptism of fire in Rommel's forthcoming attack.

By late August Rommel's armour had been reinforced to over seventy PzKw Mark III Specials, capable of outgunning all Allied tanks except the Grant, as well as twenty-seven Mark IV Specials with their long-barrelled 75mm guns, for which he also had armour-piercing ammunition. In total *Panzerarmee Afrika* had 229 tanks,[*28] while the Italian *Ariete* and *Littorio* armoured divisions disposed another 243 mediums[29] and thirty-eight lights. However, the Italian tanks were of poor quality. Axis anti-tank artillery was still powerful; Rommel had a second regiment of 88mm anti-aircraft guns that could also be used as anti-tank weapons, capable of killing any Allied tank at long range.

Montgomery's armour strength was high on paper, with almost 800 tanks available. Of these just under 700 were serviceable, but only 164 were the 75mm-armed Grants; the remainder were either British Cruisers – Crusaders or Valentines – or American Stuarts, the latter suitable only for reconnaissance. Most Cruisers were still armed with the obsolete 2-pounder, although some were being up-gunned with 6-pounders. Montgomery had but one armoured division at the end of August, the newly-arrived 10th, which temporarily replaced 1st Armoured Division, now recovering from its recent ordeals. Tenth Armoured Division's armoured brigade, 8 Armoured Brigade, under Brigadier Neville Custance, included 3rd Royal Tank Regiment, the Staffordshire Yeomanry and the Sherwood Rangers Yeomanry. Although 3 RTR was a hardened unit, neither yeomanry regiment had seen any armoured action thus far in the war.[**]

Rommel could also count on improved support from the Luftwaffe and *Regia Aeronautica*, which had been reinforced to some 700 machines, outnumbering Desert Air Force. Both sides could call on support from aircraft not directly under their command: over 200 Luftwaffe machines based in Crete could be deployed while a similar number of RAF and USAAF machines, including

---

*   The *Official History* notes that, on 30 August, *Afrikakorps* had 93 PzKw MkIIIs, 73 MkIII Specials, 10 MkIVs and 27 MkIV Specials, giving a total of 203 tanks; there were also some MkIIs.

**   The Sherwood Rangers had been in action at Tobruk during the siege of 1941 but in an artillery role.

some four-engined Halifax and Liberator bombers, were available.*[30] The situation in the air was almost equally balanced at this stage, although von Mellenthin suggests an Allied superiority of 5:1.[31] The Germans had superior fighter aircraft in the Messerschmitt Bf109, although three Spitfire squadrons had become operational in Desert Air Force. RAF aircraft caused much more damage to Rommel's forces and its supplies than the Luftwaffe inflicted on Eighth Army. However, No.208 Squadron's Hurricanes suffered considerably at the hands of German fighters. A proposal to re-equip the squadron with Spitfires was rejected by the Air Ministry who claimed that Spitfires were too valuable to use on low-altitude work. (Spitfires were being used for strategic reconnaissance work.) The Hurricanes soldiered on and during July No.208 lost eight machines and eight pilots with another fifteen aircraft damaged.[32]

ULTRA intercepts indicated Rommel's intention to attack on 26 August but he delayed this due to fuel and transport shortages. His fuel situation was not as bad as on previous occasions; there was enough for a week-long battle, including 1,500 tons from Luftwaffe stocks. Even so, Rommel considered abandoning the offensive but

> in the end he accepted Kesselring's assurance that he could fly in 90,000 gallons of gasoline a day, and we relied on a large tanker due in Tobruk at the end of August. Kesselring did in fact fulfil his promise but most of the gasoline was consumed on the long journey to the front, while the sinking of the precious tanker by a submarine off Tobruk harbour on 31 August put an end to any hope of a victorious battle.[33]

In von Mellenthin's view, Rommel was 'compelled to launch' his attack on the night of 30/31 August to take advantage of the full moon. Had he not done so, he would have had to wait three weeks, a postponement that was 'out of the question'. And so Rommel's command moved to the attack once again on the night of 30/31 August. The ensuing action, the second major battle fought on the El Alamein line, was to be known as the Battle of Alam el Halfa, from the ridge around which the most significant fighting occurred.

---

* Not all soldiers were impressed with the Halifaxes. One AA gunner, whose battery was defending a bomber airfield in Palestine, recalled that Halifaxes seemed to crash with monotonous regularity.

Although Montgomery had begun planning for an offensive, he had also to prepare for the expected Axis attack which had been alluded to in Dorman-Smith's Appreciation. Chink had suggested that the attack was unlikely before the end of the month as only then would Rommel have any hope of success. That assessment was accurate: the Desert Fox was making ready for what Heinz Werner Schmidt described as 'Rommel's Last Try'.[34] In late-August Eighth Army was alerted to

> [e]vidence accumulating that enemy intend to attack within 2/3 days South of the New Zealanders by the open South flank. To meet this 8 Army is standing to as from 2400 24 August. From this day everyone will be constantly ready. As it is confidently expected the attack will only take place by night, by day units may relax somewhat unless concentrations are seen by recce.[35]

Reinforced, but with a low margin of fuel stocks, Rommel was gambling on knocking out Eighth Army and punching through to the Delta. However, had he been able to penetrate the El Alamein line, he would have encountered such powerful opposition in the Delta that, with his fuel state, the momentum of his advance would have been lost. Montgomery was in an advantageous position, with a secure base area behind him, thanks to the efforts of his predecessors, allowing him to devote all his attention to Rommel. Eighth Army was growing in strength daily: the first 6-pounder-equipped Crusaders arrived on 25 August while troopships were disembarking thousands of reinforcements. His artillery strength was increased and there were even plans to adapt the superlative 3.7-inch heavy anti-aircraft gun for a field and anti-tank role with 'special scotches being made so that 3.7s could fire from their wheels against ground targets'.[36]

Although Montgomery inherited plans to meet an enemy attack, he modified these in several respects. Axis deployments, and the laying of minefields in the northern sector, pointed to an attack in the south, leading Monty to bolster his strength there. Identifying the Alam el Halfa ridge as crucial, he decided to relieve 21 Indian Brigade with the recently-arrived 44th Division, less 132 Brigade which came under command of 2nd New Zealand Division at Bare Ridge. Additional armour and artillery was moved up; 10th Armoured Division and 8 Armoured Brigade deployed in the Alam el Halfa area. In his *Despatch* Alexander noted the importance of this area and the fact that 'the positions had been prepared on a sound plan of defence [but] owing to the heavy casualties suffered during June and July, the forces available to man them were slender'.[37] Those forces were now not so slender. The ridge was important because

> [i]f the Germans could bypass it quickly to the east, they would have a clear run to the places on which they intended to meet and destroy the British armour. If Montgomery could hold Rommel from the Ridge then the battle was his, for the German commander would not dare to move eastwards towards the Nile so long as the undefeated Eighth Army was in a position to sever his lines of communication.[38]

Eighth Army implemented deception measures which, it was hoped, might even cause Rommel to postpone his attack. It is doubtful whether these played any significant role in the battle although, when the attack did not materialize on the night of the full moon, 26 August, the deception experts thought that they had succeeded. When *Panzerarmee* rolled into action four nights later they realized otherwise.

In essence Rommel planned a re-run of the Gazala attack with a rapid thrust round Eighth Army's southern flank. During the night 30/31 August, *Afrikakorps'* 15th and 21st Panzer Divisions would thrust through that flank, north of Himeimat, to strike south of Alam el Halfa Ridge at the rear of Eighth Army's positions. *Afrikakorps* would be flanked, to right and left respectively, by a group created from the Axis reconnaissance units and an Italian armoured force of *Ariete* and *Littorio* Divisions. This force was to be in position, facing northward, by 3.30am on the 31st and, at first light, *Afrikakorps* would attack towards the coast while the left-flank units struck the British rear about Ruweisat Ridge. Cut off from re-supply, Eighth Army would be annihilated and its armour defeated, allowing Rommel to race for Alexandria and Cairo and chase the fleeing British up the valley of the Nile.

But Montgomery had prepared well and *Afrikakorps'* advance was much slower than planned since the southern minefields, being stronger than expected, took longer to clear. The Axis armour struck northwards west of Alam el Halfa earlier than planned but did not catch Montgomery off guard. He redeployed and reinforced his armour to place 500 tanks in three brigades between Bare Ridge and Alam el Halfa with orders to fight from static positions screened by anti-tank guns. Determined not to allow Rommel a battle of movement, Montgomery was assisted by the local topography. Rommel failed to gain surprise.

Minefields delayed Rommel's armour while his supply columns were pounded by British aircraft as they made for Jebel Kalakh. When *Afrikakorps'* panzers were scheduled to be in position between Bare and Alam el Halfa Ridges, refuelled and ready to attack towards the coast, they had still not cleared the minefields.

The first contact on the ground was between Axis tanks and the anti-tank guns of 2nd Rifle Brigade and guns of F Battery RHA near Deir el Munassib, south of Bare Ridge, from which Rommel's forces retreated. This was not the sole setback to *Panzerarmee*, which was suffering heavy air attack. General Walter Nehring, *Afrikakorps'* commander, was wounded but General von Bismarck, commanding 21st Panzer Division, was killed by a mine. By 8.00am Rommel knew that his plan was going awry and considered calling off the attack. He deferred that decision and decided to watch the progress of *Afrikakorps*, now commanded by Colonel Bayerlein, its chief of staff. Instead of flanking east of Alam el Halfa, Bayerlein's men would make the ridge their objective. By contrast, reports reaching Montgomery were more positive. Although 2nd West Yorks lost a company in an attack by the Ramcke Brigade, and there were some actions in which Australians, New Zealanders and South Africans were involved, XXX Corps had enjoyed a relatively quiet night with any setbacks made good at dawn.

However, XIII Corps' front had suffered three enemy thrusts, although the enemy strength was not clear initially; a panzer division and 90th Light were certainly involved with, possibly, XX Italian Corps in these attacks which struck south of 2nd New Zealand Division, at Munassib and north of Himeimat. As the day grew older so the picture became clearer. With about 100 tanks, *Afrikakorps'* attack from Himeimat was the main effort and, once clear of the minefields and with the Reconnaissance Group pushing 4 Light Armoured Brigade off the escarpment to the south, this caused concern in 7 Motor Brigade, although it created little pressure on the brigade front. The brigade commander, Brigadier Jimmy Bosvile, ordered his units back to the area of his reserve battalion, which manoeuvre was complete by about 9.30am. By then *Afrikakorps* was some seven miles east of Himeimat, having reached the final minefield in 4 Light Armoured Brigade's area.

XIII Corps' new commander, Lieutenant General Brian Horrocks, countermanded 7 Motor Brigade's withdrawal order and made it clear that 7th Armoured Division should hold the line of that final minefield, which by then had been abandoned. In an effort to redress the situation 10th Hussars were sent forward to deploy in the Muhafid depression, north-east of Munassib, and 23 Armoured Brigade was transferred to XIII Corps from XXX Corps, although a squadron of each regiment remained with the latter formation, and into positions between 22 Armoured Brigade and the New Zealanders. Under constant air attack, Rommel had made little progress by noon. The only relief from Allied aircraft was provided by a sandstorm that blew up some thirty minutes before noon and temporarily grounded Desert Air Force.

Following refuelling, *Afrikakorps* moved forward again, north-eastwards, at one o'clock. The storm was at its worst, adding to an already confused situation. Soon *Afrikakorps* met 3rd/4th County of London Yeomanry and 1st King's Royal Rifle Corps and in the ensuing brief battle a number of Grants were knocked out, but British anti-tank gunners also accounted for several panzers. Confusion continued as elements of 4 Light Armoured and 7 Motor Brigades fought *Afrikakorps* in the sandstorm and 10th Hussars, concerned lest they be cut off, sought permission to withdraw before, following conflicting orders, the regiment was pushed back against the Alam el Halfa minefields. By then it was late afternoon and 22 Armoured Brigade[*39] under Brigadier Pip Roberts, was about to join the fray.

Roberts' brigade was positioned around Point 102, west of Alam el Halfa, with some elements on a ridge some three miles south, to which they had been ordered that morning, from where Roberts had ordered patrols from CLY and 2nd Gloucestershire Hussars to move farther south to seek information on enemy movements. Those patrols soon met enemy armour and withdrew quickly with the news that over 100 enemy tanks were on the move south of 22 Armoured. Before long 120 panzers, Mark IIIs and some Mark IVs, believed to be 21st Panzer Division, were spotted approaching a line of telegraph poles running at an angle across the front and about 1,000 yards forward of 22 Armoured Brigade's positions. On reaching the poles the panzers stopped and thirty tanks turned to the east. Soon the remainder moved off northwards before making an eastward turn that would take them across the front of the CLY positions but out of effective range of that regiment's guns. With the sandstorm still blowing, although starting to subside, the panzers seemed unaware of the presence of 22 Armoured Brigade. However, the axis of advance of the tanks was taking them straight towards the positions of 44th Division at Alam el Halfa.

---

* The brigade held all Eighth Army's Grants and was 'a motley collection of combined units'. The sole complete regiment was the Royal Scots Greys while two Royal Tank Regiments, 1st and 6th, were combined, as was 5th Royal Tanks with the Gloucestershire Hussars; 3rd and 4th County of London Yeomanry (CLY) combined as the other regiment. The formation was completed by 1st Royal Horse Artillery and 1st Rifle Brigade.

Roberts now ordered 5th Royal Tanks and the CLY to show themselves and prepare to take the enemy from the flank should their advance continue in the same direction. Just after 6.00pm his armour carried out the order and the German armour, finally aware of the presence of British tanks, adopted fighting formation and turned towards the CLY tanks. By now the dust was subsiding and visibility improving, although only an hour of daylight remained. The light favoured the British gunners, 'being slightly behind them and in the faces of the enemy'. Advancing with their right flank against A Squadron of the Yeomanry and their left against B Company 1st Rifle Brigade, the Germans were under 1,000 yards away when the Yeomanry opened fire. The panzers halted and returned the fire, concentrating on A Squadron's tanks and quickly knocked out twelve. Unable to take up hulldown positions because of their sponson-mounted main guns, the Grants made large targets. Their high-octane fuel also made them liable to combust rapidly, or explode. A Squadron's leader, Major Cameron, noted how tank after tank in his squadron, including his own, went up in flames or was otherwise disabled while 'German tanks seldom go on fire'. However, B Squadron had also engaged the panzers and that attention made the Germans pull back.

Roberts now sought to fill the gap created by the loss of A Squadron by ordering the Royal Scots Greys to move over the crest of Point 102 and deploy to the Yeomanry's right. The Germans began another advance as the Greys started their move but this time moved more slowly, heading for the gap in the British positions. Rifle Brigade anti-tank guns fired at 300 yards and claimed a number of victims, thus checking the advance. However, the panzers were soon moving again and the Greys had not arrived. Roberts ordered their CO to get the whips out as artillery engaged the panzers in their inexorable advance. At last the Greys came over the crest and charged downhill against the Germans. Daylight was fading as the clash began and the German advance in the centre was stopped.

On the left flank the thirty tanks detached from the main body had advanced on 133 Brigade to be met over open sights, and with armour-piercing shot, by B Battery 1st Royal Horse Artillery. CLY Crusaders were deployed to support 133 Brigade as soon as the Greys closed the gap in 22 Armoured Brigade's front and the Germans withdrew as darkness fell, although some panzers remained close to 133 Brigade throughout the night. Surprisingly, British casualties had been light; although the CLY lost twelve Grants and a Crusader they had only one man killed and fifteen wounded. (The CLY had only fifteen Grants, some of them manned by American servicemen, the first US soldiers to fight on African soil, who had been attached for battle experience. None were injured, 'though one or two had to bale out of burning tanks'.[40]) Other brigade units had escaped almost unscathed: 1st Rifle Brigade, with two killed, was the only other with fatalities. The brigade claimed to have destroyed nearly seventy German tanks, but the true figure for the entire day was just over twenty.

This short action at Point 102, the major engagement of the latter part of the day, marked the turning point of the battle of Alam el Halfa. That night Axis tanks went into leaguer and British aircraft and artillery pounded enemy positions with the Reconnaissance Group suffering particularly from the bombers.

Next day, 1 September, saw little action and Montgomery, realizing that the possibility of an enemy outflanking move around Alam el Halfa had all but disappeared, concentrated his three armoured brigades between the New Zealand and 44th Divisions. Soon after daybreak 21st Panzer attempted to move round 22 Armoured Brigade's left flank but was stopped by Roberts' tanks and an 8 Armoured Brigade threat from 21st Panzer's right. The Sherwood Rangers, Staffordshire Yeomanry and 3rd Royal Tanks eased the pressure on 22 Armoured and moved forward south of the minefield in front of 44th Division, ready to counter-attack the enemy's northern flank should Rommel try to thrust around Alam el Halfa. Their commander, Brigadier Neville Custance, had orders not to become too deeply involved in action or to take needless casualties, but he did advance when heavy artillery bombardment forced enemy tanks to withdraw.

During that day *Afrikakorps* lost thirteen tanks against 8 Armoured Brigade's sixteen. In the air there was much more activity with Allied aircraft harassing enemy communications and supplies. A bombing attack on *Afrikakorps* HQ resulted in seven officers being killed. Rommel again considered abandoning the offensive but deferred a decision until the next morning, by which time *Panzerarmee* had suffered another night of heavy aerial bombardment. On 2 September Rommel finally abandoned the attack, citing as his main reason the shortage of fuel and, specifically, the failure to keep him supplied with sufficient petrol: half the stocks promised by 3 September had already been lost en route in the Mediterranean.[41] At 10.30pm (German time) on 2 September, Rommel signalled to *Oberkommando des Heeres*:

The non-arrival of the petrol, oil and lubricants requested, which was the condition laid down for the successful carrying out even of limited operations, forbids a continuation of the attack.[42]

Little ground activity took place that day, although there was much air activity as Rommel's forces began withdrawing. By the morning of the 3rd Axis troops were positioned from below the New Zealanders eastward to Muhafid and then around Ragil and thus in a salient south of Alam el Halfa. Determined to cut them off, Montgomery decided to mount a set-piece infantry attack with 2nd New Zealand Division, including the British 132 Brigade, striking south towards the Munassib Depression, thereby sealing the British minefields behind Rommel's men to trap them in front of Alam el Halfa Ridge.

Operation BERESFORD was to be launched on the night of 3 September. Throughout that day, as preparations were completed, Montgomery restricted British activity to patrolling. Following the night-time infantry attack 7th Armoured Division was to enter the battle in the morning. The plan for the initial assault was for 5 NZ Brigade to attack on the east flank with 132 Brigade on the west while 6 NZ Brigade made a diversionary attack on 132 Brigade's right. Attacking on a 5,000-yard front to a depth of 6,000 yards, the division was to take the enemy positions on the northern edge of Munassib. The plan did not work out.

When 4th and 5th Royal West Kents, 132 Brigade's attacking battalions, advanced, the defenders, alerted by the diversionary attack, were waiting for them. Although the West Kents' attack was to have been 'silent' – without artillery support – this was not so and when the delayed attack was launched after midnight it was lit up by flares dropped by German aircraft and by blazing lorries. Neither battalion could make inroads into the Munassib defences. Brigadier Robertson was wounded, communications broke down and the brigade major had to re-organize the formation some 1,000 yards short of their objectives. Brigade casualties totalled 700, of whom 250 were from 4th Royal West Kents.

Brigadier Howard Kippenberger's 5 NZ Brigade had enjoyed more success, although 28th (Maori) Battalion, on the right, had veered westwards while 21st Battalion, on the left, had moved to the east. In the gap thus created Valentines of 50th Royal Tanks advanced, following what they thought were marker lamps. But the lamps were really German lights and the tanks went too far forward, coming to grief on mines and from anti-tank guns, which claimed twelve tanks and killed the squadron leader. Kippenberger's brigade lost 124 casualties while 6 Brigade lost 159 in their diversion, including George Clifton, their commander, who was captured. That evening Clifton escaped from a latrine but was recaptured some days later by German officers on a gazelle hunt.

Operation BERESFORD had failed. Rommel was able to continue his withdrawal throughout the following day, putting in several counter-attacks against the New Zealanders' new positions on an exposed forward slope. Less than two miles of desert was the total gain of the operation. Even that was given up when Montgomery, deciding that there would be no further moves to close the gap in the south, ordered Freyberg back to his original positions. Should the enemy withdraw then the British armour would follow up with patrols. But Rommel did not pull back to his original positions. His new front line in the south now encompassed the British *January* and *February* minefields which became part of the Axis defences, as was some high ground from which the British lines could be observed.

Losses at Alam el Halfa, the second battle of El Alamein, were some 3,000 men on the Axis side and 2,000 in Eighth Army; tank losses were nearly equal, under forty on each side. But the battle had been a British success and Rommel's last try had failed in its objective of striking through to the Nile. Eighth Army had achieved its objective of holding the enemy, boosting morale throughout the army. This would be a critical factor in the long-term objective of destroying *PanzerarmeeAfrika*. Montgomery's image had also improved throughout Eighth Army; his soldiers began to see him as someone who could be trusted to deliver success while he had given himself an introduction to waging battle in the desert.

His appointment of Brian Horrocks to command XIII Corps had also been proved correct 'in the Battle of Alam Halfa'.[43] Horrocks was one of a number of new commanders appointed by Montgomery who had decided that he would also relieve the commanders of X and XXX Corps, Lumsden and Ramsden respectively. Sir Oliver Leese, a Guardsman who would later succeed Montgomery as Eighth Army commander, took over XXX Corps but Alexander vetoed Monty's plan to relieve Lumsden in X Corps. John Harding, later Field Marshal Lord Harding, was brought in from GHQ to command 7th Armoured Division while Brigadier Sidney Kirkman was brought out from England to command Eighth Army's artillery. There were many other changes until Monty decided that he had the team he needed. Among those was Brigadier Francis de Guingand, whom Monty appointed as his chief of staff and who would soldier with him until the end of the war.

Eighth Army's strength was being increased and the composition of formations was adjusted. With only two infantry brigades, 2nd New Zealand Division was strengthened by the addition of 9 Armoured Brigade – 3rd Hussars, Royal

Wiltshire Yeomanry and Warwickshire Yeomanry – from 10th Armoured Division while 44th Division lost 133 Brigade to X Corps as lorried infantry but gained 151 Brigade, the surviving brigade of 50th Division, and 1 Greek Independent Brigade. Among other changes, 7th Armoured Division lost 7 Motor Brigade to 1st Armoured Division and new formations entered the line. Fourth Indian Division relieved 5th Indian Division and 51st (Highland) Division took over from 44th Division. Heavy losses in men and equipment had been sustained since June and every effort was being made to replace them but the manpower shortage was serious and led to the dilution of some units.

> ... dilution of British military personnel in the rear areas was already in progress, additional Indian and African Pioneer Battalions arrived during [August] while recruitment of Palestinian manpower continued.[44]

This policy released British personnel from units such as pioneers and anti-aircraft artillery for retraining in other roles, especially infantry, with their places being taken by African and Indian soldiers. Eighth Army was to continue to suffer a manpower shortage, particularly in the infantry arm; this was something Montgomery had to take account of when planning for the offensive.

Preparations now began for that new offensive. Alam el Halfa had convinced Montgomery that his army needed retraining: the various arms had to work together with trust and effectiveness if Eighth Army was to be a successful team. Training thus became a priority but Monty was able to build on work initiated by Auchinleck. Other priorities included consolidating the present positions as the start line for a new offensive and re-organizing Eighth Army into his preferred order of battle for that offensive.

> I had decided that in building up the Eighth Army ... I would concentrate on three essentials: leadership, equipment and training. All three were deficient. The equipment situation was well in hand and I knew that Alexander would see that we got all that we needed. Training was receiving urgent attention. I soon realized that although the Eighth Army was composed of magnificent material, it was untrained; it had done much fighting, but little training. We had just won a decisive victory, but it had been a static battle; I was not prepared to launch the troops into an all-out offensive without intensive prior training.[45]

By contrast, Rommel was now in a situation that he had wanted to avoid.

> But the main thing I had wanted to avoid was the war settling down at
> El Alamein into mechanized static warfare with a stable front, because
> this was just what the British officers and men had been trained for. The
> good points of the British soldier, his tenacity, for instance, would have the
> maximum effect and the bad points, such as his immobility and rigidity,
> none at all.[46]

Rommel would have to do his best to ensure that his opponents would have less
opportunity for displaying tenacity than for immobility and rigidity.

Chapter Four

Monty Makes his Plan

Now thrive the armourers

ighth Army's re-equipment programme received an important boost on 3 September when the first of Roosevelt's 300 Sherman tanks arrived from the United States.[1] By 11 September there were 318 Shermans in the Middle East.[*2] The standard Allied tank in the latter part of the war, the Sherman had a turret-mounted 75mm gun superior to anything then in British service, including that in the Grant. By the time Montgomery's preparations were complete Eighth Army would have over 1,300 tanks with 1,136 in the forward area, including a handful of the new Churchill I-tanks. There were also increases in artillery strength with 832 field guns in the army's inventory, as well as 554 2-pounder and 849 6-pounder anti-tank guns;[3] only in medium artillery was Eighth Army deficient, deploying but fifty-two weapons. The Desert Air Force was also reinforced, air superiority regained, and additional US Army Air Forces units had arrived.[4] (The first USAAF units arrived in late-June, followed by a pursuit (fighter) group of Curtiss P-40 Warhawks in July, a heavy bombardment group of Consolidated B-24 Liberators and a medium bombardment group of North American B-25 Mitchells in August. Under command of Major General Lewis Brereton, the USAAF elements were the nucleus of what became Ninth Air Force.)

For the first time Eighth Army included a majority of British divisions. Of the eleven divisions that Montgomery could deploy, seven were British: all four armoured divisions – 1st, 7th, 8th and 10th – were British, although 8th Armoured would be broken up before 23 October,[**] and there were three British infantry divisions – 44th, 50th (now reconstituted) and 51st. The remaining

---

* A convoy of seven fast ships left the USA on 15 July carrying the Shermans promised to Churchill by Roosevelt after the fall of Tobruk. On the 16th one ship was torpedoed and sunk but an additional shipment of fifty-two tanks made good the loss.

** The reason for breaking up 8th Armoured Division was that no infantry brigade was available for it, reflecting the shortage of infantry that prevailed even when LIGHTFOOT was launched. Its two armoured brigades, 23 and 24, saw action in the battle, the former

infantry divisions were from the Dominions or India – 2nd New Zealand, 9th Australian, 4th Indian and 1st South African, all veteran formations. However, the Dominion divisions retained a smouldering distrust of the armour and of British troops generally. Nor did the South Africans enjoy the trust of their fellows, following what was considered a less-than-tenacious showing in recent battles; the surrender of 2nd South African Division at Tobruk did little to improve matters.

As his strength grew Montgomery came under pressure, as had Auchinleck before him, to launch an early offensive. Churchill had expected the new team of Alexander and Montgomery to act quickly but was told by Alexander that Montgomery could not be ready until October, whereas Auchinleck had suggested September. This further delay was justified by Montgomery's expressed need to attack in a full-moon period.

> The minefield problem was such that the troops must be able to see what they were doing. A waning moon was not acceptable since I envisaged a real 'dogfight' for at least a week before we finally broke out; a waxing moon was essential. This limited the choice to one definite period each month. Owing to the delay caused to our preparations by Rommel's attack, we could not be ready for the September moon and be sure of success. There must be no more failures.[5]

With the October full moon due on the 24th, Montgomery planned to attack on the night of 23 October. Churchill's pressure continued and Alexander received a signal demanding that the offensive be in September to coincide with Soviet operations and precede Allied landings on the north-west African coast in November. Of this signal, Montgomery wrote:

> Alexander came to see me to discuss the reply to be sent. I said that our operations could not be completed in time for a September offensive, and an attack then would fail: if we waited until October I guaranteed complete success. In my view it would be madness to attack in September. Was I to do so? Alexander backed me up wholeheartedly as he always did, and the reply was sent on the lines I wanted. I had told Alexander privately that, in view of my promise to the soldiers, I refused to attack before October;

serving with XXX Corps and the latter, as an armoured brigade group, in 10th Armoured Division before passing to the command of 1st Armoured Division.

if a September attack was ordered by Whitehall, they would have to get someone else to do it. My stock was rather high after Alam Halfa! We heard no more about a September attack.[6]

In early-September, with the echoes of the Alam el Halfa clash still ringing, the first plans for Eighth Army's October offensive were drafted at Montgomery's headquarters. Simultaneous attacks were planned on both flanks, the main effort being in the north by Leese's XXX Corps while Horrocks' XIII Corps broke into the enemy's southern positions. This latter move was intended to draw Axis armour in that direction, thus easing the task of Lumsden's X Corps which would follow XXX Corps, using two corridors that XXX Corps would 'punch … through the enemy defences and minefields'.[7] Having cleared the corridors X Corps was then to 'position itself on ground of its own choosing astride the enemy supply routes'. With Lumsden's armour so deployed, Rommel would be forced to counter the British armour with his own and in the ensuing battle the Axis armour would be destroyed, following which their infantry would be rounded up. To prevent the Axis armoured divisions on the southern flank – 21st Panzer and *Ariete* – moving to help their northern brothers, XIII Corps would make another attack in the south, pinning down those two armoured divisions in that area. This draft plan was the basis for Operation LIGHTFOOT which, having been approved by Alexander, was outlined to a conference of corps and divisional commanders on 15 September at Eighth Army's new headquarters at Burg el Arab on the coast.

The day before, the plan for Operation LIGHTFOOT was outlined in a 'Most Secret' document issued to corps and divisional commanders, as well as senior staff officers. This paper described the object of the plan:

To destroy the enemy forces now opposing Eighth Army.
    The operations will be designed to 'trap' the enemy in his present area and to destroy him there. Should small elements escape to the West, they will be pursued and dealt with later.[8]

This broad concept became the basis for the re-organization, deployment and training of Eighth Army, and the logistic support needed to sustain the army. Desert Air Force also prepared in concert with the army and the reconnaissance aircraft were kept busy, especially No.208 Squadron's Hurricanes. Previous desert battles had followed a pattern of attempting to destroy the opposing armour before rounding up the infantry which Montgomery followed in his initial planning, but he departed from that template by planning his main effort in the north rather than the south, from which flank had been made a swinging movement in earlier battles.

Although this plan was simple it was also ambitious and likely to lead to heavy losses in the armour. However, by 6 October, Montgomery had become concerned about 'whether the troops would be able to do what was being demanded'[9] because of insufficient time to train fully Eighth Army's reinforcement and replacement troops; since its formation a year earlier, the army had suffered 80,000 casualties. Furthermore, he had reservations about the ability of many commanders to train their men. With these thoughts in mind he revised his battle plan to place an emphasis on 'crumbling', the destruction in detail of Axis infantry divisions in their defensive locations by attacks from the flank and rear. Such predatory moves against the infantry would draw the German and Italian armour into heavy counter-attacks, enticing them into battle against the British armour in position. Montgomery later wrote:

> I aimed to get my armour beyond the area of the 'crumbling' operations. I would then turn the enemy minefields to our advantage by using them to prevent the enemy armour from interfering with our operations; this would be done by closing the approaches through the minefields with our tanks, and we would then be able to proceed relentlessly with our plans.[10]

Critical to the revised plan was a successful break in to the Axis lines and creation of the minefield corridors by XXX Corps to enable X Corps' armour to pass through. To allow the leading armoured brigades to negotiate the corridors quickly, Montgomery planned to push them into those corridors in the immediate wake of XXX Corps' leading infantry divisions. Thus he would be committing his first armoured formations before knowing if the corridors were clear. If, on the morning of D+1, 24 October, the corridors were not clear, he ordered X Corps' armour to fight its way into the open beyond the minefields' western edge. For the tank crews of X Corps this made for a very different battlefield scenario which neither Lumsden nor any armoured divisional commander thought viable. In this they were supported by the three Dominion infantry commanders: Freyberg, Morshead and Pienaar told Leese that they did not believe that the armour could break out as soon as Montgomery suggested. Their comments probably owed much to the antipathy between armour and infantry.[11]

The Dominion generals predicted that Montgomery's plan for the armour's break-out could result in disaster for the tanks and, consequently, the infantry. They suggested that XXX Corps' attack should continue for longer before the armoured breakout. Carver noted that XXX Corps 'soon came to suspect that [X] Corps were not even seriously intending to try to break out'.[12] This suspicion indicates just how low had sunk trust between the two arms. When Leese reported these feelings to Montgomery the latter reiterated his order that X Corps would have to pass through XXX Corps at dawn on the first day of LIGHTFOOT. Perhaps he was concerned that any delay would only give the enemy time to strengthen his response, as had been the case in the First World War. Eighth Army certainly did not have enough infantry strength to develop the break-in any deeper without armour support.

The battle that Montgomery was planning was really a First World War battle with modern weapons. It is debatable whether Montgomery understood fully the role of armour, and the limitations of tanks, since his plan had about it much of the First World War mentality of using tanks as a screen for infantry. In his history of the British Army in the Second World War, General Sir David Fraser comments that Montgomery, at the time and in retrospect, was critical of his armoured commanders, blaming them 'for their lack of drive at Alamein, where at least part of the blame should have been directed inwards, at his own failure to comprehend what tanks can and cannot reasonably be made to do'.[13] It is arguable that Montgomery never really arrived at a true appreciation of armoured warfare and the limits of tanks, as his deployment of armour during the battle for Normandy suggests.

During the July battles Auchinleck had identified the Italian formations as the weak links in the Axis defensive chain and had worked on breaking those links. Montgomery revived that principle for his 'crumbling' operations but, typically, gave no credit to Auchinleck for the tactic. Instead he attributed it to Major Bill Williams of his intelligence staff, who had pointed out that

> German and Italian troops were ... 'corseted'; that is, Rommel had so deployed his German infantry and parachute troops that they were positioned between, and in some cases behind, his Italian troops all along the front, the latter being unreliable when it came to hard fighting. Bill Williams' idea was that if we could separate the two we would be very well placed, as we could smash through a purely Italian front without any great difficulty.[14]

Montgomery described this as 'very brilliant analysis' on the part of Williams and claimed that, as a major feature of his 'crumbling' plan, it helped pave the way to victory at El Alamein. Far from being a 'brilliant analysis', suggesting an original concept by Williams, this principle was there to see for anyone who studied the battles fought only two months earlier, as Williams doubtless did.

Not only was the identification of the Italians as the weak link in the Axis battle line not original, neither was the concept of 'crumbling'. That concept would have been familiar to generals of the First World War, for what Monty was planning was something with which he was very familiar, a battle of attrition, or 'bite and hold', on the lines of many of the clashes of that earlier war. Destroying the Axis infantry by 'crumbling' meant that Eighth Army's infantry would have to do much close-quarter fighting and would need close flexible support from the artillery as well as from the air forces.

The success of Operation LIGHTFOOT, averred Montgomery, depended on high standards in training and the closest possible co-operation between arms. Eighth Army's divisional commanders were told to arrange realistic training and ensure that individual soldiers attained high levels of weapon skills. Armoured units were to train alongside the infantry they would partner in battle so that trust could be built. Above all else, the army commander emphasized the importance of morale and fitness. His visits to many units had left him doubting the level of fitness of his soldiers.

> I am not convinced that our soldiery are really tough and hard. They are sunburnt and brown, and look very well; but they seldom move anywhere on foot and they have led a static life for many weeks.[15]

Instructions were issued that officers and men were to be made 'really fit' since the battle would last for many days and the final decision could depend on which side could better endure the strain of such prolonged fighting. Thus normal fitness would not be enough for Montgomery's purpose: the soldiers 'must be made tough and hard'. So began a programme to achieve high levels of physical fitness as well as battle skills. As they trained to become fitter individuals, Eighth Army's men would also carry out training specific to their own roles in LIGHTFOOT. In this respect also Montgomery considered the army to be deficient.

> The need for training had never been stressed. Most commanders had come to the fore by skill in fighting and because no better were available; many were above their ceiling and few were good trainers. ... If I was not careful, divisions and units would be given tasks which might end in failure because of the inadequate standard of training.[16]

Many in Eighth Army considered that having been in action for so long was the most appropriate training for future fighting; this ignored the need to absorb and train reinforcements for the tasks they would meet. It also assumed that future fighting would be as fluid as previous battles. However, such were the Axis defences that the battle would be very different: it would be one of attrition, and would have many features of First World War battles with mines and artillery playing crucial roles. Montgomery doubted if Eighth Army was ready for such a battle; this led to his change of primary objective for LIGHTFOOT from destroying the enemy armour to destroying his infantry.

The need for greater physical fitness had been demonstrated during exercises organized by many divisions. These had demonstrated the need for better co-operation between all arms, the need for everyone to know what was going on and a lack of physical fitness with soldiers falling out through simple exhaustion. This had occurred even in the New Zealand Division, regarded as one of the best of Eighth Army's formations. And we shall see how, at the end of September, an attack by XIII Corps near Deir el Munassib further emphasized the problem. Small wonder that Montgomery was calling for a higher level of physical fitness from his soldiers.

But training involved much more than Eighth Army's armour and infantry. A crucial problem facing the Army was the strength and depth of the defences it faced. *Panzerarmee Afrika* had been stopped at El Alamein since the beginning of July where, since late that month, it had been clear to Rommel that he would have to go on the defensive. Not only was the strip of land between El Alamein and the edge of the Qattara Depression ideal for defending the Nile Delta and the main cities of Egypt against an invader from the west, it was also ideal for containing an opponent wishing to burst out of Egypt and advance westwards. And there were fewer armies more skilled in preparing defences than the German, while Rommel, although noted for his risk-taking in attack, was a highly-skilled defensive commander. All those skills were put to use in preparing the line against the inevitable British offensive.

As with Montgomery, so also did Rommel have First World War experience. In fact, he had more first-hand experience than his opponent, who had spent the greater part of the war as a staff officer, having been seriously wounded in the conflict's early months. Furthermore, Rommel had written the German army handbook on infantry tactics and to do so had studied closely British battle doctrine.[17] He knew that Montgomery would have to launch a First World War-type attack on *Panzerarmee* and he knew the best methods of defence against such an attack.

One defensive method to which the El Alamein position lent itself was mining. Although mines had been used before in the desert, there had never been such prolific use as at El Alamein. Both sides made extensive use of minefields and Eighth Army would have to make its way through the heaviest such defences since 1918. Each side had already suffered from mines, Eighth Army losing many tanks to anti-tank mines in the July fighting while *Afrikakorps*' advance at Alam el Halfa was hindered by British minefields. Since July both sides had realized that large numbers of mines could play an important part in the forthcoming battle and many more were laid. By 21 October Rommel's engineer commander, Colonel Hecker, estimated that Axis minefields contained over 445,000 mines, of which about 14,000, or three per cent, were anti-personnel. The Axis intention had been for the minefields, which they dubbed 'the Devil's gardens' and the British called 'mine marshes', to contain anti-tank and anti-personnel mines in the ratio of two-to-one. Fortunately for Eighth Army's infantry this ratio was never achieved.[18] However, the anti-tank, or Teller, mines could be detonated by the footfall of a running infantryman and so the advancing infantry of XXX Corps were to move forward at a walking pace. Nor could the leading infantry carry heavy weapons, being restricted to nothing heavier than a Bren gun. Mortars, medium machine guns and anti-tank guns would follow when gaps had been cleared. The choice of the codename LIGHTFOOT for the operation was, therefore, appropriate, if not somewhat macabre.

Let us look now at those 'devil's gardens' to see one reason why the forthcoming battle was very much in the mould of those fought in France and Flanders a generation earlier. Eighth Army patrols and aerial reconnaissance had allowed Montgomery's intelligence staff to build up a good picture of the extent of enemy minefields and their basic pattern. The 'devil's eggs', as the Germans termed the mines, some of which were British from minefields at Gazala and Tobruk, had been sown in a fairly regular pattern along the front. Variations were usually the result of local topography. Along the forward edge of the Axis defensive positions was a band of mined and wired ground from

500 to 1,000 yards wide, within which were dug-in battle outposts, each held in company strength with machine-gun support and, in some cases, watchdogs. These outposts, reminiscent of German defences on the Western Front over twenty years earlier, were located at intervals of about 1,500 yards. This first line of a layered defence allowed interlocking arcs of fire for the machine gunners and would be lethal to advancing infantry.

A report on a typical minefield noted one east of Himeimat, the course of which was uncertain. The minefield was described as

> wire on angle-iron pickets (wire fallen in places and covered with sand). 100 yards inside wire: 4 rows Teller, spaced 3 yards, 8 yards, 3 yards. Blocks of 20 mines, 5 yards between mines, 50 yards between blocks. 3 yards further, second wire.[19]

A patrol on the night of 20/21 September reported the total depth of this minefield to be 135 to 150 yards. In addition, there were minefields south-west from Himeimat and 'in general it is not certain whether there is more than one field in this area'. The report's writer suggested that the main field was 'evidently encountered first, and the possibility of running into further mines once this is [passed] should be reckoned with'. It was also noted that the main field contained some S-mines – the source for this information was 7th Armoured Division's Royal Engineers – and that it was possible that the minefields continued northwards from Himeimat.[20] Although there was barbed wire this was not used to First World War levels, simply because there was not enough. At the beginning of October wire-cutting demonstrations were carried out by Brigadier Kisch's HQ and a new triple grapnel for dealing with wire was introduced.[21]

After the first band of mines came another strip of ground, anywhere between 1,000 and 2,000 yards wide that, in most places, was empty of any defences; but behind that lay another strip some 2,000 yards wide, across which were laid more mines and where each defending infantry battalion deployed its other two companies. As well as the standard firepower of rifles and machine guns, this belt also included the battalions' support weapons – heavy machine guns, mortars and anti-tank guns. But the empty zone was not completely empty. It included lateral belts of mines between inner and outer minefields, laid in the shape of narrow triangles, their points facing Eighth Army. In the median lines clear passages allowed the advance of counter-attacking infantry and the movement of reinforcements to the battle outposts. Also within the 'empty zone' were additional small haphazardly-laid minefields intended to play a part in defeating any British attack. The basic defensive concept was that any attackers who made it through the outer minefields would be forced into the areas between the lateral belts and there encounter the smaller minefields. At the same time those areas would be bombarded by Axis artillery which had already registered the areas.

Most mines, as we have seen, were anti-tank devices, each capable of blowing the track off a tank, thereby crippling it. They could also destroy wheeled vehicles, causing fatal injuries to many of their occupants. Nor did the systematic organization of Colonel Hecker's minefields end there: many mines were linked together so that a tank or lorry that detonated one would set off a line of others. Many were also booby-trapped so that anyone attempting to defuse them would be killed; only the most expert of bomb-disposal men could deal with these. In addition, some British aerial bombs and large-calibre artillery shells, part of the booty of Tobruk, were buried in apparently open areas as improvised mines, rigged to explode by tension on a trip wire.

For the infantryman it was fortunate that only about three in every hundred mines was an anti-personnel device but even that small proportion created risk. As we have seen, a heavy footfall from a running infantry soldier could detonate an anti-tank mine. Most anti-personnel mines were of the German S-mine type, a metal cylinder with small wire horns protruding from the top. Those horns were virtually invisible in the dusty conditions of the front, even in daylight, but treading on them detonated a charge that blew the mine out of the ground to explode at about waist level, scattering its contents of shrapnel and pellets. S-mines could also be linked together so that one soldier might set off a series that could inflict horrific injuries or even death not only on himself but on other members of his section. The S-mine was hated especially by the infantryman whose main dread of the device was not that it might kill him but that he might survive an explosion while losing his manhood through emasculation.[22]

The 'devil's gardens' provided a major problem for Montgomery and his planners. Since the plan called for two wide corridors to be created in the minefields for the armour and since the mine marsh was over three miles wide along most of the front, it was clear that many trained men would be needed to neutralize mines. Those men would have to work to a detailed and skilfully-crafted plan; and there was the problem of detecting the mines. Although the recently developed Polish electronic detector, so named in tribute to the nationality of its inventors, Captain J.S. Kosacki and Lieutenant Kalinowski of the Free Polish Forces,[23] would be available for the battle, almost 500 being delivered in time, these had been produced in haste; many suffered manufacturing defects as well as the inevitable problems of any new electronic machine. Using Polish detectors also required operators to stand upright, listening through earphones for changes in tone while sweeping the detector, on the end of a pole, from side to side. There could be no doubt that many operators would become casualties, while detecting tonal changes amidst the uproar of battle might also prove difficult.

Thus alternative methods of detection were sought. While special mine-destroying devices were improvised for the battle, and used to some extent, the principal method of detection was the tried and tested 'prodding' with a bayonet, or similar tool. This called for each square foot of ground to be so treated and, if metal were struck, for sand to be cleared away from the mine. Then would follow careful checking for booby traps or trip wires before the mine was detonated from a distance, or made safe by removing the detonator. Anti-personnel mines were somewhat different: these were fitted with a safety pin which was removed when the mine was laid and the hole for that pin could be fitted with a nail thereby neutralizing the mine.

> Mine detection was not going to be an easy task and would be a matter of very cool nerves and very steady hands, neither being ruffled or disturbed by the violence of battle raging on all sides. As protective infantry would have aroused the enemy at least in the battle outposts, the violence was likely to be extreme.[24]

Since there were not enough men trained for the task in Eighth Army, a School of Mine Clearance was established under Major Peter Moore, a pre-war regular officer of the Royal Engineers

> who had already distinguished himself during the first battles on Ruweisat Ridge, was one of the few men who had shot his way out of trouble with a revolver and one of the even fewer who had actually wrestled with an armed antagonist in the dark.[25]

The school was set up in mid-August near Burg el Arab and Moore, together with a New Zealand engineer, Major A.R. Currie, worked out the optimum team for mine-clearance operations and devised the drill for those teams. (The war diary of the Chief Engineer HQ Eighth Army, Brigadier Kisch, indicates that Currie was the school commandant.[26]) The first course at the school began on 26 August. Between then and 20 October seven courses passed through, each lasting eight days and catering for eight training teams from engineer units. A team included an officer and three NCOs. All students were made proficient in the mine-clearance drill with proficiency being defined as 'up to 100% reliability in deliberate mine clearance by day or night'.[27] As well as devising the standard drill for clearing mines, the school also developed a list of standard stores for the task and for lighting and marking gaps. Of the drill devised by Moore and Currie, Pitt wrote that

> even in an armchair forty years later without the slightest possibility of personal involvement, reading the drill instructions can evoke feelings of cold discomfort; how it looked and sounded to the men under training and faced with the realization that theory would become practice in but a few days requires little imagination.[28]

Pitt's comments are ones with which the author can concur, although in this instance the drill was read in an original document at Kew almost sixty years after it was written. Knowing something of the dread of the presence of an explosive device allowed the author an insight into the courage of those who passed through Eighth Army's School of Minefield Clearance.

In action, mine-clearing teams would follow the infantry with each being led by an officer and four men marching on a compass-bearing and unrolling white tape to mark the gap's axis. When the forward edge of the minefield was reached – calculated by reference to aerial photographs and information from foot patrols – a stake would be hammered into the ground and a blue light mounted on it to shine to the rear. The leading party would then move into line-abreast to advance in stooping posture with fingers brushing the ground and the backs of their hands facing to the front to feel for trip wires. All the while they would scan the ground for the horns of the hated S-mines. As this procedure was being carried out, the party's direction was controlled by the man with the compass who continued unrolling his white tape.

This party was followed by a light vehicle with sandbagged floor and extended steering column – so that the driver would not be impaled on it should the vehicle be blown up. The role of this vehicle was to ascertain that the forward edge of the minefield was where it was believed to be. If that were not the case then the vehicle would be blown up. That vehicle was followed by twenty-seven more men on foot, three teams of nine, each clearing an eight-foot-wide area to make a gap of twenty-four feet. In each team the leading three were detailed to mark the way and unroll more tape to guide their comrades while those on the gaps' outside edges planted stakes that would later support guiding lights for tanks and other heavy vehicles. (The placing of the lamps, almost 90,000, was to be carried out by military policemen.) As if this were not enough the leading trio of each team, if they had time, would also deal with any trip-wires, S-mines and booby-traps marked by the leading sappers but not made safe.

In each nine-man team, the second group of three carried out the actual mine detection, using Polish detectors if they had them or carefully prodding every square foot of ground while moving forward. Each mine detected was marked with a white cone for the teams who were to defuse the 'devil's eggs'. They scraped away the sand around the mine, checked for booby-traps or wires connecting it to other mines and, once a mine was isolated, pulled it out using a length of wire looped at the end. If it did not explode at this stage the detonator was removed and disarmed mines piled at the side of the gap to await removal.

As the team worked its way forward and the twenty-four-foot-wide gaps lengthened the lights could be lit on the stakes: green lights indicated the inside edge of the gap and orange the outside. Then, also, the infantry's heavier weapons could be taken through.

Creating the gaps would be a lengthy process. Training experience indicated that prodding could clear 100 yards in an hour while the Polish detectors could accomplish twice that rate. Thus an estimate could be made of the time, and manpower, needed to create gaps. This could only be an estimate: although the two main fields were known to be at least 500 yards and 1,000 yards deep respectively, there was no solid information on the extent of the fields inside the areas bounded by the main fields and the lateral belts.[29]

We have already noted that special mine-clearing devices were improvised and used to some extent in the battle. Dubbed 'Scorpions', these were later deployed with considerable success in north-west Europe. They did not enjoy quite so much success at El Alamein. Devised by a South African engineer named Du Toit, Scorpions were war-weary Matilda tanks fitted with auxiliary engines to drive a front-mounted rotating roller to which were attached twenty-six flails.[*][30] These would, literally, flail the ground in front of the tank, exploding any mines in its path. A number of Scorpions were built at Abbassia but there were obvious problems even at the experimental stage. The externally-

---

[*] In 1948 the Royal Commission on Awards to Inventors recommended awards totalling £20,000, tax free, to eleven officers, NCOs and civilians who had shared in the development of the Scorpion. Of the eleven men, five were members of the South African forces.

mounted engines driving the rollers became choked with sand and dust as the vehicle flailed, which caused overheating and breakdown. Sand also affected the main engine's filters. Another side effect of the dust raised by flailing was that operators became blinded by the huge columns of dust created. In spite of these problems, Scorpions manned by 42nd and 44th Royal Tanks, with RE personnel attached, were used by XIII Corps in the battle in the southern sector and had the unexpected advantage of striking terror into enemy soldiers who could not understand what was advancing towards them in the form of pillars of dust from which emanated mechanical sounds and occasional explosions. It must have appeared as if some biblical punishment was being visited upon the men of *Panzerarmee*.[31]

One other innovation used in XIII Corps was the 'Snail'. This was a lorry fitted with diesel tanks that allowed light streams of fuel to flow in its wake, it having been discovered that diesel reflected moonlight and would, therefore, leave a clearly-marked trail, akin to that of a snail and hence the codename.[32] In the battle 'Snails' were manned by sappers of 211 Field Park Company, who normally provided engineering stores, who thus led their comrades and the infantry into action. This was probably a 'first' in the history of the Royal Engineers field park companies.

The presence of the mine marshes was one factor that meant that Operation LIGHTFOOT would be fought as a battle of attrition in the manner of the First World War. Another was the concentration of artillery, although British counter-battery fire would attempt to destroy as much Axis artillery as possible in the opening phase. However, Axis anti-tank artillery would remain potent and a very real threat to Eighth Army's armour. The popular image of the desert as a huge stretch of flat sand owes more to films than to reality. Although there are no real heights around the area of the El Alamein line, there are some ridges that dominate while depressions create dead ground capable of hiding numbers of men or equipment. There are also small folds that can conceal a low-profile weapon such as the German 50mm anti-tank gun. The top of this weapon's shield is less than waist-high and a little fold in the ground can hide it. Combine that fold with darkness and the dust and smoke of battle and it can be seen that a tank could be upon such a gun before spotting it. At such short ranges the 50mm Pak 38 could destroy any British tank.

Eighth Army had a new chief gunner in Brigadier Sidney Kirkman whom Monty brought out from England to be his BRA (Brigadier Royal Artillery). Kirkman, who would end the war as a corps commander, arrived on 13

September, took over at HQ Eighth Army from Brigadier Martin on the 15th[33] and was the man behind Eighth Army's fire-plan for 23 October. This brought to bear the largest single concentration of artillery thus far in the war and the greatest since 1918. Kirkman would command 882 field and medium guns in LIGHTFOOT, firing a planned programme of destruction along the front for five and a half hours with only a ten-minute stop per hour to allow each gun to cool. Should the gunners come under enemy counter-battery fire they were neither to desist from their task nor to take shelter. The main part of the artillery programme would fall on the guns of XXX Corps whose CCRA (Corps Commander Royal Artillery), Brigadier Meade Edward Dennis, transferred from XIII Corps in September.[34] Dennis, an Irishman, was to be decorated with the DSO for his role in LIGHTFOOT.[35]

To enable the gunners to perform their task required a huge stockpile of ammunition which had to be dumped in appropriate locations, a further responsibility for each CCRA. On 10 October XIII Corps' dumps held 147,000 rounds of 25-pounder ammunition to meet the requirements of the guns taking part in the bombardment, each of which would fire 390 rounds, of which a quarter would be supercharge rounds. It would also cover the artillery of 7th Armoured Division, of which 3rd Regiment Royal Horse Artillery, 3rd Field Regiment, RA and 1st Field Regiment, Fighting French Forces, would fire 200 rounds per gun while the remainder would need only normal stocks. In addition the artillery of 50th Division, including 1st Greek Field Regiment, would fire 200 rounds per gun; all their requirements were noted as having been dumped in 44th Division's locality. Finally, the Field Maintenance Centres would hold further stocks for XIII Corps to cover four days' firing at Eighth Army rates and a further day at 30 rounds per gun.[36] During the course of the battle the guns of XIII Corps fired 578 rounds per gun, giving a daily average of forty-eight rounds for each gun.[37]

Some gunners had to learn to deal with new equipment in the prelude to LIGHTFOOT. This was the American M-7 howitzer motor carriage, a 105mm howitzer on a modified M-3 Grant chassis. Firing a 33-pound round, the first examples of this effective weapon were issued to 11th (Honourable Artillery Company) Regiment, Royal Horse Artillery, in 1st Armoured Division. This was 'Priest', an appropriate equipment for the 'galloping gunners', but it required training further to that needed to familiarize skilled gunners with a new weapon. US artillery procedure was based on that of the French army and officers and men of 11 (HAC) RHA had to absorb a new jargon in which degrees were replaced by 'mils', there were 'panoramic telescopes' and 'pro-directors', among other novelties.[38]

The Royal Artillery has long had the single battle honour 'Ubique', or *Everywhere*, and since the gunners have fought in all the Army's campaigns and battles it follows that that one word 'Ubique' sums up their service. But it also means that the Royal Artillery may lay claim to every battle honour awarded to every regiment in the Army. If those honours are compared to stars in the firmament of the Royal Artillery then, surely, the brightest of all those must be that representing the Battle of El Alamein since it was then that the Regiment proved its capability beyond doubt and demonstrated its battle-winning prowess to friend and foe alike. As Sir David Fraser writes of the Gunners: 'Now they came into their own.'[39] After El Alamein the opening bombardment became a yardstick by which to compare later bombardments: 'more guns than at Alamein'; 'as many rounds as at Alamein'; 'a sound like that at Alamein'. The philosophy for the Gunners – their mission statement in modern jargon – was expressed in the comment: 'British artillery should dominate the battlefield and should allow no enemy movement within range to remain unpunished.'[40] And that is exactly what Sidney Kirkman's artillery achieved.

The dumping in forward areas of ammunition for the artillery was but one piece of the logistical jigsaw that was Eighth Army's build-up for Operation LIGHTFOOT. A total of 286,000 rounds of 25-pounder ammunition, plus 20,000 medium shells were dumped and concealed in the battle area.[41] Stocks were buried at sites chosen as gun positions but not occupied until the very last moment. In addition to that ammunition, stocks of ammunition and equipment were also needed for the infantry battalions and armoured regiments. Fuel had to be stored and that almost priceless commodity in the desert, water, provided. A list of stores handled by the army's supply arm would be almost endless. That it was all in place in time was a tremendous tribute to that arm and a lesson to modern–day management experts.

Stores were held in field maintenance centres, although there were also specialist depots for engineers. The Royal Army Service Corps (RASC) ran the FMCs, as well as moving supplies into them from the rear areas, or the ports, and then bringing them forward for the offensive. In the northern sector Eighth Army had to hide 2,000 tons of fuel, 600 tons of food, 400 tons of engineer stores, 3,000 tons of ammunition and 600 tons of ordnance stores; the first three commodities were hidden in the El Alamein area, the others near El Imayid.[42] During the first three weeks of October the railheads in the forward area were dealing with a daily movement of 2,500 tons of supplies for Eighth Army; as well as providing a week's battle maintenance of all logistic requirements at

FMCs and on wheels, the RASC had also to keep the army supplied with the daily living requirements for its ration strength of 250,000 souls.[43] One RASC officer, Colonel William Eassie, another Irishman, had been appointed KBE for his work as Deputy Director of Supply and Transport (DDST) of XXX Corps earlier in the year and was to earn the DSO for his services at El Alamein in October.[44]

The stockpiling task involved the equivalent of thirty-six general transport (GT) companies of the RASC whose vehicles had a capacity to carry over 10,000 tons; most GT companies were equipped with 3-ton lorries but some operated 10-tonners; a GT company equipped with 3-tonners could lift 300 tons.[45] These vehicles moved materials from the railheads at Burg el Arab and Amiriya, as well as other depots in the rear area, to the forward area. Added to the GT companies were six tank-transporter companies, which performed sterling service in delivering tanks to armoured units in the forward area, and a Bulk Petrol Transport Company. Nine water-tank companies added their skills to the build-up programme. GHQ still had a reserve of seven GT companies; between 1 August and the opening of LIGHTFOOT, GHQ issued or assigned to Eighth Army a total of 8,700 general service vehicles from the 10,300 received in the Middle East.[46]

Near El Alamein three new waterpoints were built for Eighth Army and many miles of water pipeline were laid. The movement and storage of water in smaller quantities presented a cause of frustration at all levels down to the individual soldier. Since the beginning of the desert campaign the standard British container for water was a tin – basically a civilian petrol tin – made of very thin metal. So thin was that metal, and so poor the can's seams, that 'staff calculations allowed for 25 per cent loss by breakage and evaporation on a desert journey of 250 miles'.[47] British soldiers envied the Germans their petrol and water container, a strong can that would absorb considerable abuse and was much more easily handled than its British counterpart. An Eighth Army report on lessons from operations between 10 September 1941 and 25 August 1942 contained a note on the inadequacy of British water containers and a preference for the German container. It also noted that one British container, the four-gallon drum, was lead-lined which led to contamination 'after storage of saline water for about ten days'.[48] Not surprisingly, captured examples of the German container were pressed into service and dubbed 'Jerrycans', a nickname that became an accepted description of the container to the extent that 'jerrican' can now be found in English dictionaries. The 'Jerrycan' was copied by both British and US forces and became the standard container for carrying small quantities of fuel or water. But, in the build-up to El Alamein, Eighth Army still relied heavily on the British 'flimsy'.

The medical services made their own preparations for the forthcoming battle. As in every such case a medical plan was prepared and estimates made of the probable number of casualties. Among the preparations made were those for transfusing blood into wounded soldiers for which, immediately prior to the battle, 3,220 bottles of blood were flown to Eighth Army, the largest despatch in a single day being that of 366 bottles. All field medical units were supplied with plasma and 2,961 bottles of plasma were sent forward during the battle period. There was also a large demand for saline solution, exacerbated by the fact that men who would have died but a few years before were now being saved: these were the casualties who had suffered severe abdominal wounds and who were treated in the forward area.[49] The introduction of what were then known as 'chemotherapeutic' drugs, especially 'the substance now known as Penicillin', was responsible for this achievement.[50]

Blood and other medical supplies were moved by air or refrigerated truck to No.3 Field Transfusion Unit (FTU), which then supplied all other transfusion units. An additional refrigerated truck was sent forward to form an Advanced Blood Bank and, after the initial issue, all blood and other requirements were 'issued in exchange for returned empties'.[51] No.3 FTU accompanied the Advanced Air Transport Centre and was supplied daily with blood from the Base Transfusion Unit. The first 300 cases transfused in the field during the battle showed a very low level of reaction; this remained the case when the results from the transfusing of 2,500 bottles were analyzed.[52]

A further element in the medical plan was the arrangement of air evacuation for wounded, which reached a new stage in its development during the battle with more than 2,000 cases evacuated to base by air. The peak figure for one day was 200 cases. However, abdominal cases were not suitable for immediate air evacuation and were usually retained for about four days before being flown out. Chest cases were able to travel with little discomfort at about a hundred feet, the operating height of the aircraft carrying out the evacuation flights.[53]

Also within the remit of the medical services were the hygiene sections. Among their duties during the battle was the cleansing of areas captured from the enemy, including clearing fouled ground, purifying water supplies, delousing prisoners and pushing forward apparatus for the future cleanliness of their own troops. To them fell the often horrific task of removing the remains of crews from knocked-out tanks. Among the hygiene measures taken during the build-up to LIGHTFOOT was the creation of No.1 Fly Control Unit of five officers and 300 men from 1502 Mauritius Pioneer Company and soldiers from an infantry base depot to deal with a serious plague of flies. The problems had been caused by

> concentration of large forces on a narrow front in late summer, season of fly and mosquito borne diseases
> mass of Bedouins swept back behind Alamein by German advance
> slackening of unit hygiene discipline due to July withdrawal
> disturbance caused to hygiene organization by the withdrawal[54]

Some soldiers in 10th Armoured Division Signals found an unusual temporary antidote to the fly problem when a chameleon took up residence in their wireless van. 'Where he or she came from I just don't know. But the short time we had it, there were no flies on us. It was with us for about three days, then was gone, to be seen no more.'[55]

Among the many items that had to be produced for Eighth Army were maps. Large-scale and highly detailed, these were issued in their thousands. During June and July some sixty tons of paper had been used to print maps of the Delta and Egypt and, on average, the army was using about 200,000 maps each month (in October 547,169 maps were issued by 13 Field Survey Map Depot RE).[56] Units and formations were asked to reduce the numbers of maps used due to a paper shortage in India, whence came the paper on which they were printed. This policy of rationing was not helped, although it was possibly inspired, by the loss of 800 maps by one officer who went to Ikingi to draw maps for his formation. On his return journey he lost the maps which seem never to have been found. (They had still not been recovered in May 1943.) The officer responsible was not named, nor was his formation, but such carelessness was not isolated, as was shown when over 5,000 maps were found 'in chaotic state' in the waiting room of Imayid railway station. The find was reported by 4 Lines of Communication Signals Company and the maps salvaged. Such incidents led to a general exhortation to tighten security with units urged especially not to report enemy positions in clear over the air.[57]

By contrast *Panzerarmee*'s logistic arrangements were poor, principally because of the interdiction of Axis supplies as they were ferried across the Mediterranean, but also because the supply systems of the two Axis powers had never been as fine-tuned as that of the British. Had the battle depended entirely on the quartermasters of the opposing armies then it had been won by Montgomery's men before the first round was fired on the night of 23 October.

Another important element of Montgomery's overall plan was deception. Since an offensive was inevitable, the build-up of personnel, supplies and equipment through the ports obvious, and the length of the front so short, it was vital to deceive Rommel as to when and where the attack would take place. Montgomery wrote:

> I attached great importance to the arrangements for concealing our intentions from the enemy. It seemed impossible to disguise for long the fact that we were preparing to attack, so our efforts were bent mainly in achieving tactical rather than strategical surprise. The express object of the scheme of deception was to mislead the enemy as to the date of the operation and to give him the impression that the main thrust would develop in the south.[58]

Thus was born Operation BERTRAM, the tactical deception plan to mislead Rommel as far as possible about the exact timings and location of Eighth Army's attack.* The deception story behind BERTRAM was that

> owing to teething troubles with our tanks, uncertainty about the Russian front, and the desirability of synchronizing the 8th Army offensive with the passage of a Malta convoy, the attack by 8th Army will not take place before 5 November and it is expected to take place in the Southern sector.[59]

The man behind BERTRAM was Lieutenant Colonel C.L. Richardson and this basic concept was simple:

> every evidence of concentration of force would be openly displayed as quickly as possible so that, when no assault immediately developed, the enemy would grow used to its existence and notice no change when fact replaced fiction.[60]

---

* There was also a strategic deception plan, TREATMENT, which sought to create the impression that Montgomery did not intend to attack at all.

Hitherto, Rommel had enjoyed good intelligence on British intentions but both his principal sources had been removed. These were his wireless intercept service, which the Australians had captured as we saw in a previous chapter, and his 'good source' which had been identified through ULTRA intercepts on 29 June, two weeks before the wireless company was captured. This 'good source' was the US Military Attaché in Cairo, Colonel Bonner Fellows, whose regular and full reports to Washington had been read by German intelligence who had broken the American code. Even with these two intelligence sources plugged, there was still much information going back to German and Italian intelligence from Egypt, which was another reason for the creation of a deception plan.

Operation BERTRAM included a number of subsidiary operations: BRIAN, DIAMOND, MARTELLO, MELTINGPOT, MUNASSIB and MURRAYFIELD.[61] These covered concealment of stores, vehicles, ammunition, fuel and water, as well as artillery. Operation BRIAN, which seems to have been a play on Horrocks' forename, was the dummy petrol, food and ammunition dump in the southern sector, while, also in that sector, MUNASSIB was a concentration of dummy artillery which, when the battle had commenced, would be replaced by genuine artillery to support a XIII Corps attack. Operations MARTELLO, MELTINGPOT and MURRAYFIELD were complementary plans, intended to cover the move of X Corps' armour to their forward concentration areas and 'probably the most important parts of Bertram'.[62]

Soldiers were set to digging slit-trenches in the frontal area, which were left unused, while dummy vehicles, tanks, artillery and dumps were constructed in early-October to give the impression of a build-up for an attack. But, as the days passed, the vehicles either remained in position or some slight changes were made in dispositions while the real tanks, lorries and guns arrived at Wadi Natrun to be tested and allow some training in their use before moving, during the hours of darkness, into the operational area where they replaced dummies. In turn those dummies were moved to the training area to give the impression that no changes had taken place. The illusion of vehicles was created by stacking boxes of food into the shapes of lorries covered with camouflage netting. Small tents, of the kind that might be used by drivers, were erected alongside the 'lorries' and also filled with boxes of food. To reduce the chances of pilferage, the outlying 'lorries' were made up from boxes of bully beef and army biscuits, neither popular with local Arabs. From time to time, some real lorries were driven around the areas to give the impression of activity.[63]

The illusionist Jasper Maskelyne was commissioned to head a special section that dreamt up and put into effect some outstanding examples of deception. Their work included a dummy oil jetty with a ship moored alongside. From day to day the ship's appearance changed by the addition or removal of funnels or masts or the lengthening of the hull. A dummy railhead was built near a dummy oil-discharging point and inflammable materials were stacked nearby. In the piles of inflammable material remote-controlled pyrotechnic devices could be set off to create blazes whenever Luftwaffe or *Regia Aeronautica* bombers attacked the area. The fires thus started led following bombers to drop their loads on what seemed to be significant targets. A nautical flavour was continued with the construction of dummy landing craft to create the impression that Eighth Army might use a right hook and land troops behind *Panzerarmee*'s lines.[64]

When a new water pipeline was laid from Alexandria to the front the old pipeline was left undisturbed and was, apparently, still the main pipeline to the front. However, the new pipeline, which was of greater diameter than that which it replaced, was laid entirely at night and was not spotted by the enemy. At its terminal a new waterpoint was built and camouflaged at El Imayid station; this did not come into operation until the opening of the battle. By contrast, a dummy freshwater pipeline was laid from the end of a genuine pipeline at Alam el Khadim, south of El Imayid, to a point in the southern sector some four miles east of Samaket Gaballa. Along the pipeline's route three dummy pump-houses were erected with waterpoints and storage reservoirs at two pump-house locations. Work on this was also carried out during the night but arranged so that early-morning reconnaissance flights by enemy aircraft should occasionally spot evidence of the work which progressed at a rate that made it clear the pipeline would not be complete until early-November, thus suggesting that the British offensive would come at the time of the November full moon.[65] This was Operation DIAMOND.

In the northern sector real intentions were concealed while signs of considerable activity and build-up in the southern area gave the impression that the main assault would be launched there. Enemy aircraft ran less risk of being shot down in that sector and so could see much more of what was happening on the ground while, since the Alam el Halfa battle, enemy troops had occupied the twin peaks of Himeimat, allowing them to see much activity in the XIII Corps area. They were given much to observe: in Operation BRIAN dummy administration camps were built in the area south of Ruweisat ridge and existing dumps were expanded with empty tents and cases and new, empty, dumps built in between.[66] From Horrocks' point of view it was an infernal nuisance to have the enemy sitting on the hill from where he could observe everything that went on in the southern part of the sector. I should like to have driven him off Himeimat, which we could have done quite easily.[67]

But Montgomery said no to Horrocks' suggestion for an attack on Himeimat: it suited his deception plan to have the enemy observe the build-up in that sector.

On 5 October orders were issued for a party of 200 men to erect dummy tanks on the night of D-1 in two map squares in the corps area; this party was needed as 'the camouflage company will be fully occupied elsewhere'.[68] In addition XIII Corps had its own deception plan, Operation MELTINGPOT, which was 'to represent 10 Armoured Division from D-4 to morning of D+1 in areas 4686 and 4786 and possibly 4685', thus concealing the move of that division to its concentration area under X Corps. That move was to take place between 20 and 22 October. The first two map squares were those in which the dummy tanks were to be erected on the night before LIGHTFOOT. The dummy force representing 10th Armoured was to include the surplus transport of 51st (Highland) Division, have its commander supplied by that division and include a Royal Engineers camouflage company with a mobile section of 85 Camouflage Company of the South African Engineer Corps; 118th and 124th Royal Tanks, both dummy units; two batteries of dummy Bofors guns; dummy MT released from the southern assembly area with substitute MT, if available, from the northern area; and a LAA battery from XIII Corps. By the opening of LIGHTFOOT the true 10th Armoured Division included 8 and 24 Armoured Brigade Groups as well as 133 Lorried Infantry Brigade.[69]

False information was also planted to mislead enemy agents in the Delta: wireless frequencies and call-signs were changed often; only troops holding the front line were allowed to patrol in the forward area so that any taken prisoner would not have seen the build-up to the rear; those knowing the battle plan were not allowed to leave Eighth Army's area; and the plan was not passed down to officers below lieutenant colonel until 21 October and to the soldiers not until a day or two after that.[70]

Throughout September and October the build-up continued: training developed from unit level to brigade level to divisional level and all the stores needed were moved into place. The jigsaw that was LIGHTFOOT was moving towards completion. On the other side the deception plan seemed to have worked in convincing Rommel that there would be no British offensive until

November. He departed for Germany on sick leave on 23 September, handing over command to his deputy, General Georg Stumme, who was to carry out Rommel's instructions and was told that, at the first sign of British aggression, the Desert Fox would return. At much the same time, the period of the full moon, Allied air forces launched a major bombing and strafing attack on the Axis positions, designed as part of the deception process so that, when a similar attack was launched in the October full-moon period, it would be seen as routine. Montgomery had achieved surprise in his timing for Operation LIGHTFOOT.

Chapter Five

On the Eve of Battle

O God of battles! Steel my soldiers' hearts

Montgomery continued emphasizing the importance of training as D Day for LIGHTFOOT approached. The crews of the new Shermans were becoming familiar with their machines and, in the case of personnel recently arrived from Britain, the conditions in which they would be fighting. Those tankmen 'had now to learn how to take advantage of a tank whose armament, power and reliability were well above any they had previously encountered'.[1] Not only did tankmen need to become familiar with the desert and its conditions, so too did infantrymen. This was especially true for recently-arrived divisions, including 51st (Highland), which had been re-formed after the capture of the original formation in France in 1940. Since that division had surrendered to Rommel, the new 51st (Highland) Division, under Major General Douglas Wimberley, had a particular score to settle.

Wimberley, with his passionate belief in morale, averred that his division should always have 'a guid conceit o' themsels';[2] they would earn the soubriquet 'the Highway Decorators' from their practice of painting their divisional cypher everywhere they went. In late June 1942 the Highland Division sailed to join Eighth Army and uphold Scotland's pride. Nine weeks later, in August, its soldiers disembarked in Egypt, moving to concentrate at Qasassin before being deployed in the Delta defences. From the Delta 51st (Highland) Division moved to occupy defensive boxes at El Hammam, about twenty-five miles east of El Alamein. Each brigade spent a week at the front with 9th Australian Division and the Highlanders learned much from the Australians who

> had a different type of discipline from ours, but in the line our men learned very valuable lessons from those fine troops. The Aussies kept their weapons scrupulously clean and always free from sand. Their slit trenches were prepared with the utmost care, and each trench was completely equipped with such things as grenades. Before a party left on patrol each member of it was searched thoroughly for any identification marks. By night silence

was enforced and no lights were allowed. When a patrol returned from its job a complete account of its investigation and acquired information was recorded on a map, and such maps combined with air-pictures gave the most detailed information of the enemy's minefields and other defences.[3]

Some ten miles south of El Hammam was a full-scale replica of the German defences that 51st (Highland) Division would attack. Much time was spent there practising attacks through wire and minefields. To make training realistic, live ammunition was used for artillery bombardments. This cost several lives, including that of Major Sir Arthur Wilmot, second-in-command of 1st Black Watch. Operation orders were refined to the last detail before the division moved into the line, relieving the Australians.[4]

Newcomers learned quickly that it was difficult to navigate in the desert and they had to become familiar with new navigational aids. For the El Alamein attack it was essential that each company and each battalion should follow its own axis of advance. However, the difficulties of finding one's way in the desert at night were illustrated convincingly for 51st (Highland) Division's commander one night when he left his caravan to walk to the mess tent, 400 yards away. In a duststorm it took Wimberley some two hours to find the tent.[5]

So that attacking troops would not go off course, each company had a navigating officer who would advance on the line of the company axis holding a compass and keeping the men of his company on the right path. One of 7th Black Watch's navigating officers was Lieutenant George Morrison, from Crieff in Perthshire. Writing home to his mother on 29 August he informed her that he was his company navigating officer,

using sun compass, oil compass, astro and azimuth tables, protractors and all the rest. The desert is like the sea and needs deadly accurate navigation, as there is not a single landmark to help you at all, it's as flat and desolate as the moon must be. It's a big responsibility, but I'm pretty good at the sun compass now; I've been studying it since we landed. It's an eerie job going out into the unknown and very often the unmapped as well. It means that every man of these hundred men depends on me, the navigator, to guide them perhaps a hundred miles over the desert, and it's my job to keep watching and checking all the way. Still, for a Morrison, nae bother at all!![6]

The opening hours of LIGHTFOOT would demand a heavy toll of navigating officers. George Morrison would be among those to pay with their young lives.

While the training and preparations continued, XIII Corps' commander, Horrocks, decided to seize some ground near Deir el Munassib on which to deploy additional artillery during the battle. This attack would also add to the deception that Eighth Army's main offensive would be in the south. To this task Horrocks assigned 131 (Queen's) Brigade of 44th Division, a brigade untested in action which included three battalions of the Queen's Royal Regiment – 1/5th, 1/6th and 1/7th. The attack was launched on the morning of 30 September and 131 Brigade, supported by 4 Armoured Brigade tanks, advanced under cover of heavy artillery fire and dense mist. However, the shelling almost neutralized the cover of the mist. In the north neither 1/6th nor 1/7th Queen's met any serious opposition and secured their objectives, but 1/5th hit positions held by Italian and German paratroopers from *Folgore* Division and the Ramcke Brigade. The ensuing battle was hard and bitter: the defenders inflicted heavy casualties on the Queensmen who lost almost 300 dead, wounded or missing: 'two whole companies were wiped out and a third decimated.'[7]

Attempts to retrieve the situation came to naught. A 4 Armoured Brigade effort to renew the attack ended in confusion, largely due to misunderstanding and inexperience. On the morning of 1 October Horrocks called off the operation; 132 Brigade was sent to relieve 1/6th and 1/7th Queen's. Although neither battalion had seen much fighting there were casualties from heatstroke and exhaustion while some men who had lost their way were never seen again. For the trip back the ambulances had full loads.[8] The commanding officer of 1/6th Queen's, Lieutenant Colonel D.L.A. Gibbs, described the taking of the ground as 'unpleasant enough, [but] the easiest part of the operation'. He went on to note the difficulties of re-organizing on the objectives and selecting suitable positions for his companies and battalion headquarters 'in what seemed to be a very open, naked and coverless sandy arena'. Gibbs' battalion was 'in that situation, pretty visible to the enemy, and under mortar and shell fire for a couple of days or so' before being relieved.[9]

This setback gave Montgomery pause, emphasizing that some brigades were not yet fit for battle. He had to rethink his policy of keeping divisions intact as there was not enough time for sufficient training before LIGHTFOOT. A few days later, another development hastened his review of the plans.

On 5 October Montgomery's intelligence staff produced a fresh analysis of *Panzerarmee Afrika*'s defensive layout, which indicated conclusively, and for the first time, that these were especially formidable. While Monty and his planners were aware of two lines of defences, the fresh analysis warned that there might be a third. Allied to the setback in the south this analysis led to Montgomery's revision of the plan for LIGHTFOOT, which was made known on 6 October. The armoured commanders' lack of enthusiasm, and the comments of the Dominion commanders, must also have played a part in changing his mind. When he addressed conferences of officers of the three corps on 19 (XIII and XXX Corps) and 20 October, he emphasized the nature of the battle: it would be one of attrition in which Eighth Army had an overwhelming superiority in guns and tanks, but would not be a walkover. Indeed he went on to stress that every man in Eighth Army must be ready to kill the enemy and to go on killing him until the battle was won. In what Bishop Montgomery might have regarded as blasphemous, but which drew laughter from his audience, he even suggested that chaplains would need to kill enemy soldiers – one each on weekdays and two on Sundays. Montgomery's carefully structured notes for this presentation include the point that the battle would last ten days. In fact he told his listeners that it would last for twelve, a remarkably accurate prediction; the change is indicated in a pencilled amendment to the original document.

The principal difference in the revised plan was the change from a break-out by the armour to engage and destroy Rommel's armour to a deployment by X Corps, as soon as they had cleared the minefield gaps, into a screen separating Axis infantry from Axis armour, behind which would be fought the infantry battle. When the Axis armour tried to break through the British screen to assist their own infantry, X Corps would be able to support XXX Corps 'and both would be kept tightly under Montgomery's personal control'.[10] However, Lumsden was convinced that the minefield corridors could not be cleared in a single night, leaving his tanks cooped up in their narrow confines at dawn to become targets for concentrated fire from enemy anti-tank guns. The whole concept was alien to the ethos of the armour. Montgomery directed that, in the event of XXX Corps' engineers not completing the corridors in the first night, X Corps' engineers and infantry would complete the task and the corps should fight its way forward to its designated positions. Once again this instruction was anathema to Lumsden who told his brigade and regimental commanders that they were not to charge against anti-tank guns and should ensure that the corridor exits were not under anti-tank fire when they tried to debouch. However, he seems to have offered no alternative plan.

The antipathy between armour and infantry had not disappeared and Montgomery should have listened more closely to the Dominion commanders' reservations. Those were not brought to his attention immediately by Leese, to whom they were first expressed, probably because Leese, a newcomer to the desert himself, did not appreciate just how deep-seated they were. He took more cognizance of them when, about two weeks before D Day, Brigadier G.P. Walsh, his Brigadier General Staff, having attended a conference held by X Corps, informed Leese that he did not believe that X Corps intended to break out through XXX Corps at dawn on the 24th. Leese reported this to Montgomery, whose reaction was to issue 'absolutely definite orders' to X Corps that the armour must pass through XXX Corps early on the morning of the 24th.[11]

Lumsden was aware of armour's limitations and of the problems his corps was having in training for LIGHTFOOT. He had lost one armoured division, 8th, for which no infantry brigade could be found, and 10th Armoured Division had to absorb an armoured brigade from 8th Division as well as an infantry brigade from 44th Division. This latter was 133 Brigade, which converted hurriedly to being lorried infantry, a role its soldiers could not have dreamed of in Britain a few months earlier. So much for the doctrine that divisions would not be broken up. Stern reality was forcing this on Montgomery.

Additional problems were caused in the armoured regiments by the practice of concentrating tanks in squadrons by type. While this might not have caused too many problems in normal circumstances, these were far from normal days and, during the build-up, the practice caused the regular transfer of tanks and crews from squadron to squadron. Such transfers might be reversed within days or weeks, making for an unsettling time for crews. It also made it more difficult to train for the forthcoming operation, especially as there was 'no common battle drill in regiments with one Grant and two cruiser squadrons'.[12] Regimental commanders were trying to obtain Shermans for their units but were often given Grants instead, or even Crusaders. Some regiments even received Shermans on the day the battle began but with vital items of equipment missing.

Perhaps cognizant of some of the armoured units' problems, Montgomery issued a special message to all workshops in Eighth Army.

> The Army Commander wishes all ranks concerned with the repair, inspection and delivery of Tanks to know that the present is a time of critical importance. The rate at which Tanks are delivered to Units in full battleworthy condition during the next few days may determine the extent to which the Eighth Army can complete the discomfort of the enemy. He calls for a special effort from all Ranks.[13]

The workshops were working flat out and did not let Montgomery or the armoured units down.

X Corps held an exercise from 23 to 26 September to study the problems of:

moving a division into a restricted assembly area by night
moving forward from an assembly area by restricted routes through gaps
in our own minefields and thence through gaps in enemy minefields to a
deployment area beyond
deploying by night of an Armoured Brigade Group in the deployment area
deployment by day of the remainder of the armoured division in the
deployment area.[14]

The nodal point of the exercise was a series of four forty-yard-wide gaps in a
dummy minefield, each centre about 500 yards apart, four gaps being taken as
an armoured divisional front.

Training and exercises were underway in all formations. In 7th Armoured
Division, of XIII Corps, 1st Rifle Brigade's commanding officer, Lieutenant
Colonel Stephens, and his company commanders took part in a brigade scheme
on 1 October, beginning with a move to an assembly area, followed by adoption
of night formation before, from 2300 to 2359 hours, passing through a dummy
minefield. The scheme concluded on the morning of the 2nd with the adoption of
battle positions. A corps scheme followed on the 7th involving the commanding
officer, a skeleton HQ, C Company and A, B and I Companies' commanders,
alongside the affiliated armour. Once again movement through a minefield was
practised, with four gaps being cleared through a dummy minefield. Reality was
never far away as, on 9 October, a day after the corps scheme ended, eight anti-
tank guns of 65th Anti-tank Regiment were assigned to the battalion to counter
a possible raid on its front by 21st Panzer Division. No raid developed and
preparations for the offensive continued with a divisional scheme on the 18th
and 19th while a fighting patrol engaged enemy troops in a forward minefield on
the night of the 20th. During this engagement Major J.A. Persse was wounded
seriously and a rifleman was missing. Then, on the 22nd, the battalion moved to
a concentration area in readiness for its part in LIGHTFOOT.[15]

Among the constituent formations of 7th Armoured Division was 4 Light
Armoured Brigade – the Greys, 4th/8th Hussars* and 1st King's Royal Rifle

---

* A composite regiment made up from 4th Queen's Own and 8th King's Royal Irish
  Hussars. Both had sustained heavy losses in earlier fighting. In 1958 they amalgamated to
  form the Queen's Royal Irish Hussars but are now part of a new regiment, the Queen's
  Royal Hussars (Queen's Own and Royal Irish).

Corps – commanded by Brigadier Marcus Roddick. Until the afternoon of 20 October the brigade was involved in exercises, rehearsing its part in the operation. Roddick, together with his brigade major and Lieutenant Colonel Kidd of 4th/8th Hussars, attended Montgomery's conference at XIII Corps headquarters on the 19th.

The heavy brigade of 7th Armoured Division was Pip Roberts' 22 Armoured Brigade, with 1st and 5th Royal Tank Regiments plus 4th County of London Yeomanry (Sharpshooters). On 1 October the brigade held a night exercise to practise passing through minefield gaps; this was proclaimed 'a great success, considering the novelty of the manoeuvre'. Next day 22 Armoured played host to Lieutenant General Sir Oliver Leese, commander of XXX Corps, who was inspecting the recent battlefield. Thereafter the brigade resumed its training routine until moving into the assembly area for the offensive.[16]

On 22 October the war diary of Headquarters 1st Armoured Division noted:

For the past month intensive training had been carried out by units and bdes with a view to the forthcoming operations of the Div making three gaps by night through enemy minefields through which 2 Armd Bde and 7 Motor Bde could pass.[17]

Of the armoured divisions, 1st, under Major General Raymond Briggs, had the most up-to-date equipment, ninety-two of 161 tanks in 2 Armoured Brigade being Shermans. His artillery, under Brigadier Bryan John Fowler DSO MC, known as Frizz and another of the many Irishmen to be found in the higher echelons of Eighth Army, included the Priests of 11 (HAC) RHA and the SP Deacons (6-pounder anti-tank guns mounted on armour-protected AEC Matador lorries) of ZZ Battery, 76th Anti-Tank Regiment. The latter were assigned to Briggs' infantry, 7 Motor Brigade, veterans of the desert campaign; the brigade's battalions were all Green Jackets – 2nd King's Royal Rifle Corps and 2nd and 7th Rifle Brigade – with a high reputation from their days with 7th Armoured Division. Also under command of 7 Motor Brigade was a composite squadron with six of the new Churchill I-tanks. Commanded by Major Norris King, Royal Gloucestershire Hussars, this scratch sub-unit was known as Kingforce and would see action twice, under direct command of 1st Armoured Division. The divisional Minefield Task Force – and of such forces we will learn more shortly – was commanded by Lieutenant Colonel Victor Buller Turner, who was to earn the Victoria Cross in the forthcoming battle.

Brigadier Frank Fisher commanded 2 Armoured Brigade, which included The Bays, 9th Lancers and 10th Hussars with the Yorkshire Dragoons as motor battalion. On 18 October, with the aid of a sand model at divisional headquarters, Fisher explained to officers down to and including squadron leaders the general plan for the attack.[18] Next day the brigade moved to a staging area at Alam Shaltut and from there, on the night of 20/21 October, to its assembly area near El Imayid. On the 22nd Fisher held a conference of his commanding officers to discuss the brigade's final plans and on the morning of the 23rd visited his regiments 'to explain the general plan to all ranks and to stress the necessity of success in the forthcoming operations'. He also read Montgomery's special order of the day to all officers and NCOs of each unit.[19]

One of the soldiers of 2 Armoured Brigade was Jack Merewood, a tank gunner of The Bays. Following convalescence from a wound he returned to his regiment in early October to find many new faces alongside his comrades; new recruits had arrived from Britain to replace the regiment's losses in earlier battles.

The days in October were spent driving the new Shermans and firing the guns. Because of the sand it was essential to be constantly stripping down, cleaning and oiling the guns. To clean the barrel we had a long rod with a brush on the end. The rod unscrewed into two pieces, and it sometimes came in handy when making a 'bivvy' at the side of the tank. When we stopped for any length of time camouflage nets were spread over the tanks to eliminate the shadow cast by the sun, this making it more difficult to be spotted by enemy aircraft.[20]

The soldiers knew they were preparing for a major offensive. At 8.00am on the 23rd Merewood's troop leader informed his men of the details of the plan. At 9.30am there was a church parade and, following their midday meal, the crews carried out last-minute maintenance on their tanks. That afternoon Jack Merewood's crew played cards, being unable to sleep as they were supposed to.

In 10th Armoured Division 4th Royal Sussex was one of the battalions of 133 Lorried Infantry Brigade, the formation that had not only been transferred from 44th Division but also been given a change of role. The battalion war diary notes 'Normal Training, Ranges. Etc.' until the warning order to move to the staging area was received from Brigade HQ at 8.00pm on 17 October, a move which was completed next day. A move to the divisional assembly area followed on the 20th. With companies in their own assembly areas, final arrangements were made for the attack. On 22 October the battalion received eight four-wheel-drive 3-ton lorries.[21]

The same division's 8 Armoured Brigade carried out its Brigade Exercise No.12 from 30 September to 3 October and, on 1 October, Montgomery, Lumsden and Gatehouse, commanders of Eighth Army, X Corps and 10th Armoured Division respectively, attended a brigade battle practice. Exercise No.12 was no sooner complete than Neville Custance had his units undertaking Exercise No.13, from 4 to 6 October. Then, from the 7th until the 9th, Exercise No.14 took place in conjunction with Divisional Exercise No.3, followed by a sandtable exercise at divisional headquarters on the 10th. Two days later there was a signals exercise – 10th Armoured Division Signals Exercise No.7 – while reports were received from each regiment on important reconnaissances. On the same day 8 Armoured Brigade learned that it was to receive thirty-three Shermans in exchange for the same number of Grants; it was decided that eleven Shermans should go to each regiment – 3rd Royal Tanks, Sherwood Rangers and Staffordshire Yeomanry. Further signals exercises followed over the next few days, at both divisional and corps level. On the 17th senior officers attended a conference at X Corps HQ and fifteen Shermans were delivered to the brigade.[22]

In 51st (Highland) Division the training programme was rising to a crescendo. One battalion, 7th Argyll and Sutherland Highlanders, produced an account of their part in the battle and the preparations beforehand. The writer noted that everyone knew that something major was afoot, although place and date, 'and even the probability of a night attack', were closely guarded secrets.

> In the month before the battle we took part in five full-scale rehearsals, all slightly different, but all of approximately the same operation. Finally, during our spell in the sector of the front a little South of Tel el Eisa station which the three brigades held in turn, we were ordered to dig and camouflage slit trenches for the whole battalion about a mile behind the front line, nominally as a new defensive position, actually for our assembly area before the attack.[23]

One element of the divisional training programme was preparation for making eleven gaps through the British minefields, a task assigned to 152 Brigade. The first gaps cleared were codenamed, from north to south, Sun, Moon and Star. Within the brigade 5th Seaforth were to provide 'the firm base from which the attack would be launched, to lay out the Divisional start line and to mark the routes leading forward to it'.[24] There would be nine such lines.

The battalion had already evolved a drill for the task and those involved began their work on the night of 19/20 October. Their first problem was ascertaining the exact spots for the ends of the start line; an error would knock awry the entire layout. Since the ground was as featureless as the ocean 'map references were useful as a general guide only' and navigating officers were called upon to exercise their skills. A number of officers began to pace forwards from known points, each holding a compass, following a bearing until they converged. With the end points of the start line defined, an initial, but concealed, marking was laid down using signal cable fixed at ground level to metal angle-iron pickets at fifty-yard intervals. Even if German or Italian patrols found the cable they were unlikely to deduce its purpose; they were more likely to consider it to be a trip-wire. The work of marking the start line was completed in a night by a party of sixty who saw no enemy but 'narrowly missed being shot up by the New Zealanders on the left of the battalion who "Stood To" when the working party … began to come in'.[25] The routes forward depended on the points at which the sappers had made gaps in the minefield. This was complete two nights later and the work party went out again to plot and mark the nine approach lines. Once more the work was completed in a night. This left the night of the 22nd, on which

> representatives from several units walked the line with the Officer Commanding 5 Seaforth [Lieutenant Colonel J.S. Stirling] to see the layout and to mark their own battalion boundaries and centre points. It was found, by pacing from north to south, that the forward routes delivered units upon the start line very accurately throughout its length.[26]

There remained the task of marking the layout with tape, which would be carried out after dark on the evening of the 23rd. Before that an officer of X Corps' Engineers met Colonel Stirling at a forward minefield and pointed out that a gap from which one forward route had been fixed had since been altered. The route now lay through a minefield and had to be changed in the few hours before H Hour.[27] It was a perfect example of the wisdom of the adage that 'time spent in reconnaissance is seldom wasted', since the Seaforth commanding officer had not otherwise been notified of the change. (Stirling's battalion formed part of 152 Brigade alongside 2nd Seaforth and 5th Cameron Highlanders.)

Ninth Australian Division ensured that training was directed to further toughening and hardening of the soldiers, already regarded by most observers as Eighth Army's toughest soldiers, while developing battle drills suited to the operation. Exercises were designed to be so similar to the role the division would play in the initial attack 'that every man and officer unwittingly became familiar with the part he was to play'.[28] An Australian officer wrote that 'if the preliminary work has been thorough and competent, every aspect should have been investigated, and the only possibility of failure should be that of Divine Intervention'.[29] One wonders what Montgomery's reaction might have been to that comment on Divine Intervention since he was to call for just such intervention, but on his side, in his personal message to the men of Eighth Army on the eve of battle.

As the great day drew nearer, final touches were put to plans and Montgomery's orders and intentions were passed down to the soldiers who would execute them. At the two corps conferences, Montgomery spoke to officers and outlined the operation about to take place. In Horrocks' words,

> the effect on this occasion was electrifying. Clear, and full of confidence, he explained that the initial attack would be made by the 9th Australian, 51st Highland, 2nd New Zealand and 1st South African Divisions from right to left. He then described the enemy situation, the deep minefields, anti-tank guns and so on. He stressed that there would be some very hard fighting, a dog-fight, in fact, which might last for up to ten days. After giving details about our great strength he drummed in the fact that everyone must kill Germans.[30]

Horrocks noted that Montgomery stated that the battle might last ten days, which suggests that he may have used this figure at the first conference on 19 October, changing his estimate to twelve days for the next day's conference.

We have already noted the existence of minefield task forces and it might now be appropriate to look at those. As indicated on page 86, the Minefield Task Force of 1st Armoured Division was commanded by Lieutenant Colonel Victor Buller Turner of 2nd Rifle Brigade. In addition to his own battalion, Turner commanded the division's sapper squadrons, three tank troops, and detachments of the divisional Military Police and Royal Signals. The format of 1st Armoured's Minefield Task Force became the accepted model for Eighth Army, being taught as such at the Staff College at Haifa. Turner's force was responsible for clearing minefield gaps for the armour and for traffic control, communications and providing an information centre.

The control of traffic in both directions was of the first importance to operations and the coolness with which the 'redcaps' performed this and other duties in the minefields under fire, immaculate in their daily turn-out until they became smothered in dust, was one of the star performances of Alamein.[31]

Although it would become the standard for Eighth Army, this was not the sole format of a minefield task force at Alamein. In the south XIII Corps had a force with a very different configuration, built around 44th Reconnaissance Regiment, the 'eyes' of 44th (Home Counties) Division. Commanded by yet another Green Jacket, Lieutenant Colonel J.L. Corbett-Winder, 44 Recce provided the covering force for the sappers and was equipped entirely with Bren-gun carriers. The regiment was even redesignated 44th Divisional Reconnaissance Carrier Regiment; its light recce cars were sent to the rear and the new organization included a strong carrier squadron, formed from all the regiment's own carriers, plus two other carrier squadrons composed of men and machines from 132 and 151 Brigades. (Although an infantry reconnaissance regiment, 44 Recce, in common with all units of the Reconnaissance Corps, adopted cavalry nomenclature in June 1942.[32]) Six Scorpions were also issued and the regiment devised a minefield clearance drill that was practised to perfection. The force was to work for 7th Armoured Division and, by the opening of the battle, had absorbed all that division's carriers. It also included 4 Field Squadron Royal Engineers and a squadron of Greys with Stuarts (although it had been intended to use Matildas), a battery of anti-tank guns and two companies of 1st King's Royal Rifle Corps. As training progressed, the regiment was re-formed into two carrier squadrons and an assault squadron. It was told that its role would be to clear four gaps for the armour and, while doing so, be prepared to seize and hold ground, 'to carry out reconnaissance in force and in so doing to be prepared to overcome minor resistance'. [33]

Among final preparations being made was the construction of operational tracks for the movement forward of assaulting formations. To deceive the enemy as long as possible, it was essential that these tracks not be built too early. The building, by Royal Engineers and Pioneers, was carried out successfully. However, following a blinding dust-storm that began in the afternoon of 16 October, followed by high winds and overnight heavy rain, it was felt that the tracks might have been damaged. An inspection was carried out by Brigadier Kisch and Colonel Shannon, the Deputy Chief Engineer responsible for roads, on the 17th who discovered that the tracks 'had been improved by [the] rain'.[34] On the 18th Monty expressed his appreciation to the sappers for the work they had done in building about 120 miles of operational tracks.

Since the assaulting formations would be moving forward at night, the tracks had to be marked for such use. Marking was by symbols and lamps; each track was code-named and lights, fixed to trackside posts, had the appropriate symbols cut into their sides. This required thousands of oil lamps along the tracks: in the Australian area tracks were called Diamond, Boomerang, Two-bar and Square; those in the Highland Division's area were, as we have seen, Sun, Moon and Star; a spur off Star, plus Bottle and Boat led to the New Zealanders' area while Hat was the sole track for 1st South African Division. Lest there be any confusion between Sun and Moon in the Highland Division area, a crescent moon symbol was used. Traffic control along these routes was the task of the Corps of Military Police, whose soldiers would perform their duties coolly under fire. The Military Police, the 'Redcaps', were also responsible for ensuring that marking lights were working. In the battle's prelude, as formations moved into position under cover of darkness, Redcaps spent the hours of darkness directing

> the blacked-out convoys in ever-increasingly complicated moves through ever-thickening dust-clouds hastily snatching up the pickets holding the guiding lamps, while alongside them engineers replaced the fence lines, the dummy huts and dummy minefields which they had removed a few hours before, to disguise once again the very existence of the tracks to the front.[35]

That task complete, the Redcaps then had to ensure that any sign of the passage of a vehicle along the secret tracks was brushed away before daylight.

On 18 October Brigadier Kisch issued a secret note to sapper officers stressing the importance of their role in the battle ahead. He covered several points, including minefield clearance, noting that the detectors would be affected by heavy rain – obviously thinking of the previous night's downpour – and that the Engineers must 'be prepared if necessary to use the crude methods of locating mines'. Another topic covered in Kisch's note was tank-busting: he commented that

> Eighth Army Sappers have been pioneers in 'tank-busting' on the battlefield. The Army Commander has ordered that we are to have free hands and every facility for destroying enemy tanks and guns whenever

and wherever we can get at them. Units will be prepared to seize every opportunity that presents itself, and will seek the co-operation of other arms in creating such opportunities.[36]

Kisch concluded with a reference to the existence of assault engineers in the German army, something for which the British Army had no equivalent.

> The reason for this is that every Sapper is an Assault Engineer.
>
> This is our privilege and our pride.
>
> The Eighth Army is confronted at the moment by fairly strong defensive positions of considerable length and some depth.
>
> It falls to the Sappers to open up the way for the Army to advance; and whatever gaps have to be cleared there must be no failure. An immense amount depends on the resolution and skill with which this task is tackled.
>
> The Army Commander is confident that his Sappers will do all that is required of them in this first step to the coming victory.[37]

This message was to be passed to every sapper in Eighth Army.

Kisch was not the only commander issuing such messages. The commander of 133 Lorried Infantry Brigade produced one on 21 October in which he referred to the numerical advantage that Eighth Army enjoyed but went on to advise:

> But a superiority of weapons and tanks and equipment will avail us nothing, unless the men behind those weapons and in those tanks also possess a superiority of will-power to fight them harder, more ruthlessly, more daringly, and, most important, longer than the enemy. Thus the success or failure of this forthcoming battle depends, in the end, upon us, each and every one of us, from the Commander-in-Chief down to the individual private, individually and collectively. Let us see to it that the 133rd Royal Sussex Lorried Infantry Brigade provides an extra surprise to Master Rommel in the hardness of its hitting and its lasting power. Let us make him say 'Gott straffe these men of Sussex – do they *never* tire?'[38]

Secrecy was being observed at all levels and in many ways. A subsequent report on the battle by 9th Australian Division noted:

In order that the stoppage of contracts for fresh rations would not give warning of the imminence of the battle, contracts were stopped and the force went on hard rations for a short period early in October.[39]

This report went on to note that no officer or man who 'had the slightest chance of being taken prisoner prior to the battle' was informed of the plan until that possibility had passed. Nor was any officer who was aware of the plan allowed to leave the forward area. Even so, the usual pattern of six-day leave continued, but arranged so that the last leave parties before D Day would consist of those to be 'left out of battle'. Thus all units were up to strength on D Day and no attention was drawn to the fact that the offensive was about to begin through the absence of Australians on leave in Alexandria or Cairo.[40]

On 18 October the units of X Corps began their move. Eight Armoured Brigade moved to a staging area where it spent the 19th before beginning its move to the assembly area on the 20th. That move continued the following day but the brigade

was still short of many items of equipment and parties [were] sent in all directions to collect vehicles etc. that had been made available at the last moment. Had these items been made available one week earlier it would have made this part of the operation a great deal easier.[41]

Not until the 23rd – D Day – was the brigade complete in its assembly area. By then Custance and his senior officers had attended Monty's conference at Amiriya and Custance had divulged the final details of the plan to his commanding officers. By 3am on the 23rd 8 Armoured Brigade was in its assembly area with thirty-two of the promised thirty-three Shermans. Final preparations were now being made by officers and men alike.

The initial moves by X Corps on the 18th were a further part of the deception plan. Some 450 tanks and 2,000 lorries of the corps moved openly to the staging area south of Alam el Halfa ridge and behind the headquarters of XIII Corps. They carried canvas replicas of their vehicles which were erected to give the impression that the main body of the British armour was still in place in the south as it really made its way north again, under cover of darkness, to its final assembly area around El Imayid. There it occupied the dummy positions that had been present for some weeks. All traces of the move were cleared.

Bearing in mind the difficulties of desert navigation, the Intelligence Officer of 2 Armoured Brigade issued a note on 21 October detailing locations of several derelicts that might be 'useful land marks for navigational purposes'.[42] Included were a Bren-gun carrier, two knocked-out Valentine tanks, an 8-ton Fiat vehicle, another Italian lorry, a British 3-tonner, a tank of undefined type, the wreckage of an aircraft, an unserviceable ambulance, a half-burnt-out ambulance and another half-burnt-out vehicle.

We have looked at the final preparations of some of the formations and units that would take part in the opening phase of the Battle of El Alamein. But other preparations were being made at a personal level. Soldiers did not have to make wills; they simply signed a standard will form supplied by the Army. Of those who had not done so already, many now made good that oversight. Others wrote letters home and for some these would be the last they would ever write. That was the case with Lieutenant George Morrison of 7th Black Watch. On 16 October the 21-year-old subaltern from Perthshire wrote to his mother.

> I am writing this wee letter to you in case I become a casualty in this action I am entering now. It may be that I will be killed, and if so, then I have left instructions that this letter will be sent on to you – you are the sort of person who can stand these things better than most people and I know you'd like to hear from me – and so I am now writing this last letter to be posted only if I am killed.
>
> I feel excessively cheery and optimistic right now and this death business doesn't worry me in the least! So if I do get one – don't be too sad – it's too late to be sad and I wouldn't like it. If you would just get the organist to play Handel's Largo in my memory in the kirk one Sunday morning – then that's as far as you should grieve for me. Even in heaven, or hell – I'll be all right, never fear!! I'll send you a bit of ambrosia or alternatively a piece of glowing coal!! So don't be sad please – remember this war is being fought to protect people like you from horrible things, and it's only right that some should have the privilege – yes, the privilege, to give themselves for the cause of the good and the right.[43]

It would not be entirely accurate to say that this letter was George Morrison's final communication with home. He later sent Christmas greetings to his family and may have posted that greeting himself. But the missive to his mother represents his final letter home and suggests that the young officer had a premonition that he would not survive. As a navigating officer his chances of 'getting one' were very high. George's letter was not delivered to his home in Crieff until 22 February 1943. Long before then his parents would have received the War Office notification that he had been killed in action – perhaps they had a 'missing' telegram followed by one confirming his death – and then his Christmas greetings. Christmas 1942 in the Morrison household must have been very sad. George Morrison's parents had divorced some years before; his father was a clergyman.[44]

In what Barrie Pitt has described as being 'as significant a piece of administrational expertise as the modern world had seen up to that time, the move of the Eighth Army into position for the Second Battle of Alamein'[45] was complete in good time. Gunners occupied sites that had been reconnoitred beforehand and surveyed for their fire plans; their ammunition had been buried close at hand. It remained only for them to make their final arrangements, check their guns and carry out final adjustments. In XXX Corps many guns had been moved forward from an area between El Alamein and El Imayid, where they had been disguised as lorries by the simple expedient of fitting a cover shaped as a lorry over each gun and limber; these were known as 'cannibals'. Other guns had, of course, been firing at the Axis positions over the previous weeks, but the pattern of their fire hardly altered during that time.

The infantry occupied their slit trenches by dawn on 23 October. They would spend the day in them, sweating in the intense heat of the desert and, perhaps, thanking God that it was not mid-summer. They would also curse the omnipresent flies and try not to think of what lay ahead. And they would check their weapons again and again. For on them, the poor bloody infantry, as ever, would fall the greatest weight of this battle. And they would pay the larger portion of what Wellington called the butcher's bill.

Let us now consider the dispositions of the opposing armies in those final hours before battle. In the north Eighth Army deployed XXX Corps with its infantry divisions assigned to the task of leading the armour through the minefields. The initial intention had been to assign three infantry divisions to this role but it had been 'decided that additional infantry was required to create the bridgehead'[46] and thus 2nd New Zealand Division, formerly part of X Corps, was transferred to XXX Corps, which now included 9th Australian, 51st (Highland), the New Zealanders, 1st South African and 4th Indian Divisions, from north to south, i.e. from right to left of the corps front line, with 23 Armoured Brigade in support. The first four divisions of XXX Corps were to attack in the northern sector with a regiment of 23 Armoured Brigade supporting each division except the New Zealanders who included 9 Armoured Brigade in their order of battle. Fourth Indian Division would hold XXX Corps' flank to the junction with XIII Corps, a distance of some dozen miles across Ruweisat Ridge.

These divisions were commanded by some remarkable men. Leslie Morshead, a shipping executive in civilian life, commanded the Australians – and the respect of soldiers who did not easily give their respect, and certainly did not give it on the basis of rank alone. That respect had to be earned and Morshead earned it as one of Australia's finest commanders. Alongside the Australians were the Jocks of the Highland Division. Their commander, Douglas Wimberley, we have already met. Himself a Cameron, he understood the nature of the highland fighting man, and of the Irish, fellow Gaels, and Sassenachs included in his division. His machine-gun battalion was from the Middlesex and, in his special order before the battle, Wimberley added to a Scottish exhortation a special word for his 'Diehards' – 'For ever England!' The New Zealanders were commanded by one of the most famous divisional commanders of the war, Sir Bernard Freyberg VC, an inspiring figure in every sense, who was forthright in his criticism of the armoured commanders for their previous performances and stolid in his support of his Kiwis. Freyberg had a rare battlefield instinct and great empathy with the soldier on the ground. Dan Pienaar commanded the South Africans and was perhaps the least gifted of the Dominion commanders, noted for his truculence in the days before Monty's arrival. The Australians were especially suspicious of his Springboks and there had been one famous riot in Cairo when an Australian commented that a South African who had just entered a bar looked tired and queried, 'Run all the way from Tobruk, mate?' Perhaps for this reason the South Africans would play a smaller part in LIGHTFOOT than the Australians, Scots and New Zealanders. Committed to a holding operation, 'Gertie' Tuker's Indians might have expected to play a much greater role than was assigned to them. Desert veterans under a gifted commander who was 'an intellectual soldier of the highest standing',[47] they would have made an excellent assault formation but Montgomery was no admirer of the Indian Army.

Tuker's Indians had, on their left, 50th (Northumbrian) Division, a formation that had seen much service in a relatively short time and suffered heavily. The division had lost a brigade in earlier struggles; its place was now taken by a Greek Brigade. At one stage 50th Division had only one British brigade, Brigadier Percy's 151 (Durham) Brigade, its strength being completed by the Greeks and a Fighting French brigade group. General J.S. 'Crasher' Nichols, its commander, enjoyed a fine reputation which probably had much to do with the division's survival in Eighth Army's order of battle. By 23 October the division had its own 69 Brigade, with a battalion of East Yorkshires and two of Green Howards, restored. Its task was to hold the line from the junction with XXX Corps astride Alam el Nayil and southwards to Deir el Munassib. From there XIII Corps' line was held by 44th Division, commanded by Major General Ivor Hughes (it had once been commanded by Brian Horrocks, now its corps commander). It had already suffered heavily, having been committed to the Alam el Halfa defences before being desertworthy and then suffering in Horrocks' attack at Munassib. It had also lost a brigade as lorried infantry for 10th Armoured Division and would soon lose another. Not surprisingly, 44th Division was disbanded after the battle.

XIII Corps also possessed an armoured division, the famous Desert Rats of 7th Armoured, who had been in the desert from the beginning. Their presence in the southern sector was due to the fact that the division had taken a mauling, but also served the subsidiary purpose of adding to the deception plan: that this most-respected British armoured formation was in the southern area must surely have pointed, in German eyes, to an attack from there. However, 7th Armoured, now commanded by Major General A.F. (John) Harding, one of the outstanding British commanders of the war, would not play a leading role in the battle. With two armoured brigades – 4 Light and 22 Armoured – it possessed just over 200 tanks and, although it had no infantry as yet, also included about 170 armoured cars. Its lack of infantry would end when another 44th Division brigade – 131 – transferred to Harding's command at the beginning of November.

The final element of XIII Corps was based in the extreme south of the line, near Himeimat. This was General Koenig's Fighting French Brigade Group, composed of French and African soldiers, under command of 7th Armoured Division.

Both 1st and 10th Armoured Divisions constituted X Corps, which had lost the New Zealanders. Raymond Briggs' 1st Armoured included 2 Armoured Brigade and 7 Motor Brigade while Alec Gatehouse's 10th Armoured was stronger, with two armoured brigades – 8 and 24 – and 133 Lorried Infantry Brigade. Under overall command of Herbert Lumsden, these were the formations that would pass through the minefield gaps in XXX Corps' area and take the battle to the enemy armour.

We have already seen that X Corps should have had a third armoured division but that it lost 8th Armoured since no infantry brigade could be found for it. However, the division still had a role to play in the battle, and especially in the deception plan, since the divisional signals provided the apparent signals traffic of X Corps headquarters in the southern sector when that corps moved to its final assembly area. In addition, the division's armoured brigade joined 10th Armoured Division and other elements provided part of Hammerforce, under command of 1st Armoured Division.

This was Eighth Army's strength on the ground. In the air its partner, Desert Air Force, had gained complete superiority over the battlefield and aircraft of the RAF, Royal Australian Air Force, Royal Canadian Air Force, Rhodesian Air Force, South African Air Force, US Army Air Forces and Royal Hellenic Air Force, as well as the Fleet Air Arm, ranged far and wide to wreak havoc and destruction on Axis forces and lines of supply. Each day the aircraft flew an average of over 550 sorties and their contribution was obvious to, and appreciated by, the soldier on the ground. Air Chief Marshal Tedder, commanding the equivalent of 104 squadrons, was able to allocate some of his strategic and maritime aircraft to support Desert Air Force. In the DAF squadrons were some 750 machines, of which 530 were serviceable. Against this power the Axis had about 350 serviceable aircraft, of which 150 were German, including eighty dive-bombers. Another 130 serviceable German aircraft, from a total of 225, were available from bases in Greece, Crete, Sicily and Sardinia; these were long-range bombers. There were also some 300 German and Italian transport aircraft.

During the five days and nights in which Eighth Army moved to its final assembly positions Desert Air Force, with its attached US squadrons, launched its own offensive. This, it was hoped, would be seen as a parallel to the air offensive around the September full moon, which had not led to a major ground attack. Air Vice Marshal Coningham had two principal aims: lessen the possibility of enemy air attacks on Eighth Army; and win air superiority over the battle area. DAF fighters patrolled the line between El Alamein and Himeimat while light bombers and fighter-bombers struck at enemy landing grounds at El Daba and Fuka. These attacks were continued by night bombers, and the USAAF long-range Liberators struck farther to the west, while Fleet Air Arm aircraft patrolled the coastal waters.

Their operations were so successful in protecting the British staging and assembly areas and preventing reconnaissance by hostile aircraft that the 8th Army was unmolested during its concentration and no information reached the enemy from aerial reconnaissance.[48]

By contrast Allied airmen were of particular value to Eighth Army in providing information from aerial reconnaissance. The Hurricanes of No.208 Squadron provided a mass of such information from their tactical reconnaissance operations, including photographs that were immensely valuable to Eighth Army's artillery in developing its fire-plan for the opening of LIGHTFOOT.

> The value of vertical air photos prior to and throughout the battle was immense. Practically all CB [counter-battery] locations and the exact whereabouts of enemy defended localities were based on air photos, though in the latter case the information was taken from overprinted maps prepared from photos prior to the battle by an RE Photo Survey Section. In a desert of the type in which the battle was fought, oblique photos are of no use to the gunner as it is impossible to correlate the photo with the ground.[49]

A proportion of No.208's Hurricane IIs were fitted with multiple cameras, including oblique cameras. Prior to the battle the squadron's main role was photo reconnaissance but after D Day 'the task changed to spotting Armour, vehicles, movement and likely bombing targets'.[50] Between 1 October and 7 November the squadron flew 233 sorties for the loss of a single machine. In normal circumstances the recce aircraft flew with a fighter escort. Sorties were flown at varying heights: area sorties for information of a general nature were carried out at between 3,000 and 6,000 feet; those with a specific, limited task, such as identifying armour in a certain area, were carried out at very low altitude; vertical photos were taken from heights between 15,000 and 25,000 feet, the lower height being considered 'dangerously low' for this task. Oblique photos were usually taken at heights between 4,000 and 6,000 feet.

Examples of the work of No.208 Squadron include some missions carried out on 25 October. Tac/R No.4, from 3.45–4.30pm, was

> a recce of the area QARET EL ABD, DEIR EL QATTARA and DEIR EL MUNASSIB. Visibility was very bad due to sandstorms and only one medium concentration of MET [mechanized enemy transport] was seen. This was 300 MET some 5 miles N.N.W. of DEIR EL MUNASSIB. 30 MET were also seen moving towards MUNASSIB from the S.W.[51]

while Tac/R No.5, from 5.35–6.20pm,

was twice recalled by Controller 211 Group on account of enemy fighters. After this it was considered too late to achieve reasonable visibility.[52]

but Tac/R No.6, from 3.45–4.30pm, was

a last light recce of the Southern Area and a look at Lake Maghra area. 350 MET were observed dispersed in Wadi KALAKH. ... 300 MET were observed dispersed in depression off track running N.W. about 2 miles W. of MUNASSIB. At DEIR EL QATTARA there were 300 MET. No general movement observed.[53]

In the days before and during the battle of El Alamein, No.208's Hurricanes and their pilots and ground crew proved an invaluable asset to Eighth Army. With their comrades in Desert Air Force and the other air elements under Tedder's command they proved the power of army/air co-operation and reaped the harvest of the seeds sown by Sir Claude Auchinleck.

With the battle about to begin, Eighth Army enjoyed superiority over the enemy in many ways. Ready for action with their units were 435 armoured cars, against the Axis total of 192; 1,029 tanks, excluding lights, against 496; 908 field and medium artillery pieces against an Axis total of, at most, 500 (200 German and between 260 and 300 Italian) with eighteen German heavy howitzers; 1,451 anti-tank guns, of which 849 were the new and highly effective 6-pounders, against 850 Axis pieces (which included eighty-six of the lethal 88s), made up of 550 German and 300 Italian guns. A contemporary British report assessed Axis anti-tank gun strength at 1,063 pieces.[54] Thus it was that only in anti-tank weapons did the Axis enjoy anything near parity; this was to be felt as the battle unfolded. Interestingly, one of the most feared German anti-tank guns was the 76mm PAK36, a captured Russian weapon pressed into service by the German forces. When an example was captured in the desert some British artillery officers were amazed to see that the weapon was not Russian at all, but British. It was the obsolete 3-inch anti-aircraft gun, hundreds of which had been gifted to the USSR after withdrawal from British service. The Soviets had taken the gun from its AA mounting and adapted it to other uses, including anti-tank. In turn the Germans had produced a new carriage for the gun and proved its lethality as an anti-armour weapon, in which role it was second only to the 88, another anti-aircraft weapon.[55] What an opportunity was lost to provide the

British Army with a superb anti-tank weapon when those guns were sent to Stalin.

In terms of manpower Eighth Army also held the advantage with a fighting strength on the morning of 23 October of 174,000 men. In contrast Axis forces disposed at most 108,000 men, of whom 60,000 were German.[56] The British *Official History* puts Eighth Army's strength at almost 200,000 while Pitt states that it was 220,000 on the morning of D Day,[57] both figures that suggest that support services had been taken into account. Whether Eighth Army had the strength needed to defeat *Panzerarmee* in a dog-fight, as Montgomery described what was about to begin, was a moot point. Only time would tell.

Panzerarmee was deployed in a lamination of German and Italian units, with the Germans intended to advise and strengthen their allies. For the Italians, considerable war-weariness had set in and the average *soldato* was not inclined to make any great effort other than for self-preservation, such as digging trenches and shelters or sowing additional mines. As for burying the dead, or clearing waste from their positions, or even washing, they seemed to care little so that they added to the grimness of life at the front. Lice infestation was a matter of course for both German and Italian soldiers. Perhaps the latter at least had the consolation of contributing 'to the additional discomfort of their enemies wherever the opposing lines were close together'[58] in an unintentional form of biological warfare.

Between the coast and the end of Miteiriya Ridge, opposing XXX Corps in what would be the main area of attack, were the Italian *Trento* and the German 164th Infantry Divisions, with their units intermingled so that the Germans might control all, although the theory was that it was an equal partnership. The same situation prevailed as we look southwards where *Bologna* Division was intermingled with Groups Heydte and Schweiger of the Ramcke Brigade to face 4th Indian Division. Groups Burckhardt and Hubner of Ramcke were farther south, now facing XIII Corps, with *Brescia* and *Pavia* Divisions holding the line opposite 50th and 44th Divisions. Finally, the paratroopers of *Folgore* Division held the southern end of the Axis line down to the Qattara Depression, supported by the German 33rd Reconnaissance Battalion.

The German and Italian armour was held behind the line but, contrary to Rommel's usual practice, dispersed. This had often been the failing of British armour, which Rommel had criticized, so why disperse his own armour? It has been suggested that these dispositions were made by Stumme who had relieved Rommel in late-September.[59] But Stumme merely implemented Rommel's orders and those dispositions were dictated by *Panzerarmee*'s precarious fuel situation rather than by any change in tactical doctrine. However, Rommel's consideration of what Montgomery might do also played a part. He thought that Eighth Army's commander would put in a number of powerful attacks at many points along the line, until he made up his mind about which attack was most likely to succeed. (One is tempted to conclude that Rommel had read Montgomery's submission to the Bartholomew Committee on the BEF, as the latter describes the German method of attack in similar words.[60]) That attack would then be reinforced but this would lead to a redeployment that, in typically British fashion, would be slow: thus Rommel would have time to move his armour to meet that thrust. But he could move the armour only once since there would not be enough fuel to return divisions to their original locations. And so 15th Panzer and *Littorio* were held behind the northern sector with 21st Panzer and *Ariete* behind the southern sector. The headquarters of the divisions were so close as to be combined commands. Finally, *Panzerarmee* held two divisions in reserve: 90th Light and *Trieste* were along the coast from Sidi Abd el Rahman to the area of Ras el Kinayis.

When he left Africa for his convalescence, Rommel had attempted to extract from the Italians, with whom overall command in North Africa still lay, promises of improvements to roads and communications as well as an assault on Kuffra oasis to deny it to the British as a base for what he called commando operations but which were actually raids by the SAS, Long Range Desert Group and other groups. Promises were made, but none were kept: the raids continued throughout the battle.

Promises were also made in Germany where Rommel met Hitler and was amazed at the lack of reality in the Führer's headquarters. Göring, the Luftwaffe chief, assured Rommel that his airmen dominated the African skies, in spite of what Rommel had seen with his own eyes, and also told him that America would not be able to give significant aid to the Allies. However, Hitler listened with apparent interest to Rommel and promised that he would receive reinforcements, transported on Siebel ferries, of such shallow draft that they would not be vulnerable to torpedo attacks. He would also let Rommel have a heavy mortar, or *Nebelwerfer*, brigade, forty of the new Mark VI Tiger tanks and a number of assault gun (SPG) units. An Eighth Army intelligence report suggests that news of the *Nebelwerfern* had reached Axis troops in North Africa: 'Information from PWs and from Censorship sources tend to indicate the imminent use in the WESTERN DESERT of the SCHWERE WURFGERAT and the NEBELWERFER d'.[61] The *Nebelwerfer* was described as a six-barrelled mortar firing 15cm rounds to a maximum range of 4,500 yards. It was a weapon that *Panzerarmee* would have appreciated at Alamein but Axis forces in Africa would not see examples of it until after the battle. The same intelligence reports also suggest the imminent appearance in Africa of a self-propelled variant of the 88, perhaps the assault guns to which Hitler referred. But Hitler's promises were not to lead to any solace for Rommel's command.

As October drew on the Axis troops had no immediate worries about a British offensive. Routine prevailed, patrols were carried out, defences strengthened, maintenance of vehicles and weapons went on as usual while staff officers spent their time on plans and in trying to resolve the problems of supplying an army whose lines of communication were under such severe pressure. The morning of 23 October dawned as did any other day and the usual routine was followed. As the heat of the day diminished and the cool breezes of evening sprang up, the soldiers of *Panzerarmee* left their trenches to ease their limbs, prepare meals and carry out the many duties that were possible only under cover of darkness. Some moved forward to relieve their comrades in the forward battle posts. But there was no sign of urgency, no sense that this night would be different from any other. That evening the *Panzerarmee* daily report to *OKH* stated simply 'Feindlage unverändert' – Enemy situation unchanged.[62] By contrast, the Italian Capitano Giacomo Guiglia, head of *Panzerarmee*'s radio intercept unit had noted changes in British radio traffic and had warned, on the 22nd, that it was a 'question of hours, not days' before the British would launch their offensive.[63]

Montgomery, confident of victory, had done his utmost to improve training and raise morale. Among the factors affecting morale was the feeling of belonging to a unit and formation. An earlier regulation had forbidden divisional emblems on clothing but, on 29 September, Monty wrote to corps commanders to lay down the composition and affiliation of each division. All units belonging to the division, including divisional troops such as gunners and engineers, would display divisional signs on clothing and vehicles. This was welcomed especially in 51st (Highland) Division which had brought out from home thousands of cloth divisional emblems for stitching on to uniforms; these were now displayed proudly.[64]

Eighth Army had the best possible equipment, including Sherman tanks and Priest SPGs, and enjoyed a significant numerical superiority over the enemy – although whether that superiority was quite enough was another question. On 23 October Monty's personal message to Eighth Army was read to all soldiers. In that message he exhorted every officer and soldier to enter the battle determined to see it through, in which case Eighth Army would knock the enemy for 'six' out of North Africa. And he called on 'the Lord mighty in battle' to give Eighth Army victory.

Immediately after dark on that evening of 23 October, B Company, 5th Seaforth Highlanders moved forward with rolls of white tape to mark the routes forward to the divisional start line and the start line itself. The tape was fixed to the angle-iron pickets. The task, requiring nine miles of tape, was completed in ninety minutes and by 8.45pm the start line and all routes forward were marked clearly. Although operating well in advance of the forward positions B Company sustained no casualties, having enjoyed the protection of defence patrols from D and HQ Companies of the battalion which had been operating forward of the start line. In the other attacking divisions of XXX Corps similar parties completed the same task.[65]

On the other side, at 8 o'clock German time, the sounds of artillery fire were heard from the northern sector and a raid by the Australians was expected – a nuisance, but typical of the Australians. Then, forty minutes later, the peace of that evening was shattered as the eastern horizon erupted into a fireworks display such as had not been seen before by anyone in *Panzerarmee*. And the silence of the night was broken by the almighty roar of the guns of Eighth Army. As with the Missionary Franciscan Sisters in Sacred Heart Convent, sixty miles away in Alexandria, the men of *Panzerarmee* knew that they were listening to the sound of history.

Chapter Six

The First Clash

The day, my friends and all things stay for me

In Eighth Army's gun lines officers checked their watches as the minutes ticked down to H Hour. Over 800 guns stood ready to fire as one, delivering a steel storm of death and destruction such as Africa had never before known. Detachments stood by their weapons, with the first rounds of the bombardment in the breaches, awaiting the command to fire. Battery command post officers had before them the tables for the fire-plan for each battery, with adjustments for individual weapons and for batches of shells and charges that differed from the normal. Along the thirty-eight miles from El Alamein to the Qattara Depression Eighth Army's gunners knew what was required of them: to fire for over five hours with but a ten-minute break each hour to allow the guns to cool. Then, at 9.40pm exactly, Egyptian Summer Time, the order was given – FIRE! Under the gentle light of the full moon, on a cool Mediterranean evening, the guns began hammering the Axis gun lines in a massive counter-battery programme to neutralize the enemy artillery.

On XXX Corps' front of some seven miles almost 500 field and medium guns – all XXX Corps' artillery, plus some 'borrowed' from X Corps (Dennis had 336 field guns – 25-pounders – plus seventy-two from X Corps) – engaged known Axis artillery positions, of which it was believed that there were 200 field, forty medium and fourteen heavy guns. Their positions had been plotted carefully, thanks to the tactical reconnaissance aircraft and ground observation, including sound-ranging and flash-spotting. The forty-eight mediums, including sixteen of the new 5.5-inch weapons, in XXX Corps' area unleashed 1,800 shells in fifteen minutes; each Axis battery was smitten with ninety-six shells in two minutes. In biblical times this land of the pharaohs had been afflicted by a series of seven plagues. That night, in the modern age, a new plague was being visited on Europeans in Egypt.

The storm of fire from the guns was added to by bombing from RAF Wellingtons, striking at targets illuminated by flares dropped by Fleet Air Arm Albacores while low-flying Hurricane night-fighters added their contribution in thirty sorties against gun areas, camps and transport, strafing with cannon and machine-gun fire. Specially-equipped Wellingtons jammed enemy radio transmissions, thus increasing confusion on the ground. Nowhere in the enemy gun lines was there respite for the German and Italian artillerymen: the thunderbolts of Saint Barbara, patron saint of gunners, were descending on them. Major Anthony 'Rex' Wingfield MC, second in command of 10th Hussars, described the opening of the attack in a letter to his father:

> The whole affair was perfectly stage-managed and preceded by an artillery barrage such as this country has never known, in this war at any rate. In fact one chap said that it was as intense as anything he'd ever known in France during the last. It certainly was an incredible sight as we trundled up through it.[1]

Then, as suddenly as it had begun, the bombardment ceased. Shocked and stunned Axis gunners wondered at the havoc wrought in their positions: many guns had been reduced to scrap metal; many gunners lay dead or dying. Save for those who had served in the previous war, and they were few, none had ever experienced anything comparable. Return fire was almost non-existent, partly due to the disruption of the bombardment and the Wellingtons' signal jamming, but also to General Stumme's order, twice given, that the guns should fire only at known targets and should not fire too soon.[2] The war diarist of 153 Brigade in 51st (Highland) Division noted that all the guns fired on counter-battery tasks in a bombardment that appeared to be very effective 'as there was no reply from the enemy batteries either during the C.B. programme or for sometime thereafter'.[3]

Eighth Army's guns remained silent for only five minutes. Then, at 10.00pm, they opened fire again, switching attention to the forward Axis infantry positions. This was the signal for XXX Corps' infantry to advance. Some time before they had left their trenches, eaten their meals and stretched their limbs. Now, behind the curtain of fire provided by the guns, they closed up to the bursting shells. Already the earlier clearness of the evening was giving way to the dust and haze of battle, as shells, vehicles and men created their own fog over the battlefield. Visibility was reduced to a very short distance. To aid the infantry in direction finding, Bofors light anti-aircraft guns fired tracer on fixed lines and searchlights shone into the sky as beacons.

This second part of XXX Corps' fire-plan lasted for seven minutes before subordinate divisional fire-plans began taking precedence. Save for two places, where the fire took the form of a bombardment, fire support was usually concentrations lifting at exact times from locality to locality.

> Thereafter, as the infantry moved forward, accompanied by Gunner OP parties, the artillery concentrated their fire on all known or suspected enemy company areas and strong-points.[4]

It would continue thus for five and a half hours. As the official historian notes, 'This was artillery support indeed'.[5] It was exhausting work for those who manned the guns.

> A Gunner participant described the night's work as 'impressive at first, then exhausting, then rather maddening'; the ammunition numbers probably used more vigorous terms.[6]

As the infantry moved off, the savage skirl of the great highland pipes could be heard even above the roar of the guns. Certainly Wimberley's Jocks had no difficulty in hearing their pipers and the Australians and New Zealanders to either side of them could also catch snatches of this most primal of musical instruments, which in Scottish and Irish regiments were often also regarded as weapons. Before following the infantry of XXX Corps into battle, let us first ascertain what Montgomery expected of them that first night.

> The objective was the MITEIRIYA ridge … believed to be the limit of the depth of the enemy position, some 6000 yards from our front line. NZ Div was then to be prepared to exploit SW and the AUSTRALIAN Div Northwards so as to widen the gap. 4 Ind Div was to carry out raids along RUWEISAT ridge.[7]

Once the infantry took that objective, the armour of X Corps was to pass through gaps created by the sappers, with 1st Armoured Division in the Highlanders' sector and 10th Armoured in the New Zealanders' sector to 'secure the high ground about AQQAQIR as soon after daylight as possible'[8] on ground astride *Panzerarmee*'s line of communications from the coast road to their positions about Qattara. Seizing that ground would 'almost certainly force the enemy armour to attack ours to remove this threat to his communications'.[9] Montgomery hoped that X Corps could neutralize 15th Panzer and *Littorio* before 21st Panzer and *Ariete* arrived from the south.

While XXX Corps and X Corps were carrying out their parts in the operation XIII Corps would clear a gap in the southern mine-marsh through which 7th Armoured Division would advance with two objectives: to maintain the delusion that the main attack was being made in the south and prevent 21st Panzer and *Ariete*, or any other Axis forces, moving north.

XXX Corps' four attacking divisions were, from north to south, 9th Australian, 51st (Highland), 2nd New Zealand and 1st South African. Their first objective was codenamed *Oxalic* and their front extended for about six miles. Within the ground that they were to take that assigned to the Australians was almost rectangular, their objective line being similar in length to their start line. For the Highlanders, their area was a reverse wedge, their operational area widening as they advanced. The New Zealanders' ground also widened, to an even greater extent than that of the Highlanders, while the South Africans' objective line was also longer than their start line.

One of the three Australian brigades – 24 – was assigned to what was really a feint to keep the enemy guessing. The brigade attack, between the coast and Tel el Eisa, was supported by a new weapon, the 4.2-inch mortars of 66 Chemical Warfare Company, Royal Engineers, two sections of which were positioned in front of the infantry; these supplemented 3-inch and 2-inch mortars. During the course of the night 66 Company fired off 1,600 rounds, the entire Middle Eastern stock of high-explosive bombs for the 4.2-inch.[10] (The weapon was a rifled mortar originally intended as a retaliatory weapon firing poison gas, should the enemy fire poison gas first. Since that did not occur the mortar was assigned to normal duties.) This mortar fire was reinforced by fire from captured Italian Breda guns and machine guns. Raids were made on enemy positions and dummy figures raised by remote control in front of such positions. Flares were used to guide a Boston light bomber laying a smoke-screen along the main road while two searchlights lit up the coastal strip and revealed the groups of dummies from time to time. So effective was this feint that enemy defensive fire continued for four hours while prisoners later stated that they were convinced that they had beaten off part of the main Eighth Army attack.

The real Australian attack was made by 26 Brigade on the right and 20 Brigade on the left, the soldiers of both having four miles to cover to reach *Oxalic*. Complete success attended the attack of 26 Brigade, which had a much narrower front than its fellow, since it would also have to provide right-flank protection for the entire army. As the brigade's leading battalion, 2/24th, moved forward it created an open shoulder that stretched eventually for 7,000 yards, of which

3,000 had been in no man's land. Only on the left flank did the brigade meet any serious opposition – from one enemy outpost that was soon overcome. Barbed wire caused no problems and, at this stage, so bright was the moonlight that many anti-personnel mines were spotted by infantrymen who were thus able to avoid them. The second phase of the attack, undertaken by 2/48th Battalion, made good progress for almost a mile before meeting opposition from strongly-wired posts protected by deep minefields and anti-personnel mines. Following some hard fighting the battalion took its first objective by 2.10am. The corps objective, *Oxalic*, was reached thirty-five minutes later.

Since 26 Brigade had to cover its section of the new front line and the exposed flank, Brigadier Whitehead used a special grouping, known as Composite Force, under Lieutenant Colonel Ted Macarthur-Onslow, equipped with machine guns and anti-tank guns, to cover 3,000 yards of the flank. Macarthur-Onslow deployed his force on the German model, in six defensive posts covered by wire and mines and supported by light tanks of the Divisional Cavalry. Composite Force was in place by 2.00am on the 24th. Although the Germans tapped against this sector on the morning of the 24th, no attempt was made to attack it; but shelling lasted throughout the night.

However, 20 Brigade did not achieve the same level of success as Whitehead's men. The first phase of the advance was straightforward, as nowhere did Rommel's forward battle posts present a real problem for XXX Corps' infantry. That phase was carried out by 2/15th and 2/17th Battalions.[*] As with 2/24th Battalion, these two battalions suffered few casualties and most of their prisoners were Italian, thereby confirming the view that the most determined resistance would come from Germans in the next line.

The leading three Australian battalions crossed minefields in their advance, with 2/17th Battalion traversing four. All three had achieved their first objectives by ten minutes past midnight, fifteen minutes later than estimated for this phase. After an hour's pause the battalions carrying out the next phase took over.

The two battalions of 20 Brigade were relieved by a single battalion, 2/13th, recruited from New South Wales, supported by Valentine tanks of 40th Royal

---

[*] The use of the prefix '2' in Australian infantry battalions of the Second World War, e.g. 2/15th, indicated a battalion raised in the First World War and now raised for the second time. Similarly, the Australian expeditionary force, known as 2nd Australian Imperial Force, acknowledged that there had been a 1st AIF in the earlier war. New Zealand nomenclature followed similar logic: Freyberg commanded 2nd NZ Expeditionary Force, but battalion nomenclature did not follow the Australian model.

Tanks. However, the tanks had to wait for paths to be cleared through the minefields and Lieutenant Colonel Turner, with 2,600 yards to cover, decided to advance in two stages. Two companies, C and D, would make for an intermediate line, while the remaining companies, A and B, would advance on *Oxalic*.

For the first mile of its advance 2/13th Battalion made good headway against little opposition. The battle outposts in the sector were held mainly by Italian troops who withdrew under the British bombardment. After almost a mile the battalion ran into German-held posts but had succeeded in taking these and gaining their first objective soon after 3 o'clock. By then the Valentines were moving forward but their progress was delayed further when a track had to be cleared through a 1,500-yard-deep minefield. In the clearance operation two Scorpions were employed but, after a short period, their auxiliary engines seized, putting both out of action. As 2/13th Battalion continued its advance, meeting fierce opposition, losses were heavy and the advance was held up until the Valentines finally arrived at 5.15am. Thereafter some progress was made but, with the onset of dawn, the infantry had to re-organize and dig in. The battalion was over 1,000 yards short of its objective. The tanks took their places in the new Australian forward defended localities, suppressing enemy aggression with their guns.

The situation at dawn was that 26 Brigade, on the right, had pushed through the enemy lines to a depth of 5,000 yards on a single-battalion front, taken all its objectives, established the northern flank and re-organized to meet any possible counter-attack. Composite Force had closed the gap between the northern flank and the firm base on the coast. However, the southern flank of 26 Brigade was not yet locked securely to 20 Brigade on the left. As a result of the minefields and the problems of operating without their tank support, 2/13th Battalion had not reached its final objective. On the brigade left the southern flank was open: although small parties had reached their final objective, 51st (Highland) Division was not in full possession of that line and the lane for 1st Armoured Division – the northern corridor – had not been cleared.

The Highlanders encountered a number of strong pockets of resistance and reached *Oxalic* only on the extreme left flank. They also had had problems with their supporting Valentines, which had been held up by mines. Wimberley's right brigade had suffered considerable casualties in heavy fighting during which there had been much use of artillery, mortars and light machine guns. As the division crossed its start line, pipers played at the front of each battalion, stirring the soldiers to readiness for battle and encouraging them with their own special brand of courage. Regimental marches filled the air, as did tunes that had special significance for the attacking battalions. On the extreme right of the division were the leading soldiers of 5th Black Watch. The men of this proudest of highland regiments – its full title was the Black Watch (Royal Highland Regiment)* – were piped into battle by their pipers, all of them kilted and one of whom, 19-year-old Piper Duncan McIntyre, was to become a legend in the regiment and the Highland Division. As his company moved to battle, McIntyre piped as men fell 'all around him in the intense concentration of enemy artillery, mortar and small-arms fire'.[11] Although twice wounded he continued piping and when it came to the moment of the assault broke into the regimental march. His complete disregard for his own safety was an inspiring example to his comrades in that deadly advance. The objective was taken but young McIntyre was hit for the third time, by a mortar bomb that knocked him to the ground. Still he continued to play, his life ebbing from him. When his body was found 'the bag was still in his oxter and his fingers still upon the chanter'.[12]

Within the Highland Division XXX Corps' objective line *Oxalic* was known as the Blue line and there were three intermediate lines on which the attacking battalions would pause to re-organize: Green, Red and Black lines. Across the divisional front were five attacking infantry battalions, plus the divisional reconnaissance regiment, making six discrete attacks; 50th Royal Tanks supported the Division. From right to left the first phase fell to 5th Black Watch, 5th/7th Gordon Highlanders, 1st Black Watch, 7th Argyll and Sutherland Highlanders, 51st Reconnaissance Regiment and 5th Cameron Highlanders. In four areas the plan was for attacking battalions to go all the way to the final objective but the flanking battalions, 5th Black Watch and 5th Camerons, would be relieved on Red line by 1st Gordons and 7th Black Watch respectively. Along Blue line were four of the enemy's strongest defensive points, code-named *Aberdeen*, *Stirling*, *Nairn* and *Kirkcaldy*. The first lay at the feature known as the Kidney, from its shape on the map, and the last was the north-west end of Miteiriya Ridge. Intermediate enemy strongpoints were also assigned Scottish codenames, including *Kintore*, *Braemar* and *Dundee*.

---

* Formed in 1725 as independent companies but known as The Black Watch because of its dark tartan sett, it became The Highland Regiment in 1739 and was granted the Royal prefix in 1758. From 1881 to 1934 the official title was The Black Watch (Royal Highlanders) but this changed to The Black Watch (Royal Highland Regiment) in that year. Today it is The Black Watch, 3rd Bn Royal Regiment of Scotland.

A squadron of Valentines from 50th Royal Tanks was allotted to 1st Gordons to assist in capturing *Aberdeen* while a second squadron would help 7th Argylls take *Stirling*, each squadron carrying a platoon of infantry. The remainder of 50th Royal Tanks, under their commanding officer, John Cairns, would operate with 51 Recce for the assault on *Nairn*. With their pipers playing 'Monymusk', C and D Companies of 7th Argylls began their advance and by 11.00pm had taken their first objective. Thirty minutes later, having re-organized, they set off for Red line, on which they were ensconced at midnight. Thereafter, opposition stiffened and enemy artillery began to find the Argylls' range while some of their own shells were falling short. The attackers dug in but, at 1 o'clock, they advanced on the Italian-held *Greenock*. Although the defenders initially put up their arms in a gesture of surrender, they then attacked the Argylls and a bloody skirmish, in which bayonets were used, ensued, from which the Highlanders emerged victorious. But C and D Companies had suffered heavily, D Company losing all its officers and an entire platoon being wiped out in an explosion; their supporting machine gunners, the Sassenachs of the Middlesex, had also suffered badly. However, Black line was secure although the battalion was too weak to advance to *Stirling* on Blue line. As with the Australians, their supporting tanks had been delayed by mines and the Argylls' commanding officer, Lorne Campbell, who would earn the Victoria Cross before the North African campaign was over, decided to dig in.

On the division's right flank 5th Black Watch had reached their objective, Red line, where Piper McIntyre was killed. From there the advance was resumed by 1st Gordons who moved on towards Black line. However, C Company suffered severe casualties from shellfire and German machine-gun fire while D Company, who came forward on tanks to link up with B Company, ran into an uncharted minefield in which five tanks were blown up. With one company reduced to an officer and eighteen men, the Gordons were also forced to dig in. Thus the right flank of 51st (Highland) Division, in common with the left flank of 9th Australian, was short of the Corps' objective.

To the left of the line of attack of 5th Black Watch and 1st Gordons were 5th/7th Gordons. They moved forward so quickly that they almost ran into their own bombardment and had to lie down behind it. Then they took Green line and made for Red, which was also taken, following which C and D Companies advanced towards Black line only to run into intense machine-gun fire which all but wiped out a company; this came from the enemy post codenamed *Strichen*. This was the limit of the battalion's advance and they dug in, although they took *Strichen* next day. To their left, 1st Black Watch reached Black line having overcome all opposition. They too almost ran into their own artillery, so swift was their advance.

In the weeks preceding LIGHTFOOT there had been much debate about the role of 51st (Highland) Reconnaissance Regiment in the desert. Suggestions that the regiment be re-organized as a divisional cavalry regiment or as a carrier regiment – as with 44 Recce – were turned down and, eventually, it re-formed with two squadrons: a composite squadron and an infantry squadron; in common with all reconnaissance regiments, cavalry nomenclature had been adopted in June: thus squadrons and troops rather than companies and platoons.* It was in this latter guise that the regiment fought at Alamein. The composite squadron suffered its first casualties almost as soon as it moved off when one man was killed. Two assault troops covering sappers gapping the minefields had a particularly active night. The regiment's objective was *Nairn* on Blue line but, although assault troops reached the lying-up positions from which the attack on *Nairn* was to take place, the final objective was not achieved. Tanks of 50th Royal Tanks were to 'attack, capture and annihilate' *Nairn* but the German anti-tank gunners had other ideas. At 3.00am, as the Valentines began their advance, the leaders were knocked out by anti-tank fire; as one withdrew it put down smoke to obscure the gunners' view. German gunners also turned their attention to 51 Recce's carriers, four of which were knocked out in seconds. When the smoke cleared, the tanks had withdrawn, save for three crippled Valentines that had been abandoned. One scout troop of 51 Recce had only one carrier left. The attack on *Nairn* had come to a stop.

On the right flank 5th Camerons had advanced with their pipers playing 'The Inverness Gathering'. They took their objectives and the advance on that flank was passed to 7th Black Watch. In spite of all the difficulties facing them the battalion reached its final objective, *Kirkcaldy*, a piece of ground about thirty feet high but significant since it dominated the land around it. Many casualties were suffered from enemy shelling, especially in A and D Companies. This was the battalion in which served George Morrison, the 21-year-old subaltern from Perthshire, who, on 16 October, had written 'this wee letter' to his mother lest he became a casualty in the battle. As 7th Black Watch moved out the navigating

---

* Although the regiment took part in the early stage of the pursuit after Alamein, it was withdrawn in mid-November and sent to Cairo to retrain as a motorized infantry battalion. On 14 January 1943 it was redesignated as 14th Highland Light Infantry, a highly unpopular decision as the HLI, in spite of its title, was a lowland regiment. At the parade to mark their conversion the regiment responded to the call for three cheers with three hearty boos.

officers led their companies, marching with their compasses, marking the route to be followed. Not surprisingly, navigating officers suffered a high casualty rate. Within an hour, six of them had been killed or wounded. Among the dead was George Morrison, who had told his mother that 'this death business didn't worry me in the least'. The young officer had kept faith with his men to the end and had carried out without question a job he knew carried a very high risk of costing him his life; but he had been prepared to take that risk 'for the good and the right'.

George Morrison's battalion suffered heavily and by the time Black line was reached both leading companies were reduced to little more than platoon strength. Yet this battalion had one advantage: because *Kirkcaldy* lay on the end of Miteiriya Ridge it was easily identifiable, especially with enemy fire coming from it – in other areas there had been confusion over the exact locations of objective lines. Captain Charles Cathcart, of Pitcairlie, was given command of the two composite companies that the battalion mustered for the final assault to continue the advance. A cautious advance transformed into a charge that would have been worthy of highlanders two centuries before and Cathcart's men were in among the defenders of *Kirkcaldy*, fighting with the bayonet and hand-to-hand. By 4.00am the objective was in the hands of 7th Black Watch. It was the sole part of *Oxalic* that 51st (Highland) Division took that night. At the end only fifty men were left standing of Cathcart's little force.

As the left flank of its division 7th Black Watch had the interdivisional boundary with 2nd New Zealand Division as its own left flank. However, on their objective, the survivors of 7th Black Watch's assaulting companies wondered where the New Zealanders were. They need not have worried: Freyberg's division had the most successful advance of the night and, by dawn, the New Zealanders were ensconced firmly on the objective. The entire Miteiriya Ridge was in XXX Corps' hands. When Howard Kippenberger, commanding 5 New Zealand Brigade, went across to see if there had been 'a proper tie-up on the inter-brigade boundary'[13] he discovered a 'very depleted Black Watch company' which was in touch with his own brigade. The Scottish brigade commander, George Murray of 152 Brigade, told Kippenberger that his losses had been heavy but that his brigade had done what had been asked of it. Returning to his own brigade HQ by a different route, Kippenberger saw 'an extraordinary number of dead Highlanders who must have strayed into our area'. In front of one enemy post lay the bodies of a complete section, a corporal and his seven men, all of whom were lying in line, and on their faces; they had died facing the enemy.[14]

The reasons for the New Zealanders' success were several. Pitt suggests that 'their long experience of desert fighting and their undoubted ardour' had led to their following close behind the artillery curtain, and even passing through it. Thus high morale was one factor in their success. Another was that they were well trained. Once again their experience helped, but there is little doubt that Freyberg was a firm believer in training and he subsequently commented that:

> The value of well-trained infantry capable of attacking by night with the bayonet against any form of defence was fully proved. This is the difference at present between our own and the German infantry. Owing to the success of Blitz tactics the German infantry appear to have become holders of weapons and 'tank followers' by daylight.[15]

Freyberg's division was also unique in having its own integral armoured brigade and tanks and infantry worked together extremely well. In training, John Currie's 9 Armoured Brigade had built up an excellent rapport with Freyberg's two infantry brigades and Currie had no qualms about operating under Freyberg's command. This is especially notable since it was the New Zealanders who had expressed the highest level of concern about the armour in the battles of the summer months. Freyberg summarized the situation when he wrote that:

> in an attack against an organized defensive position tanks in support of infantry should work along the same axis and should be under the command of the infantry commander until the infantry have re-organized.[16]

That support, co-operation and trust had been demonstrated in the most positive fashion during the New Zealanders' attack. Of course, the initial advances were made by infantry, with 23rd Battalion on the right and 24th on the left; these battalions, with 28th (Maori) mopping up behind them, took the divisional advance as far as the first objective, the intermediate Red line. From there 21st and 22nd Battalions relieved 23rd, while 26th and 25th Battalions took over from 24th. Behind were the mine-clearing parties, then the support vehicles that would bring up the infantry's mortars and anti-tank guns. Next in line of advance – confirmation had been received at 3.00am that gaps had been cleared in the first minefield – were the Crusader squadrons of John Currie's brigade, followed by the heavy squadrons with their Grants and Shermans. The order of advance of the brigade placed the Royal Wiltshire Yeomanry on the right with Kippenberger's 5 Brigade, Warwickshire Yeomanry on the left with Gentry's 6 Brigade, and 3rd Hussars following up. Then would come 8 Armoured Brigade from Gatehouse's 10th Armoured Division. Lieutenant Colonel Reginald Romans, commanding 23rd Battalion, led his battalion on to its objective with very little opposition and almost to the minute scheduled for arrival there. Romans then decided that he could go farther and did so, advancing past several strong enemy posts to Miteiriya Ridge, the objective for the second phase of the attack, from which they had to return to the first objective. Such was the spirit of the New Zealanders. In the first phase on the left flank some platoons of 24th Battalion, and a Maori company, had even crossed the inter-divisional boundary into the South Africans' area, where progress was slower, to clear up enemy posts.

The relieving battalions followed so close to their own artillery that several enemy posts were overrun while the occupants were still sheltering from the shellfire. As the battalions advanced the divisional frontage widened and gaps between them increased. Nonetheless they pressed on so that, by 2.00am, 25th Battalion was on Miteiriya Ridge. Thus the extreme left of the objective had been taken. The battalion dug in on the crest in front of a deep minefield but soon discovered that 26th Battalion was about 600 yards to the right; the gap between was quickly filled by two Maori companies. Kippenberger's battalions achieved even more success: 21st and 22nd Battalions were either on the crest of the ridge or on its forward slope with both digging in. This was why the men of Cathcart's little force from 7th Black Watch wondered where the New Zealanders were. In fact their neighbours were some distance in front of them. Arrangements had been made between 7th Black Watch and 21st Battalion for the subalterns who commanded the flanking platoons of each, and who knew each other, to communicate, using passwords agreed beforehand. However, both had been killed, as was the first New Zealand runner sent out to make contact. However, the man had been seen by a wounded Black Watch soldier who went out under fire to retrieve his message and take it to Captain Cathcart. The wounded highlander then went out again to let the New Zealanders know that the Scots were on their right flank. And so, from the north-west extremity of Miteiriya Ridge, across the three-mile frontage of Freyberg's division, the crest and much of the forward slope of the ridge was held by XXX Corps before dawn.

The tanks of 9 Armoured Brigade had done sterling work, although they suffered many casualties on mines, especially when the heavies attempted to avoid stalled Scorpions, which had been working with the New Zealand sappers. However, the crews of the crippled Grants and Shermans remained with their charges to fire on enemy posts that were harassing mine-clearing parties. But in daylight the stranded tanks became easy targets and soon most were blazing after being struck by enemy anti-tank gunners. The Scorpions were ordered to withdraw as soon as they reached the crest of Miteiriya Ridge where, it was believed, the minefields ended; but such was not the case and many more mines awaited X Corps' armour as it broke through. By first light tanks were up in forward battle positions but too late to carry out the task expected of them; elements of the Wiltshire Yeomanry were in front of the New Zealand Division on the forward slope of the ridge and engaging the enemy; the Warwicks had been brought to a halt on the crest. As the Wiltshires engaged enemy posts, they in turn came under fire from leading elements of 21st Panzer Division as these moved into the battle area. The British tanks retraced their way up the slope and, as daylight spread over the desert, Currie's tanks, refuelled and ammunition replenished, were behind the infantry and behind the crest, ready to meet any counter-attack. Thus the Wiltshires were the sole armoured unit to break out beyond the infantry's final objective on this first day of the battle. As Freyberg and others had believed, not enough time had been allowed for clearing the minefield gaps. Nor had all the infantry divisions achieved their objectives along the entire front. Such was the case with 1st South African Division.

Pienaar's Division had attacked with 2 Brigade on the right, flanking the New Zealanders, and 3 Brigade on the left, creating the southern flank of the corps advance. In the first phase of 2 Brigade's attack the Natal Mounted Rifles had little difficulty reaching Red line. They had had almost a clear run with few posts in their line of advance and casualties were light. However, when they handed over to the Cape Town Highlanders for the next phase a different story developed. In their path was a strong German-held post that had not been detected from aerial photographs, the garrison of which was fresh and unshaken, having suffered little attention from the artillery. This post engaged the Highlanders who were soon pinned down by concentrated fire; both leading company commanders were killed. The forward platoons were forced to ground until a reserve company was brought up, after which re-organization began for the advance from Red line. As a result the artillery programme had to be delayed; it was 2.00am before the guns began an effective creeping bombardment. Not for another two hours did the Highlanders clear their original start line.

Paradoxically, Cape Town Highlanders then had a much easier move, aided by those forays into their area by the New Zealanders and, by dawn, had reached the ridge and were in contact with the New Zealanders about 600 yards to their right. On the left of the South African Division the 1st/2nd Field Force Battalion suffered an absolute purgatory, running into an uncharted minefield and a very strong German post that had been misidentified as a dump by the aerial photograph analysts. This post was manned by men of 164th Division who had also escaped the worst of the British artillery and were determined not to give ground. The leading platoons of the Field Force, encountering the full fury of a well-disciplined German defence, were all but destroyed. Attempts at outflanking the post failed because of mines, booby-traps and machine-gun fire. Although a single platoon partially outflanked the post, its efforts came to an end when it was cut off and hammered by mortar and machine-gun fire, reducing it to section strength.

The fifty men of the assaulting 1st/2nd Field Force companies still on their feet were bolstered by a company of Natal Mounted Rifles and, under cover of mortar and machine-gun fire from their own brigade, charged the post. In a quarter hour of vicious hand-to-hand fighting they overcame the defenders. Thirty-six 'exhausted but defiant' Germans were captured while the attacking battalion had suffered 189 casualties.[17] This was the hardest battle the battalion had fought in two years in the desert. The delay meant that 2 Brigade's advance came to an end a mile short of their objective where the survivors dug in before dawn.

Yet another undiscovered German strongpoint lay in the way of 1st Rand Light Infantry who led 3 Brigade's advance on the left flank. The battalion used Bangalore torpedoes to tear apart the wire around the post before three platoons charged with bayonet and bomb into a short but brutal battle to overcome the defenders; platoons on the flanks ensured that no Germans escaped. By the time it reached Red line the battalion was much weakened and the follow-up battalions – Royal Durban LI and Imperial Light Horse – had been delayed by mines and by-passed enemy posts. Although the bombardment was delayed to allow re-organization for the second phase of the advance, the Royal Durbans had to form a defensive flank because of the travails of 1st/2nd Field Force. That flank was still in situ when the advance towards Miteiriya Ridge stepped off at 2.00am. In this final phase the infantry tried to stay close behind the bombardment and generally succeeded. Although the Light Horse were delayed by yet another German post, both battalions were on their objective by 4.30am. The eastern end of the ridge was in South African hands.

At the end of XXX Corps' advance the assaulting divisions held *Oxalic* at both extremities, held about three-quarters of the ridge crest and were a mile short of the line in the southern half of the Australian sector, in the right half of the South African sector and in three-quarters of the Highlanders' sector. In the New Zealanders' right sector attacking infantry and armour had gone as far as the bottom of the ridge's forward slope. Two small raids, Operations KOONJA and BEN NEVIS, and a mock attack near Ruweisat Ridge, Operation BLUFF, carried out by 4th Indian Division, had probably helped their fellow infantrymen of XXX Corps by ensuring that some enemy troops were pinned down and unable to reinforce elsewhere. Divisional casualties were light.

In the previous chapter we noted that two Axis divisions, 90th Light and *Trieste* Motorized, were being held in reserve along the coast behind the front, between Sidi Abd el Rahman and Ras el Kanayis. To keep those divisions tied down, and to confuse the enemy, the Royal Navy carried out a feint seaborne landing, Operation SLENDER, in which three Hunt-class destroyers, HM Ships *Belvoir*, *Exmoor* and *Hurworth*, with a dozen landing craft tanks (LCTs), two motor launches and eight motor torpedo boats (MTBs) sailed from Alexandria on 23 October. Four merchantmen also put out of Port Said to pass Alexandria in daylight. However, these movements appear to have been missed by enemy aircraft. A further naval diversion was provided by the cruiser HMS *Arethusa* and the Greek destroyer *Queen Olga* which left Port Said during daylight on the 23rd but returned to harbour after dark. After dark on the 23rd the vessels of the first force also returned to Alexandria although the eight MTBs continued westwards to be seen, and shadowed, by enemy aircraft. The MTBs made no attempts to conceal their presence and, west of Ras el Kanayis, came close into shore and, from about 400 yards, opened fire with machine guns and discharged flares. There was neither return fire nor any alarm signal and the MTBs withdrew but, sailing back to Alexandria, came under attack from German and Italian bombers with one vessel being damaged by cannon fire. However, no casualties were suffered and the boats reached Alexandria safely. On 24 October *Fliegerführer Afrika*, the senior German air officer, reported that Italian aircraft had 'attacked and destroyed the British naval units reported north of El Daba'. This air action appears to have been the sole Axis response to Operation SLENDER, since no troop movements were noted behind *Panzerarmee*'s front line.[18]

As dawn broke on 24 October XXX Corps had almost achieved what had been asked of it. But what of X Corps' armour? Their advance had depended on two elements: progress made by the infantry and progress by the mine-clearing parties. But, as already noted, there were those who considered that not enough time had been allowed for the sappers' task. Among those who had espoused that belief was Freyberg. The situation at dawn was proof positive that they had been right.

There can be no doubting the courage and dedication of the sappers. Theirs was one of the most difficult jobs in the battle and was carried out with all the professionalism of their corps. But they simply did not have enough time. Not only did they have to clear two main corridors for X Corps, but also gaps for the tanks supporting the infantry. Tenth Armoured Division's mine-clearing force was composed largely of Royal Engineers, with detachments of Royal Signals and Military Police, commanded by Lieutenant Colonel Gilbert McMeekan, the divisional Commander Royal Engineers. The sappers under his command included 2 and 3 Field Squadrons and 141 Field Park Squadron; 3 Field Squadron was commanded by Major Peter Moore, who had organized the minefield clearance training school. Since these three squadrons were not enough for the job ahead, McMeekan had been assigned 571 and 573 Field Squadrons, while 6 Field Squadron was under command of 24 Armoured Brigade. On the first night 2 Field Squadron was not deployed and the three Scorpions assigned to 10th Armoured were on loan to the New Zealanders. To clear four sixteen-yard gaps, McMeekan had three squadrons, with a reserve held behind. The four gaps continued Bottle, Hat and Boat tracks as well as a spare track, called Ink. Delayed by twenty minutes at the start, when a pilot vehicle blew up, the sappers moved forward to put all their training into practice. Initially there was little interference from the opposition but this could not be expected to continue and soon a heavy machine gun opened fire from the left. This was silenced by a group of men under a young sapper officer and the clearance work continued. Then two Military Police lorries, carrying pickets for gap marking, were blown up with all but a single lance-corporal killed or wounded: that single Redcap, Lance Corporal J. Eeles, carried on and with the help of some sappers, marked the path for the armour, ignoring the bullets constantly sweeping around him. For his gallantry Corporal Eeles was awarded the Distinguished Conduct Medal. A Victoria Cross would have been a more appropriate recognition of the gallantry of this young policeman; and would also have been the only VC awarded to the Corps of Military Police. After the war the gallantry of men such as Corporal Eeles, and many other military policemen, received formal recognition through the granting of the prefix 'Royal' to the Corps.[19]

Thus the sappers continued on this most dangerous of tasks, standing up when common-sense and every human instinct demanded that they take cover.

Casualties were heavy and it was little wonder that the work took much longer than planned. There were communications problems, more attention from the enemy and it was 4.30am before three gaps were swept with a fourth almost halfway through. In spite of the efforts of the sappers, and few men showed more courage that night, it was too late for the armour to achieve what was demanded of it by dawn. No other armour would achieve what the Wiltshires of Currie's brigade had done in this opening clash of LIGHTFOOT.

Chapter Seven

The Armour is Stalled

The sun shall greet them

XCorps' two armoured divisions were to leave their assembly areas after dark on the 23rd and move forward until their leading units reached Springbok track thirty minutes after midnight. After topping up their fuel tanks they would begin their advance at 2.00am with 1st Armoured travelling by Sun, Moon and Star tracks to reach the northern corridor, straddling the divisional boundary between 9th Australian and 51st (Highland); 2 Armoured Brigade would lead with 7 Motor Brigade following. Tenth Armoured Division would use Bottle, Boat and Hat tracks to reach the southern corridor through the New Zealand sector, with 8 Armoured Brigade leading 24 Armoured and 133 Lorried Infantry Brigades.

Montgomery's plan called for 2 Armoured Brigade's leading tanks to break out in the north between Morshead's and Wimberley's men into positions about a mile to the west. In the south 8 and 24 Armoured, in that order, would pass through Freyberg's division to swing west and join 2 Armoured, thereby creating line *Pierson*, about a mile forward of the infantry line, *Oxalic*, in the north and two miles forward of it in the south. The infantry brigades, 7 Motored and 133 Lorried, were to establish northern and southern flank guards respectively, for which they would deploy their heavy weapons. With the three armoured brigades between, this would create a formidable guard for XXX Corps, against which the panzers would be destroyed should they attack. Such was Montgomery's theory.

Thereafter X Corps was to advance some three or four miles into an area lying across the Rahman track, codenamed *Skinflint*, from which armoured cars would probe northward to find 15th Panzer Division and southward to provide early warning should 21st Panzer start moving north. However, the plan was complicated by the fact that neither the Australian left flank nor the Highlanders' right flank had reached *Oxalic*. Montgomery's directive, that X Corps should, therefore, fight through to its objective, would come into operation as a result. That directive was to prove immaterial as 1st Armoured

Division would have difficulty reaching even Red line by dawn. In the New Zealand sector 10th Armoured Division also faced problems; but these were of a different nature to those of their northern comrades. Gatehouse's armour had a fairly clear run as far as the crest of Miteiriya Ridge which was in XXX Corps' hands for the entire frontage of the armoured thrust. Gatehouse's main problem was that he had two armoured brigades and a lorried infantry brigade trying to pass through a relatively narrow minefield corridor to reach *Pierson* and take up positions at much the same time. Thanks to the work of the Divisional Minefield Task Force, the corridor was cleared and marked all the way to *Oxalic* by dawn. But *Pierson* was beyond *Oxalic* and the sappers had to make their way towards it to make safe the route to be followed by the leading tanks of 8 Armoured Brigade.

Although the New Zealand infantry had gone forward of *Oxalic* on the right, advancing to the bottom of the slope, the infantry on the left had been held up by a minefield forward of the crest. That minefield now had to be cleared by X Corps' sappers and would present a real problem to them since using Polish detectors would mean standing upright under fire from machine guns and, later, shells. To carry out the task, Lieutenant Colonel McMeekan, who had earlier survived an 88 airburst which had left him almost deaf, gathered together a party of six, including himself, to probe ahead of *Oxalic* and clear a path for Custance's tanks. This was just after 3.30am; the tanks were due to start through at 4 o'clock.

Going down the slope in a jeep, McMeekan passed though the foremost New Zealand infantry, from the Maori Battalion, and soon had the good fortune to find a German gap in the minefield, discovered when he dismounted to remove a wire that was entangled in his jeep's rear axle. He also found 571 Field Company's recce party, equipped with a 'pram', a detector mounted on bicycle wheels, and with them he moved on, marking the gap whilst doing so. By this stage McMeekan's little party were the leading men of Eighth Army. When they had got some 150 yards beyond the crest they were pinned down by machine-gun fire. McMeekan decided that, with three gaps clear and a fourth cleared to about halfway, he could call forward the armour. He crawled back through the minefield to the shelter of the crest to do so and found that his signals set had been destroyed by the airburst that had deafened him. Efforts to pass his message on met with both misfortune and an almost unbelievable element of bureaucratic inertia that is rare among front-line troops. When, finally, Gilbert McMeekan was brought to Neville Custance's headquarters, it was too late: the Sherwood Rangers, under Flash Kellett, had already been sent forward.

Guided by Peter Moore, the tanks of the Rangers moved onto the crest of the ridge, there to be silhouetted by the lightening sky in the east. Ahead a screen of anti-tank guns, dug in and camouflaged effectively in the German manner, awaited them. Six Crusaders were knocked out in as many minutes in a furious engagement. The following Grants attempted to deploy into battle formation but ran onto the minefield as the markers placed by the sappers had been knocked down by shellfire. Soon sixteen Rangers' tanks were wrecks. Trooper Philip Foster recalled the chaos of the advance:

The tanks had fallen foul of savage cross-fire from 88mm guns and machine guns. Everywhere there was a crisscrossing of coloured tracer, accompanied by the ear-splitting crescendo of explosion and the bark of small-arms fire. Green, red and whitish balls of brilliant fire raced through the air at colossal speed, seeking their targets. The whole column ... had been forced to halt owing to this powerful opposition. Tanks began to 'brew up' right and left. I glanced forward at other lines of tanks extended in battle order like ships of a fleet. It was extraordinary how in this half-light of dawn these armoured monsters suggested the silhouettes of battleships floating dispassionately in a calm sea. Armour-piercing thermite shells ricocheted close to the echelon, cracking viciously as they smacked the deck.[1]

A Squadron's Crusaders took the brunt of the enemy fire but B Squadron also lost tanks as it broke out. In all, sixteen Rangers' tanks, seven from A Squadron, had been hit.[2] Kellett, who would be killed while second-in-command of 8 Armoured Brigade in Tunisia, attempted to retrieve the situation by calling forward the machine gunners of 1st Buffs, part of his regimental group, to tackle the enemy anti-tank gunners. But he could not get through to the Buffs on the radio and, therefore, asked his Gunner officer, Major David Egerton, to bring his B Battery 1st Royal Horse Artillery into action.

Egerton told Kellett that he would have a try and issued orders to the battery, who were still in the column of march on Boat track, sandwiched between two tank squadrons. They could not deploy in such a confined situation and so Captain Peter Jackson decided to go forward. The eight guns pulled out of line and drove about 300 yards beyond the minefield where Downham and Sahagon Troops deployed to right and left. They were in front of almost the entire army and so close to the enemy anti-tank guns that one German 50mm was attacked and knocked out with hand grenades.

Firing over open sights the 25-pounders attempted to engage the enemy. But their only targets were the flashes of fire in the darkness from German muzzles; these were poor targets and their own fall of shot could not be observed. Worse still, the 25-pounders were being illuminated by the pale grey light of dawn from the east. As they became clearer to the Germans, more and more fire was poured into the gun line, with anti-tank guns, machine guns, rifles and heavier shellfire all being directed upon them. Still the gunners served their weapons, engaging the foe. Egerton's tank, some 200 yards ahead, was hit and his communications wiped out. He walked back to B Battery through the horror of battle and found both Troops still firing, although casualties were mounting with men falling by the minute. But their fire was having an effect: the flashes from the anti-tank guns were reducing. However, the brightening eastern sky brought the action to an end. As the Sherwood Rangers survivors withdrew to positions behind the ridge, Egerton gave the order for his guns to cease fire and withdraw.

The hump-backed 'quads' drove up in the dissolving gloom, led by the Troop-sergeants with the steadiness of a drill-order. Their distinctive shapes, familiar to the enemy in many a lively action, brought a new access of fire. The quads drove on, wheeled right and left of their Troops, hooked on to their guns and drove back, very fortunate that only one of them was knocked out.[3]

It was almost complete daylight before the wounded of B Battery were evacuated, one of their Troop leaders, David Mann of Downham Troop, being wounded fatally while organizing the removal to safety of his men. The last to evacuate B Battery's positions were Egerton and Jackson, the latter being wounded when a 50mm round burst between the pair as they walked calmly away from the site.

McMeekan then withdrew his sappers and the tanks settled behind the ridge. The Sherwood Rangers found their Staffordshire Yeomanry comrades sheltered there, alongside the tanks of 9 Armoured Brigade.[4] The third regiment of 8 Armoured Brigade – 3rd Royal Tanks – arrived eventually to extend the line on the Sherwoods' left flank. When 3rd Royal Tanks arrived it was almost clear daylight: they had been delayed by minefields much thicker than expected. Now the gaps had been revealed to the enemy who directed fire on them and a long-range duel between tanks and anti-tank guns commenced.

As the growing light of day brightened Miteiriya Ridge, and the area behind it, there could be seen the enormous tail of an armoured brigade, the fuel and ammunition trucks, artillery, staff cars, water lorries and all the impedimenta needed to get an armoured brigade into battle. Behind that scene stretched the entire 24 Armoured Brigade, all 140 tanks and logistical tail, reaching through what had been no man's land to the original British minefields. And there was 133 Lorried Infantry Brigade. Remember that this brigade had been intended to form the southern flank screen of *Pierson*, for which it was to be in place by dawn. But it had moved hardly any distance at all. Dawn, when its soldiers should have been the left shoulder of *Pierson*, found 133 Brigade still around Springbok track, some three miles south of El Alamein station. As day broke they were ordered to disperse, orders accepted with the frustration of men who had anticipated being in action and the inevitable and fatalistic resignation of the front-line soldier.

Kenchington's 24 Armoured Brigade also received orders to disperse but in their ranks, as Pitt, notes, these orders were received with an air of disbelief for, not only was there precious little space in which to disperse, but whatever space existed seemed to be taken up with slit trenches, or was sown with mines for which, of course, there were, as yet, no charts. And the area was shrouded in dust, and wounded men still lay awaiting evacuation. What made matters worse was the inherent weakness of the LIGHTFOOT plan, with one corps superimposed upon another: 24 Armoured Brigade had to disperse on the same ground as the tail of 2nd New Zealand Division. Since the armour was also sitting on the New Zealanders' lines of communication and supply, the infantrymen were not best pleased with their armoured colleagues, a frustration exacerbated when the former recalled that the latter should have been out in front defending the men upon whose supply lines they were now encamped. In fact, 24 Armoured was also encroaching upon the tail of the South African Division in their attempts to disperse, while elements of the tail of 8 Armoured Brigade were involved in this traffic congestion too.

> Dispersion, as far as it was possible at all, was a hazardous business, as mines were by no means confined to regular fields and slit trenches abounded. The congestion was appalling and the confusion considerable. The whole area looked like a badly organized car park at an immense race meeting, held in a dust bowl.[5]

Frustration went to the very top of 2nd New Zealand Division. Freyberg had already gone to Miteiriya Ridge and was anxious to see his soldiers' achievements exploited to the full. Naturally, he also wanted to see his men protected – and by more than the armour currently at the front. Not long after 7 o'clock on the morning of the 24th, Freyberg contacted Leese to say that he considered that 10th Armoured Division should try to break out and make for *Pierson*. He contacted XXX Corps headquarters again, less than an hour later, to ask why nothing was happening, to be told that the armour was held up by the congestion on the eastern side of Miteiriya Ridge, a situation worsened by the fact that Freyberg's supply services had commandeered the sole completely mine-free lane. When, two hours later, there was still no sign of movement by X Corps, Freyberg's chief of staff told his opposite number at Leese's headquarters that 9 Armoured Brigade had been ordered over the ridge and down through the foremost infantry positions and, since Currie's men would be outnumbered greatly, would Lumsden provide support by ordering 8 Armoured Brigade forward in their wake? Lumsden's answer was no: he considered that 10th Armoured must remain in position, re-organize and clear wider paths for its movement forward. Furthermore, any attempt by armour to cross the ridge in daylight would be suicidal: night, or a sandstorm, was essential to cover such an advance.

Lumsden was accurate in his assessment, which was proved emphatically by the experience of Currie's tanks. Every appearance on the crest by British armour was met with withering and accurate anti-tank fire. By midday only one Sherman and three Grants of the Wiltshire Yeomanry survived after the regiment made several attempts to repeat their earlier success.

The situation on XXX Corps' front demanded a rethink. But, before looking at Montgomery's reaction to it, we should consider also the other developments of the first night of LIGHTFOOT. In the southern part of XXX Corps' area, 4th Indian Division had carried out diversionary raids and such a raid was also executed by 1 Greek Brigade, under command of 50th (Northumbrian) Division in XIII Corps' area. As well as creating a diversion, the Greek operation had been intended to take prisoners and identify formations, distract the enemy and create alarm and despondency. It was

carried out at 2200 on 23 October by 1 company plus 1 platoon of infantry and 1 section of engineers, aided by artillery support. The Greeks claimed to have killed or wounded 50 of the enemy, but this figure is certainly excessive.[6]

The Italians showed little fight and the raiders returned with eighteen Italian prisoners from 1st and 2nd Battalions, 20th Infantry Regiment of *Brescia*

Division, having lost one man killed and three wounded. Thereafter 1 Greek Brigade maintained its position throughout the night and was not otherwise engaged.

XIII Corps had a task that might be described as ambiguous: to create sufficient pressure to keep 21st Panzer Division in the south but without hazarding the tanks of 7th Armoured Division. The latter included Grants, Crusaders and Stuarts but no Shermans. This must have been extremely frustrating for Horrocks, especially as he had initially been told that he was to command X Corps but had lost out on this appointment to Lumsden. Effectively, Horrocks was commanding a large-scale feint which he describes in his memoirs:

> On the night of the attack it was arranged for the wireless sets of a complete armoured division [HQ 8th Armoured Division, which lay in XIII Corps' area] to operate so as to suggest that large armoured forces were moving forward in this sector. In fact, I had the somewhat invidious task of trying to attract the enemy's attention to the place where I was due to attack.[7]

Horrocks had hoped that XIII Corps could break through in the south but this hope was dashed when Montgomery told him emphatically that he was not to incur tank casualties. Thus Horrocks might 'make faces at the enemy, but offensive operations on my front were to be restricted to small-scale raids'.[8] Yet the army commander also expected XIII Corps to exploit any weaknesses demonstrated by those raids.

There was a further factor that would help to frustrate XIII Corps. Their picture of the enemy defences in the south was inaccurate: Rommel had re-aligned the main defensive line in that sector along the old British minefield codenamed *February*, the most westerly of the minefields now covering *Panzerarmee*'s front. But it was believed that the main enemy defensive line was still that from which they had advanced towards Alam el Halfa, and the defences included the best of the Italian infantry, *Folgore* Parachute Division, with elements of the Ramcke Brigade. Horrocks' plan of attack called for 22 Armoured Brigade of 7th Armoured Division, its way cleared by its minefield task force, and under cover of a creeping bombardment from 7th Armoured and 44th Divisions' artillery, to break through the *January* and *February* minefields south of Deir el Munassib. Having done so, they would form a bridgehead into which would flow the armour of 4 Light Armoured Brigade and 44th Division's infantry. At the same time 1 Fighting French Brigade, under command of 7th Armoured, would make a flanking attack south of Himeimat and seize ground to the west and, perhaps, the peaks of Himeimat. With the bridgehead secure, both armoured brigades and the French would thrust westwards to Jebel Kalakh and the Taqa Plateau. North of this action both 50th and 44th Divisions would attack to straighten out the line.

It was a complicated plan for a feint and involved attacking formations, especially the armour, in long approach marches. The tanks had to travel over ten miles, traversing two new minefields, *Nuts* and *May*, laid by the Royal Engineers after the Alam el Halfa battle. Of course, the minefield task force, built around 44th Reconnaissance Regiment, had the same journey to make before beginning the process of clearing four gaps for the armour. The *January* field was 500 yards wide while *February*, two miles on, was believed to be twice that width. Although Roberts sent 22 Armoured Brigade forward at 6.45pm, they made such good time through their own minefields that he stopped them at 8.00pm to avoid congestion on the start line. But the minefield task force continued on its way, six Scorpions clattering along behind the carriers of 44 Recce, the sappers and the two infantry companies that were to protect them. On their left flank 1/7th Queen's moved towards the start line.

As the bombardment crashed out along the front the men of 1/7th Queen's awaited the order to advance. Their task was to establish themselves on the ground between *January* and *February* to protect 22 Armoured's right flank. But before they even left the start line they were hit by enemy shelling. In the southern sector the reaction of the Axis artillery was much faster than in the north, so much so that the Queensmen believed that their own gunners were firing short – a demoralizing belief. Three officers, including the second-in-command, were killed but the commanding officer rallied his men and led them through *January* into the gap before *February*. There more misfortune befell them as they ran into outposts manned by *Folgore* and Ramcke soldiers who inflicted heavy losses upon them. Many men were killed or wounded, all the company commanders were lost and the commanding officer was captured; he was later shot while trying to escape. Early on the morning of the 24th the adjutant rallied the survivors to form small bridgeheads to guard the exits of the gaps that, by then, had been cleared through *January*. The suffering of 1/7th Queen's was, however, but a precursor of the purgatory to be suffered by the Queen's Brigade in XIII Corps' battle.

The minefield task force, under Lieutenant Colonel Lyon Corbett-Winder of 44th Reconnaissance Regiment, had varied fortune. Led by B and C Squadrons the regiment moved into *January* ten minutes behind schedule, having been delayed as a result of many of the lamps lighting their approach route being extinguished. Further difficulties and mistakes beset the squadrons. Number 2 gap was cleared by C Squadron by 1.40am although the assigned Scorpion had been damaged first by a mine and then by anti-tank fire, leaving the sappers to clear the gap by hand. C Squadron also cleared Number 1 gap, a task completed almost three hours later at 4.30am. However, just west of the exit from that gap was an enemy post. Numbers 3 and 4 gaps, to the south, were the responsibility of B Squadron which, soon after leaving its start line, ran onto mines in a deep sandy wadi. Three carriers were lost at this point and, believing this to be the eastern edge of *January*, the squadron leader ordered flailing to begin. However, these were mines that had been laid in front of *January*. One Scorpion overheated on a number of occasions and broke down while enemy machine-gun, mortar and artillery fire was directed on the squadron which suffered heavy casualties before reaching the minefield's eastern edge. By then their crews had managed to restore all the Scorpions to working order. Although clear by 2.15am, Number 3 gap was unusable for wheeled vehicles due to soft sand; one Scorpion was disabled at the western end of the gap. The last gap, Number 4, was cleared by hand half an hour after midnight, the Scorpion assigned to it having been knocked out three-quarters of the way through.

The minefields had been a tougher proposition than expected and losses were severe. B Squadron was reduced to fewer than six carriers and Corbett-Winder told Roberts that his men would only be able to clear two gaps in *February* instead of the planned four: each squadron could muster only one column rather than two. The attack through *February* had to be called off as dawn was breaking and it would have been suicidal to attempt to clear minefields in daylight. In fact, one gapping party was unable to get to *February* and, although the other reached there it came under heavy enemy fire. One Scorpion, struck by anti-tank fire, had to be abandoned.

The armour had also suffered in its passage through the gaps. Although the tanks reached their start line on time they found that guides had gone on, many lights were already out, and enemy artillery was firing on the supply lines, causing casualties among the soft-skinned vehicles. When the tanks cleared *January* they also found themselves in a badly-congested area. Elements of Roberts' brigade were deployed on either side of the minefield by daylight. Those on the western edge, 5th Royal Tanks, had begun their approach to *February* behind Corbett-Winder's men before it became clear that an advance through *February* would have to be cancelled. Thus began the task of consolidating between the minefields, a situation that would leave 7th Armoured Division exposed to enemy positions on Himeimat unless the Fighting French had achieved their objectives.

However, the French had been beaten off Himeimat. Koenig had created two groups, one of which, Group A, included two infantry battalions of the Foreign Legion commanded by Colonel Amilakvari, while the other, under his own command, included a squadron of Moroccan *Spahis* with Crusader tanks and an anti-tank gun company. Although having to contend with soft going and deep wadis, the force reached its forming-up areas, south-west of Himeimat, on schedule and, under cover of an artillery bombardment – although this was but a shadow of other bombardments that night – and smoke put down by aircraft, made their advance. On the right 1st Battalion faced strong opposition but went forward until their left flank was exposed at which point Amilakvari ordered 2nd Battalion to support them. Unfortunately, at that stage, 2nd Battalion was attacked by the German Kiel Group, using captured Stuart tanks. These had not been spotted by Koenig's Crusaders, which had been held back by the bad going. The intervention of the tanks spelt disaster for Group A, since it had neither tanks nor anti-tank guns and Amilakvari was forced to order a withdrawal. His soldiers were reluctant to do so and when the Legionnaires came back together it was broad daylight, they were in open desert and sitting targets. They lost all their vehicles and over 100 men but, worst of all for their morale, Amilakvari was killed. Such was the quality of his leadership that his death was akin to a major defeat for the Legion and it was several days before his men took any further part in the fighting.

Thus the Germans remained in control of Himeimat's peaks and 7th Armoured Division would be under their eyes all through the daylight hours of the 24th. The divisional commander, John Harding, later said that his men were disappointed but by no means cast down following that first night: prisoners had been taken, overall divisional casualties were not heavy and nor were the French losses as bad as initially thought. The day was spent planning that night's operations, including an attack by 131 Brigade, and Harding 'looked forward hopefully to the next night's operation'.[9]

Thus on the morning of 24 October Eighth Army had not achieved what its commander had intended. Montgomery was critical of the armour, writing that he considered them to be 'pursuing a policy of inactivity'. Furthermore, he thought that their commanders, fearing tank casualties, were reluctant to 'push on'.[10] At 9.15am on the 24th he issued orders for tasks to be carried out by XXX and XIII Corps. The former was to clear the northern lanes on its front; 2nd New Zealand Division was to exploit south-westwards while 51st (Highland) Division took over from the New Zealanders on Miteiriya Ridge – but probably not before the evening – 9th Australian Division would exploit northwards during the day, but plan a crumbling operation for that night, and 4th Indian Division would raid Ruweisat Ridge with a single battalion and, if possible, hold their gains.

In XIII Corps' area 7th Armoured Division was to attempt to break through the *February* minefield but, if this proved impossible, to continue crumbling operations between *January* and *February* while using a brigade of 44th Division to break through *February* that night. Those orders were relayed to Eighth Army's main headquarters at 9.45am. Montgomery later wrote that he sent for Lumsden and told him to drive his armoured commanders: should there be 'any more hanging back' he threatened to sack those commanders and bring in 'more energetic personalities'.[11] Later that morning, after meeting Leese, Lumsden and Freyberg at the latter's headquarters, Montgomery decided to follow the original concept of 'first deploying the armour on Pierson'. Accordingly, 10th Armoured Division was to attack that night, through the New Zealand front, and with the full support of XXX Corps' artillery.[12] Montgomery told Lumsden that he was prepared to accept casualties if the armour broke through, so that they might protect the New Zealanders in their southwards exploitation.[13]

Was Montgomery fair to his armoured commanders? He continued to see the armour providing a screen in front of the infantry, thereby exposing his tanks to the fire of German anti-tank guns while bringing them to battle against the enemy tanks. In its conception, this idea belonged to the First World War with tanks seen as protectors of infantry while failing to appreciate the vulnerability of tanks to effective counter-measures. Sir David Fraser suggests that although Montgomery blamed his armoured commanders for their lack of drive, he ought to have directed 'at least part' of the blame on himself as he failed to appreciate what, in reason, tanks might be made to do.[14] (This failing was still present in Normandy when Montgomery told soldiers of 2nd Armoured Battalion Irish Guards that their tanks [Shermans] were superior to the Germans', while the guardsmen had already seen the evidence of what German tanks could do to the Sherman and wondered if Monty was talking about the same armoured warfare in which they were engaged.[15])

Another comment on Montgomery's handling of the battle came from General Sir Richard McCreery, chief of staff to Alexander and later commander of Eighth Army. McCreery considered that Montgomery erred even before the battle began. His 'big tactical mistake' was in trying to push his infantry through Rommel's defences which had too much depth for a single infantry attack to penetrate beyond the minefields, a fact that was clear well before D Day. Far simpler, in McCreery's view, to have given the infantry 'two bites of the cherry' with a second set-piece battle either the second night or, if it proved necessary to move the artillery, on the third night. Such a plan would have cost less in infantry casualties and may have caused less ill-feeling between infantry and armour.[16]

However, as Fraser points out, Montgomery was resilient and began demonstrating that resilience in the following days, in what he himself called the dog-fight phase of the battle.

The North African campaign began in June 1940 when Italy declared war on the United Kingdom. Italian forces invaded Egypt in September but stopped at Sidi Barrani. A counter-offensive, Operation COMPASS, in December 1940 led to the destruction of Tenth Italian Army and the loss of Cyrenaica. These graves are those of Italian soldiers killed at Sidi Barrani. (*9th HAA Regiment Archive*)

The Western Desert is a harsh environment in which to live and fight but these two gunners have made themselves as comfortable as possible with a makeshift shelter in the summer of 1941. (*9th HAA Regiment Archive*)

Another foe thrown up by nature was the fly. Swarms gathering around food, waste, open wounds and dirt were a threat to health that demanded strict hygiene discipline. A 'brew' has attracted a swarm. (*9th HAA Regiment Archive/6 LAA Bty OCA*)

The Axis offensive in 1942 aimed to break into the Nile Delta and take Alexandria and Cairo. Alexandria, a major port and home to part of the Mediterranean Fleet, was also a cosmopolitan city as this contemporary image shows. (*9th HAA Regiment Archive*)

Khamsin. Both sides had to contend with nature as well as each other and one natural foe was the *khamsin*, or sandstorm. As well as blotting out visibility it created intense discomfort. (*9th HAA Regiment Archive*)

A detachment of LAA gunners watch a Bristol Beaufort of the RAF flying low overhead. Beauforts deployed as torpedo-bombers played a major role in sinking tankers carrying fuel to Libya for *Panzerarmee Afrika*. (*9th HAA Regiment Archive / 6 LAA Bty OCA*)

In June 1941 General Sir Claude Auchinleck (left) relieved General Sir Archibald Wavell as Commander-in-Chief, Middle East. The two commanders confer during the handover. (*IWM E5448*)

By June 1942 Eighth Army was retreating to the El Alamein line. Auchinleck is seen here in a command car in the desert as the army made its way back to the prepared defences. (*9th HAA Regiment Archive*)

Field Marshal Erwin Rommel, commanding *Panzerarmee Afrika*, hoped to smash through Eighth Army's positions into the Nile Delta. He was stopped by the resolute defence mounted by Auchinleck in which 25-pounder field guns played a major part. (*9th HAA Regiment Archive*)

The situation in Egypt prompted Winston Churchill to visit the theatre. General Sir Alan Brooke, Chief of the Imperial General Staff, had hoped to visit Middle East Command alone but found the prime minister there as well. Churchill decided to remove Auchinleck from command but he and Brooke disagreed over who should assume command of Eighth Army. (*NARA*)

To Churchill, nothing mattered but 'beating Rommel'. Erwin Rommel, promoted to field marshal after his capture of Tobruk in June, had created a legend amongst soldiers on both sides in the desert conflict. Known as the Desert Fox, he believed in taking risks and leading from the front. His attack on the El Alamein line on 1 July 1942 proved to be a risk too many. (*NARA*)

To Rommel, the man who stopped his advance and turned the course of the desert war was General Sir Claude Auchinleck. But Auchinleck's reputation was to suffer from comments made by the new commander of Eighth Army, Lieutenant General Bernard Law Montgomery. (*NARA*)

Montgomery in the turret of a Grant tank adapted as a command vehicle. Although the two men had disagreed in the UK, Auchinleck had suggested Montgomery as a commander for Eighth Army. Brooke also supported him, but Churchill favoured 'Strafer' Gott who was killed before he could take over, leading to Montgomery's appointment. (*NARA*)

The main cruiser tank in Eighth Army was the Crusader, which was under-gunned with a 2-pounder weapon. However, the Crusader Mark III, armed with a 6-pounder, was arriving in North Africa to re-equip armoured regiments. Unfortunately, it retained many of the earlier Crusaders' mechanical problems. (*Author's collection*)

Other new equipment reaching Eighth Army included the American M7 howitzer motor carriage, a self-propelled gun (SPG) in British parlance. Mounting a 105mm howitzer, it was dubbed 'Priest' in British service, due to the pulpit-style mounting for an anti-aircraft machine gun, seen here. Issued to Royal Horse Artillery regiments in the armoured divisions, the Priest superseded the improvised Bishop SPG. (*9th HAA Regiment Archive*)

Heavier artillery equipments were also arriving in North Africa, including the 5.5-inch medium gun. However, by the opening of Operation LIGHTFOOT, fewer than fifty medium guns, either 4.5- or 5.5-inch, were with Eighth Army. (*9th HAA Regiment Archive*)

The 3.7-inch heavy anti-aircraft gun had been used as an anti-tank weapon at Tobruk and on the retreat to El Alamein. It proved very effective and some of 69th HAA Regiment's guns deployed during the Alamein battles engaged ground targets. (*9th HAA Regiment Archive*)

Churchill had been in Washington when he heard the news of the fall of Tobruk. President Roosevelt, who gave him the bad news, also promised 300 of the new US M4 Sherman tanks. The first Shermans arrived in Egypt in September and the regiments to which they were issued included the Queen's Bays. (*Private collection*)

As preparations were made for Operation LIGHTFOOT in late October, measures were taken to deceive Axis intelligence about Eighth Army's dispositions, including the whereabouts of the armoured divisions. Deception measures included disguising tanks as lorries. Elsewhere lorries were disguised as tanks while dummy tanks were also used in fictional regiments. (*Private collection*)

Following the repulse of the Axis offensive in July, Rommel had begun a programme of laying minefields, the 'devil's gardens'. To reduce the risk to attacking infantry and armour, mine countermeasures included the development of mine-clearing equipment such as this Scorpion, a modified Matilda tank with an auxiliary engine to drive the jib-mounted flails. (*IWM E19019*)

At the Battle of Alam el Halfa, the second battle of El Alamein, American M3 Grant tanks had played a crucial role, with their sponson-mounted 75mm guns proving a shock to German and Italian tank crews. Grants continued playing their part in Eighth Army's armoured formations alongside M4 Shermans and Crusaders. (*Private collection*)

Lieutenant General Herbert Lumsden commanded X Corps in Eighth Army. This was Montgomery's armoured corps but the army commander and Lumsden clashed over the role of armour with the result that Lumsden was relieved of his command after the battle. He was killed by a Japanese kamikaze aircraft on the bridge of the USS *New Mexico* in 1945, the highest-ranking British officer to die in action during the war. (*Private collection*)

Marking the tracks to be used by the attacking formations required considerable preparation, including the provision of thousands of lamps by personnel of the Corps of Military Police, who also directed traffic in very difficult conditions. (*IWM E 18384*)

The opening onslaught of Operation LIGHTFOOT was an attack by RAF Wellington bombers on Axis positions. Ground crew are 'bombing up' Wellingtons at RAF Cairo West, a process that continued into the pursuit that followed the battle. (*IWM CM3949*)

The Royal Artillery came into its own during Operations LIGHTFOOT and SUPERCHARGE, firing the heaviest bombardments since the First World War. Personnel at a command post check their calculations as they prepare a 'shoot'. (*9th HAA Regiment Archive*)

RAF aircraft involved in the battle included the Hawker Hurricane IIDs of No.6 Squadron. The Hurricane IID was fitted with a pair of 40mm cannon, one under each wing, capable of penetrating tank armour. Known as the 'Flying Can Openers', the squadron was allowed to adopt the Royal Artillery's St Barbara's lightning flash. (*IWM CM4957*)

Treating the wounded. The officer giving a drink to a wounded man is a doctor or a chaplain of 51st (Highland) Division. (*Private collection*)

Two Shermans of C Squadron, 9th Queen's Royal Lancers, move forward carefully. Known as the Delhi Spearmen, 9th Lancers had trained intensively with their Shermans and took a heavy toll of Axis tanks during the battle at Tel el Aqqaqir. The regiment served in 2 Armoured Brigade of 1st Armoured Division. (*Private collection*)

Posed photographs of infantry of 9th Australian Division advancing. The images give a very good impression of the conditions under which they fought. (*IWM E18474*)

Commanding *Deutsches Afrikakorps* in *Panzerarmee Afrika* was General Wilhelm Ritter von Thoma who was to surrender to Eighth Army in the closing stages of Operation SUPERCHARGE. (*9th HAA Regiment Archive*)

With the Axis retreating a crew of the Bays replenish their Sherman with ammunition in readiness for the pursuit. (*Private collection*)

Right: A Crusader is filled with petrol from 'flimsies'; a slow process. (*Private collection*)

Below: Sherwood Rangers Yeomanry crews pose for the camera. The regiment had been in Palestine as part of 1st Cavalry Division before being mechanized, although it also served as a defensive unit at Tobruk in 1941. In its armoured role it distinguished itself at El Alamein and would continue to do so in North Africa and Europe. (*Sherwood Rangers Yeomanry OCA*)

The price of victory. The temporary graves of a Scottish soldier and officer who died for the 'good and the right'. (*IWM E18952*)

And defeat. Axis prisoners of war, captured by 51st (Highland) Division march into captivity. (*Private collection*)

The detritus of war. Examining the remains of a knocked-out tank. (*Private collection*)

'We knew that we were listening to the sound of history.' Sister Mary Richard Coyle OSF, a missionary sister in Alexandria, heard the guns roar at El Alamein and felt their thunder sixty miles away. This photograph was taken in New York in 1964 on the 25th anniversary of her profession in the Franciscan Order. (*Author's collection*)

We remember. Ex-servicemen mark the twentieth anniversary of the battle. They served throughout the desert campaign but were not present at the Battle of El Alamein. That did not stop them commemorating the occasion. The author's father is third from right in the fourth row of diners, looking back at the camera. (*Author's collection*)

Chapter Eight

Rivers of Blood

He'll remember with advantages what feats he did that day

Throughout the 24th the main area of operations was in the air, ground operations being limited to those of 1st Armoured and 51st (Highland) Divisions in the northern corridor. Montgomery asked for intense air support on XXX Corps' front and, throughout the day, light bombers and fighter-bombers harassed enemy positions. Attacks were made on the battlegroups of 15th Panzer and *Littorio* Divisions; eight bombers were lost and twenty-seven damaged. Both British and American aircraft were involved in these operations on a day when Desert Air Force flew almost 1,000 sorties, most supporting ground forces, while the United States Army Air Forces flew another 147. RAF aircraft intercepted an air convoy of Junkers Ju52 transports, escorted by Messerschmitt Bf110s, destroying five transports and damaging severely another six. Sorties were also flown in XIII Corps' sector with cannon-armed tankbuster Hurricanes strafing a German armoured unit operating captured British tanks. In this action, near Naqb Rala, in the far south, seven Stuarts were destroyed and five damaged. Other Allied aircraft attacked enemy landing grounds at El Daba and Qotafiya. Dust put two fighter strips out of action in the early afternoon, leading to fighter patrols over Axis forward landing strips and the battle area being cancelled so that escorts could be provided for the many bombers in the air.[1]

Air reconnaissance by No.208 Squadron showed little change in enemy dispositions at first light and during the day the Intelligence staff reported no signs of 15th Panzer, 21st Panzer or 90th Light Divisions moving.[2] Leese, who had been up to Miteiriya Ridge with Freyberg, was satisfied that his infantry were positioned to meet any counter-attack but, although signs of counter-attacks were reported, none developed. However, the Axis artillery became active everywhere, although this was no surprise to 7th Armoured Division in the south who had already experienced considerable harassment from those guns.

In the meantime operations by 1st Armoured and Highland Divisions were taking place to improve the northern corridor. There had, however, been some confusion in communications, due to the presence of formations and units from two corps in the same area. Freyberg had asked for 8 Armoured Brigade to support his own 9 Armoured Brigade to restore the momentum of the battle but his request had to be routed from his tactical headquarters to XXX Corps headquarters and thence via X Corps to 10th Armoured Division, returning, needless to say, by the same circuitous route. This bureaucracy was exacerbated by the fact that the two principal individuals concerned, Lumsden and Gatehouse, were both out of contact for a time. Lumsden was in the northern corridor while Gatehouse was on Miteiriya Ridge where he witnessed the losses incurred by 9 Armoured Brigade in the move down the ridge's forward slope. Seeing evidence also of possible counter-attacks, Gatehouse considered that his armour should give all possible defensive support to the New Zealanders. He learned from Freyberg that there was a clear gap that would allow tanks to move to the New Zealanders' right flank, although this was contrary to what Lumsden had said, and so Gatehouse ordered 24 Armoured Brigade to cross behind 8 Armoured and onto the ridge on their right. Eventually 47th Royal Tanks led this move.

Then came a contrary order from Lumsden who, unable to contact Gatehouse, sent his order directly to 24 Armoured's headquarters. Kenchington's regiments were to cross behind 8 Armoured and move into and across the Highlanders' sector to help 1st Armoured Division in the northern gap; they were not to move to the right of the New Zealanders. Confusion resulted and momentum was lost, which was probably fortunate for 51st (Highland) Division since, had 24 Armoured carried out Lumsden's order, there might have been even more – and disastrous – confusion in the division's sector.

The Highlanders had almost lost their commander that morning. Setting out to visit the front, Wimberley's jeep was blown up while he was trying to find 1st Black Watch's commanding officer. His driver and another soldier were killed, another officer very seriously wounded and Wimberley hurled from the jeep and knocked unconscious, thinking for a time that he was dead. He was out of action for the rest of the morning and left the division without overall control. Returning in the afternoon, Wimberley found disagreements between his brigade and battalion commanders and those of 2 Armoured Brigade about the positions each had reached.

great difficulty was experienced in locating the position of units in terms of map reference ... largely due to the complete absence of any natural features which could be recognized as unmistakable landmarks. The difference in map locations of the same unit as given by 51 Division and 1 Armoured Division was as great as 1000 or 1200 yards, and even the two Divisional Artilleries could not agree on this matter.

Shortly after 1000 hours 24 October, Corps Royal Artillery contacted 51 Division and offered the assistance of Royal Artillery observation posts in overcoming this difficulty, but at 1135 hours the offer was declined. At 1920 hours the Commander, Corps Royal Artillery again suggested that leading units which were uncertain of their location should, after giving half an hour's warning, fire five green [Very] lights at an agreed time, and that the Flash spotting posts would then plot their positions accurately.[3]

Such disagreements over locations would influence some of the phases of the developing battle. Not only was there disagreement about the location of features, there was even confusion over the nature of one of the best-known features of the battleground: Kidney 'Ridge' was really a depression but, due to a misreading of map symbols, was referred to in the manner that has since become familiar.

While Montgomery was prodding at his armoured commanders, what was happening on 'the other side of the hill'? For some time all that Axis commanders could be certain of was that an artillery bombardment of First World War proportions had opened all along the front, smashing their communications network. As a result Stumme was virtually blind. On his orders the Axis artillery did not retaliate immediately, since he was concerned about their low stocks of ammunition, although their ability to respond effectively following the pounding they had received must be doubted. One Italian unit, 62nd Infantry Regiment of *Trento* Division, was hit so hard that many of its soldiers fled to the rear. Most Axis infantry heavy weapons were destroyed by the shellfire and *Panzerarmee* headquarters believed that British tanks were assaulting their positions and had destroyed 62nd Infantry Regiment and two battalions of 164th Division. In spite of Stumme's order to his artillery, it was also believed that a British breakthrough in the north had been stopped by Axis artillery concentrations, while 7th Armoured Division in the south was believed to have broken through the outposts only to be stopped by the main defence line.

To clarify the situation Stumme decided to carry out his own reconnaissance in the Rommel fashion. He refused an escort or a wireless vehicle since, he said, he was travelling only as far as 90th Light Division. Thus he set out in a car accompanied only by Colonel Büchting and his driver, Corporal Wolf. For both Stumme and Büchting it was to be their last journey. The trio overshot 90th Light's positions and drove right up to the front where they were fired on by Allied troops, probably Australians. Büchting received a fatal head wound and Wolf turned the car around and accelerated away. He did not realize that Stumme had been about to jump out but, apparently, hung on to the side of the vehicle where he suffered a heart attack and fell off: he was known to have had high blood pressure. Only when Wolf eased off his accelerator did he realize that he had lost *Panzerarmee*'s temporary commander. Stumme's body was not found until next day. Needless to say, the loss of Stumme had an adverse effect on *Panzerarmee*'s headquarters. General Ritter von Thoma, commander of *Afrikakorps*, took over but decided that any British penetrations could be sealed off by local counter-attacks. He also decided to keep 21st Panzer and *Ariete* in the south and maintain 90th Light in reserve. Thus no decisive counter-action was ordered at this stage.

So it was that, in the early afternoon, de Guingand was able to say that there were no signs of either 21st Panzer or 90th Light Divisions having moved and that about 1,000 prisoners, some two-thirds of them Italian, had been taken. Casualties in Eighth Army were uncertain but did not exceed 3,000, mostly in XXX Corps: Highland Division losses were about 1,000 while the New Zealanders had lost about 800 men and the Australians and South Africans some 700 in total, almost evenly divided between the two divisions. Wimberley was now bringing forward from reserve 2nd Seaforth who, supported by 50th Royal Tanks and the entire mass of the divisional artillery, would clear the northern lane by attacking the enemy outposts codenamed *Strichen* and *Keith*, short of Black line.

Three companies of the Seaforth passed through 1st Black Watch to advance and form a bridgehead through the minefield that was holding up 2 Armoured Brigade. Lieutenant Colonel MacKessack had been given very little time to prepare his battalion for this operation, the purpose of which was to permit sappers to clear the way for 2 Armoured Brigade's tanks. Nonetheless the Seaforth went forward and, in spite of heavy casualties, achieved their objective. Eighty-five men had been lost with B Company losing every officer and its company sergeant-major; it was rallied and led forward in a successful charge on its objective by the company clerk. Soon after reaching its objective B Company was reinforced by a platoon of A Company which also brought up the battalion medical officer, food, water and reserve ammunition. Both *Strichen* and *Keith* were taken. Casualties included men hit by British artillery fire, 'almost certainly due to the uncertainty as to the real location of the troops'.[4] Both 9th

Lancers and 10th Hussars had followed the Seaforth but the Bays, taking a wrong turning, ended up in the Australian sector.

However, 9th Lancers also lost contact with the Seaforth and slewed towards the Australians. Soon they ran into the Bays, returning after running into minefields and being engaged by anti-tank guns, to which they had lost six Shermans. Both regiments then moved forward through the minefields, their sappers leading them carefully along the boundary between Australians and Highlanders. Eventually 9th Lancers and 10th Hussars were ordered to 'advance in support of 51 Div and not to wait for MTF'.[5] At 3.50pm 9th Lancers reported that they had passed through the first minefield and had encountered enemy tanks. These, from 15th Panzer and *Littorio* Divisions, had the advantage of having the sun behind them. Meanwhile, 10th Hussars had also encountered Axis tanks and a sharp tank battle developed with 2 Armoured Brigade supported by the Priests of 11 (HAC) RHA. As darkness fell the enemy withdrew, leaving twenty-one tanks burning on the battlefield.[6] British losses were similar but *Stirling* had been overrun, aided by a diversionary attack mounted by 50th Royal Tanks which drew fire from 88s in *Stirling*. In this operation 50th Royal Tanks lost nine tanks to mines.

That confusion over locations then began to play a major part: Brigadier Fisher, believing that his brigade start line was about 3,000 yards, or more, farther west than was the case, now considered two of his regiments to be on the northern hinge of *Pierson*, with the other just short of the objective. Still under this impression, 2 Armoured Brigade withdrew some 500 yards after dark; they had lost twenty Shermans in all and were, in truth, far short of *Pierson*. Fisher's report to 1st Armoured Division's headquarters led Briggs to order forward the battalions of 7 Motor Brigade; by midnight Briggs' infantry were close behind the forward positions. That evening reports reaching Montgomery suggested satisfactory progress in the northern corridor.

Some of that day's air effort had been devoted to supporting the Australians who were 'allotted the first heavy bombing attack of 24 October'[7] to assist in their securing the army's long northern flank. In their new positions the Australians had endured enemy shelling throughout the day while Axis tanks also made reconnaissances. The bombing raid, at 8.00am, hit targets marked with smoke by the Australian gunners while the northernmost limit of 9th Australian Division's positions was marked by blue smoke candles captured from the Germans. However, the German smoke was effective only to a height of 6,500 feet and Allied bombers were flying much higher so that some 2,000lb bombs fell in the area of 2/13th Battalion, causing casualties. However, the problem was resolved for further raids and there were no repeats of the error in subsequent attacks with the bombing appearing 'to be effective and the placing of the bombs along an uneven front line … accomplished most skilfully without endangering our troops'.[8] Although the infantry made no further advance during the day, 20 Brigade was ordered to advance to its final objective that night and the artillery was kept busy discouraging a series of what appeared to be planned enemy counter-attacks, six of which were dispersed by artillery concentrations, the last at 6.00pm.

Montgomery described the events of that night as the time 'when the real crisis in the battle occurred'.[9] The plans for the night 24/25 October, the night of the full moon, included a breakout by 10th Armoured Division in the southern corridor; Currie's brigade was to be withdrawn to allow Kenchington's 24 Armoured Brigade to attack south-westward, its axis on the northern boundary of the original divisional breakthrough sector. South of 24 Brigade, Custance's 8 Armoured Brigade would also attack and both brigades would punch through to *Pierson* to join Fisher's brigade. During the day the plan was altered to bring Currie's brigade and the New Zealand Divisional Cavalry in on the left while 133 Lorried Infantry Brigade took over the positions hitherto held by 8 and 9 Armoured Brigades and 5 New Zealand Brigade. The last-named would then follow 9 Armoured Brigade in an exploiting role. Likewise, 133 Lorried Infantry were to follow their armour towards *Pierson*. For this operation the divisional engineers were to clear as many sixteen-yard gaps in the minefield on the ridge as possible. In their own sectors 9th Australian and 51st (Highland) Divisions were due to undertake less ambitious operations.

Freyberg was not convinced that 10th Armoured Division 'was being properly set up for its attack'[10] and, in a phone call shortly after dusk, reported his misgivings to Leese. Part of Freyberg's problem was that he and Gatehouse had been unable to make more than the briefest contact during the afternoon, so mobile was the latter's tactical headquarters. Moreover, 10th Armoured's main headquarters were so far back that Gatehouse's staff were often unaware of the latest developments, news of which reached them through XXX Corps and X Corps headquarters. Leese passed Freyberg's comments to Lumsden whose reaction was to say that he was not surprised by the New Zealand commander's misgivings since neither he nor anyone else in the armoured command had much confidence in the plans for that night. Leese felt obliged to report these feelings to army headquarters. By the time Leese made that decision Montgomery had gone to bed for the night and Leese spoke to de Guingand who hoped that matters might improve as the night wore on. That hope was misplaced.

When daylight faded Miteiriya Ridge became a hive of activity as infantrymen left their trenches to improve their defences, parties came forward with food and supplies and X Corps' sappers began clearing more lanes for the armoured advance, scheduled to begin just after 10.00pm. Suddenly, into this busy scene fell a hail of enemy shells as von Thoma's gunners, certain that the British armour would attempt to cross the ridge under cover of darkness, began a bombardment aimed at making such a move as difficult as possible.

The Axis gunners succeeded in their aim. Freyberg's engineers had made an early start in their efforts to clear gaps for the Divisional Cavalry's advance but were delayed by the Axis bombardment and then caught in their own bombardment, which killed the sapper commander and caused other casualties. Some forward infantry positions were also hit by this 'friendly' fire and a company of 26th Battalion was forced to abandon its positions. However, two Divisional Cavalry squadrons did move forward, passing carefully through the minefield gaps in their light tanks and Bren-gun carriers. One squadron advanced almost two miles before stopping to await support. Both had suffered losses from mines, anti-tank guns and small-arms fire.

Behind the Cavalry, however, confusion reigned as 9 Armoured Brigade's tanks were blocked by the Staffordshire Yeomanry, who were using the wrong gap. Having driven forward, the Staffordshires' Crusaders then moved in the wrong direction before stopping to await the other squadrons of 8 Armoured Brigade. Currie reconnoitred another route for his tanks which later came upon the Staffordshires, helped them to knock out some enemy machine-gun posts, and then set off after the Divisional Cavalry. As the Sherwood Rangers attempted to get out and join the Staffordshires, one of their soft-skinned supply vehicles was struck by a shell or mortar bomb and its cargo of petrol ignited, starting a fire that spread through the double-banked, nose-to-tail column and attracting the attention of enemy artillery and aircraft. Soon more than two dozen vehicles were blazing and the Sherwood Rangers' tanks could not move forward, nor could those of the brigade's third regiment, 3rd Royal Tanks. Custance ordered both to disperse as widely as possible and await further orders.

Misfortune had also overtaken 24 Armoured Brigade. Their minefield reconnaissance party had come under heavy fire and retired while the sappers began clearing a gap through the wrong minefield and lost contact with the recce party. Thus the sappers began their appointed task about an hour after they were supposed to have finished it. Even then their litany of sorrows had not ended: erroneous warning of an enemy counter-attack in their area reached their commanding officer who ordered a withdrawal during which he lost contact with his infantry protection party and wireless truck. Such a catalogue of disasters proves the old military axiom that no plan survives first contact although, in this instance, it hardly survived the first men crossing the start line.

Once again Freyberg telephoned Leese, this time to tell him that 10th Armoured Division were sitting about doing nothing – hardly a fair analysis. Then Custance contacted Gatehouse to suggest that the advance be abandoned due to the disorganization of his brigade, a suggestion that Gatehouse passed to Lumsden with his own recommendation that it should be accepted. It seems that Freyberg overheard this conversation and rang Leese again. The latter reported this development to de Guingand.

> But although the New Zealand Divisional Cavalry had led the way across the Miteiriya Ridge followed by their supporting armoured brigade, 10th Armoured Division held back. The Chief of Staff of the Eighth Army, General de Guingand, who had been closely monitoring the situation, decided that, notwithstanding the Army Commander's edict about not being woken in the night, this was a crisis only Montgomery could resolve.[11]

And so the two corps commanders were summoned to a meeting in Montgomery's caravan at 3.30am 'to galvanize the whole show into action'. Having established the locations of the various formations, Montgomery

> told both corps commanders that my orders were unchanged; there would be no departure from my plan. I kept Lumsden behind when the others had left and spoke very plainly to him. I said I was determined that the armoured divisions would get out of the minefield area and into the open where they could manoeuvre; any wavering or lack of firmness now would be fatal. If he himself, or the Commander 10th Armoured Division, was not 'for it', then I would appoint others who were.[12]

In his *Memoirs* Montgomery claims that all the armour was out in the open by 8.00am and that Eighth Army was in the position he had intended to have achieved a full twenty-four hours earlier. This was far from true.

There had been forward movement by some of the armour and Freyberg seems to have inspired this. Custance, having received no reply to his request to abandon the advance, re-assembled the Sherwood Rangers and 3rd Royal

Tanks and ordered them out to support the Staffordshires. The advance began at around 3.30am. By the time the pale light of dawn was lightening the eastern sky both regiments were deploying alongside Currie's brigade, with 3rd Royal Tanks filling in between the Staffordshires and 3rd Hussars. Kenchington's brigade was also moving and his leading squadrons were clearing the ridge by about 5.00am. Their intention was to link up with 2 Armoured Brigade on the right and Sherwood Rangers on the left. As day dawned they saw Shermans and Crusaders to the north and assumed these to be 2 Armoured Brigade, an assumption that proved correct. A further assumption, that they were on *Pierson*, was not correct. As the heavy armour moved into position, the Stuarts and Bren-gun carriers of the New Zealand Cavalry withdrew to the cover of the ridge.

In fact Gatehouse had sent an order to Custance telling him to send only one regiment forward, but this order only reached the latter when all three regiments had moved. When the order reached the regiments, they obeyed it and 7 o'clock saw the entire brigade in cover of the ridge, with some 3rd Hussar tanks joining them in error. Thus 9 Armoured Brigade was once again out in front and alone. Currie's brigade disposed only two regiments, 3rd Hussars and Warwickshire Yeomanry: such had been the Wiltshires' losses the previous day that they had handed their few surviving tanks to the Warwicks and withdrawn to re-equip and re-organize. As the sun rose Currie's squadrons faced south and south-west with an unsupported right flank. Although they were deployed in low ground overlooked by Axis artillery Currie considered there to be no well-organized opposition ahead of him and decided an advance would be his safest course of action. But he needed fuel and ammunition and when he requested permission from Freyberg to send a squadron back behind the ridge for re-supply the latter, now aware that Currie was alone, ordered him to remain in position for the time being to discourage any enemy counter-attacks. This was the situation when Montgomery believed that his tanks were where he had wanted them to be at 8.00am the day before.

More success had greeted the Australian effort of that night in which 20 Brigade had been ordered to advance to its final objective. During the afternoon 2/17th Battalion lost its commanding officer, Lieutenant Colonel Bob Turner, who was wounded fatally by enemy fire while talking to the CO of 40th Royal Tanks; his adjutant, Captain Ronald Leach, was also killed. Initially planned to have the same artillery support as the original attack, this bombardment was cancelled after dark when patrols reported little opposition on the brigade front. The attack, by 2/17th and 2/13th Battalions, was, therefore, 'silent'.

Both battalions reached their objectives 'with small opposition and proceeded to reorganize'.[13] Australian engineers then drove gaps through the remaining minefields to complete Diamond, Boomerang, Double Bar and Square tracks to the final objective, linking them with a lateral track in that area.

In the Highland Division sector there had also been some more progress: 1st Gordons, who had their two forward companies cut off, were re-united on the night of the 24th on Black line from which, under Major James Hay, they began an advance to secure *Aberdeen*, on the north-eastern rim of Kidney. The advance was led by D Company with a platoon of 1/7th Middlesex, the divisional machine gunners, in support. While negotiating some barbed wire they were spotted by a German patrol which, receiving no response to its challenge, simply turned about and drove off. Some minutes later flares went up and they were greeted with mortar and small-arms fire before, to their surprise, meeting up with soldiers of 7th Rifle Brigade (The London Rifle Brigade), one of 1st Armoured Division's motor battalions. The riflemen had advanced by Sun route through the Australian sector and were to deploy in support of 2 Armoured Brigade but their vehicles had been blown up on mines and they were pinned down by fire from *Aberdeen*. The Gordons and Middlesex had no option but to dig in alongside the riflemen; the ground was almost solid rock and they were unable to dig trenches any more than a foot deep. There they were on almost open ground when dawn broke on the 25th: in fact, the Middlesex gun crews and the anti-tank gunners of the London riflemen *were* on open ground; they suffered heavily from enemy fire during that day.

In XIII Corps' sector on the second night 7th Armoured Division's attempt to break through the *February* minefield failed. The two battalions – 1/5th and 1/6th Queen's – of 131 Brigade assigned to 7th Armoured for the operation were warned at midday to leave their positions in the north of the sector and move down to join Corbett-Winder's minefield task force. Not until 10.30pm did the infantry move off their start line and into *February*. Initially their endeavours seemed to be crowned with success as they passed through the minefield and nearly half a mile beyond its western edge. Their problems started as they attempted to dig in and wait for the armour to pass through the minefield: once again the ground was so hard that digging was virtually impossible. Nor was building sangars practicable; the infantry suffered rifle and machine-gun fire and mortaring as they awaited the tanks' arrival.

Behind the Queen's Brigade, the men of 44 Recce and the sappers cleared the planned two gaps by 2.30am; but enemy fire was so heavy that the sappers were unable to mark the sides with dannert wire, and the lights were too far apart. Thus the leading tanks of 4th County of London Yeomanry had difficulty in passing through the northern gap, with some losing their way and blundering into the minefield to be blown up on mines while others were hit by fire from anti-tank guns deployed to cover the exit from the gap. In all the CLY lost twenty-six tanks: their commanding officer and second-in-command were among the casualties. At the other gap an 88 was hitting tanks of 1st Royal Tanks in the flank as they passed through. Harding's division was suffering heavily and the confusion led to a belief that the northern gap had not been cleared properly.

Aware of that rumour, Harding ordered Lieutenant Colonel Withers, the sapper commander, to check that the gap had been cleared. Withers protested the order but called for volunteers to carry it out. When they reached the entrance to the gap they came under such heavy fire that Withers dispersed them before commandeering two tanks in which he and another officer set off to drive through the gap. The first tank was struck five times but not penetrated and both emerged from the western end of *February*, turned around and drove back. On the return one lost a track and was abandoned close to the home end of the gap. Withers told Harding that the gap was clear and that the tanks lost had either wandered off into the minefield or been hit by the very effective anti-tank fire being poured into anything that moved in the gap. Harding was forced to call off the effort to pass the armour through *February*: 22 Armoured Brigade was to remain between the two minefields, the remains of 4 CLY were withdrawn to join 4 Light Armoured Brigade and the Queensmen were left on their own more than a mile in front of their nearest support. Corbett-Winder's 44 Recce was pulled back to a reserve position at Deir el Regil, where it would remain until 2 November; the regiment had lost thirteen officers and over 100 men killed or wounded, and was reduced to four carriers from thirty-eight.

In the morning Horrocks and Harding agreed not to pursue the original plan in daylight but to either try to pass 22 Armoured through *February* on the night of the 25th or use 50th Division, supported by 4 Light Armoured Brigade – as yet virtually unblooded – to attack the western end of the Munassib Depression. Both plans were passed to de Guingand for Montgomery's attention: the second was the preferred option. The Queen's Brigade would have to rely on the other brigade of 44th Division to come to their assistance since 7th Armoured Division's tanks were to be preserved for the pursuit after the breakout.

On the morning of the 25th Montgomery was still certain that events had gone according to plan, that X Corps had broken out through the minefields and was on *Pierson* and that the next phase of operations could begin. At 8 o'clock that morning he issued detailed orders for X Corps' further deployment: Lumsden's men would locate and destroy the Axis battlegroups while covering 2nd New Zealand Division's operations from enemy armour from the west. It would be some time before he discovered the truth. One writer on the battle described the situation thus:

> On the morning of 25 October … XXX Corps had blasted a gap six miles wide and five deep into the strongest part of the enemy's line. A total of five armoured brigades were out in front of this gap, trying to provoke the counter-attacks which they were well-placed to smash.[14]

Still convinced that such was the case, Montgomery issued a further set of orders for X Corps at 10.30am. Having been assured by Briggs that 2 Armoured Brigade of his 1st Armoured Division was on *Pierson* at the northern end, with 24 Armoured Brigade to its left, he assigned the latter brigade to Briggs' command to act offensively against any enemy battlegroups they might encounter. To the south 8 Armoured Brigade would form a line down to the junction with 9 Armoured, which would continue facing south, protecting the flank of XXX Corps' salient; Montgomery was unaware that 8 Armoured had retired behind the ridge. Gatehouse was to command the southern armour; 5 New Zealand Brigade and 9 Armoured would exploit to the south and 133 Lorried Infantry Brigade would hold the positions along the ridge.

As Montgomery was issuing those orders General Alexander arrived to visit him and while the army commander and C-in-C were conferring came the first adverse news of the previous night's fighting. Montgomery learned that 7th Armoured Division had failed to penetrate *February* and of Horrocks' decision not to pursue that advance in daylight. It was then that Montgomery approved the attack on Munassib. Soon further bad tidings arrived: 2 Armoured Brigade were not on the end of *Pierson* but at least 1,000 yards east of Kidney. Fisher had attempted to retrieve the situation on realizing his error and sent the Bays and 9th Lancers forward through the infantry. Both regiments ran into anti-tank fire from Kidney and the Bays lost eight Shermans in eight minutes, probably to 88s, while 9th Lancers lost two Crusaders. Attempts by 10th Hussars to take the guns from the flank faded with the threat of enemy counter-attack. Before long Fisher's brigade was behind *Oxalic* again and Montgomery soon had an accurate report of its positions.

As Alexander left Montgomery's headquarters to return to his own, Eighth Army's commander was aware that his armour was not where he had thought it was and that some of his plans were not developing as he had expected. Just before noon he arrived at Freyberg's headquarters on Miteiriya Ridge to meet Leese and Lumsden, who had been called to confer with him there. By noon Montgomery was aware of even more of the grit that had entered the machinery of his plans. The infantry had done almost all that had been asked of them; most of their objectives had been achieved at considerable cost; but the armour remained stalled and 'nowhere along the front had the British armour penetrated the enemy lines beyond the infantry positions'.[15] LIGHTFOOT was losing momentum and Montgomery needed to review his plans to regain that momentum before the enemy could further strengthen his defences and build new ones. Should that be allowed to happen, the gains made since the first infantry crossed their start lines on the night of the 23rd would be for nothing and Eighth Army would have all to do again.

> It became clear that the movement south-west of the N.Z. Division would be a very costly operation and I decided to abandon it at once. Instead, I ordered the 'crumbling' operations to be switched to the area of the 9th Australian Division, working northwards towards the coast; this new thrust line, or axis of operations, involved a switch of 180 degrees which I hoped might catch the enemy unawares.[16]

In fact, the others present, including Freyberg, were not in full agreement with Montgomery, arguing that, although the proposed New Zealand exploitation should be postponed, the battle should continue using the same methods as before with another massive artillery bombardment and an infantry attack to seize the ground along XXX Corps' front up to a depth of 4,000 yards, thus giving the armour another opportunity to break out. But Montgomery's will prevailed.

As Montgomery prepared for this change in operations, Rommel was crossing the Mediterranean in his Storch. He reached *Panzerarmee* headquarters as dark fell that evening to find that '[r]ivers of blood were poured out over miserable strips of land which, in normal times, not even the poorest Arab would have bothered his head about'.[17] Half an hour before midnight, German time, he sent a signal to his command: 'I have taken command of the army again. Rommel.' With the return of the Desert Fox a new factor had been added to the battle.

Chapter Nine

Rommel's Battle without Hope

Dying like men ... they shall be famed

Since the conference at Freyberg's headquarters Montgomery had been giving deep and careful consideration to his future plans. In the meantime XXX Corps was to hold Miteiriya Ridge firmly, 9th Australian Division was preparing for its 'crumbling' operations to the north, and X Corps was to continue 'to make ground west and north-west', according to the orders issued at the conference at Montgomery's caravan at 3.30 that morning, while 51st (Highland) Division was to mop up parties of the enemy still in its sector. However, there were some changes in Lumsden's command: 10th Armoured Division was withdrawn from the New Zealand sector for re-organization but Kenchington's 24 Armoured Brigade was to come under command of 1st Armoured Division, which was to push forward to its original objectives. Freyberg's battalions were to reconnoitre along their front to investigate signs of Axis withdrawal. In the south 50th Division, supported by 4 Light Armoured Brigade, was to attack Deir el Munassib.

Morshead, the Australian commander, had suspected that his division might be given this new task and, with remarkable prescience, had told Brigadier Whitehead of 26 Brigade to be ready to seize a spur to the north ending in the feature known as Point 29. Amazingly, Morshead had advised Whitehead to prepare for this on the morning of the 24th.[1] Although not more than twenty feet high, Point 29 dominated the division's area and, overlooking the ground to the north as far as the railway, constituted a valuable observation post for whoever might hold it.

Its excellent observation was likely to be turned to good account if left in enemy hands on the flank of the initial attack. For this reason careful consideration was given to the plan to see if the objective [on the first night] could be extended northwards to include Trig 29. It was decided that this could not be done, as the depth of the attack and the frontages allotted to each division were already the maximum that the available assaulting troops could capture, so it was selected as the first exploitation task.[2]

As 26 Brigade prepared for the attack the Australian division and its armoured support had to deal with enemy counter-attacks. The first occurred at 7.10am when twelve tanks and fifty troop-carrying vehicles began forming up opposite 20 Brigade for an attack that eventually came in against 2 Armoured Brigade, whose tanks and soft-skinned vehicles were still grouped among 2/13th Battalion's posts. This attack was beaten off by 'defensive fire and action by 40 R Tanks'. The next serious attack developed along the entire front of 20 Brigade at 2.00pm when forty tanks, mostly Italian, reached the divisional forward defended localities. The attackers withdrew after seventeen tanks had been destroyed by Australian anti-tank guns. Thirty minutes later came another threat, this time on 26 Brigade's front, as tanks formed up west of Point 29; defensive fire broke this up before the Australian infantry became involved. At 4 o'clock three enemy groups, each of ten tanks and ten troop carriers, attacked 20 Brigade but withdrew in the face of intense and accurate anti-tank and machine-gun fire.

> Throughout the day, 2 Armd Bde was unable to fight its way westward through the German positions. Its situation and that of 153 Bde on the left of 20 Aust Inf Bde remained obscure but it was clear that the armour had not emerged into open country.[3]

However, the Australians were not obscure about their intentions. Reconnaissance patrols established that there were no mines between 2/48th Battalion and the spur; the attacking battalion had been relieved in its defensive positions by 20 Brigade. Then at dusk an enemy recce party, spotted approaching 2/48th Battalion's positions, was allowed to come close before being fired on. Prisoners were taken, including the acting commanders of 125th Panzergrenadier Regiment and its 2nd Battalion.

> Both officers carried sketches of the enemy dispositions, minefields and the proposed reinforcement of the area. The battalion commander spoke freely when interrogated and confirmed the information that the track northwards to Trig 29 was free of mines.[4]

Prisoners taken by 2/24th Battalion also carried a map of the minefield. This information was passed to the engineers and a new route through the minefield for 2/48th's attack was plotted, covering a distance of only 200 yards.

Both 2/24th and 2/48th Battalions would attack, the latter northwards astride the track leading to Point 29 to capture the spur; for this the commanding officer planned to use a mobile company for the final assault and capture of Point 29. This company, C, would be led by two platoons in ten carriers, towing 37mm anti-tank guns. Following up would be a troop of 6-pounder anti-tank guns on whose portees the reserve platoon would travel. After 2/48th Battalion had gone in, 2/24th would form up and attack north-eastwards to the feature known as the Fig Garden where the battalion would re-organize and establish a line between the objectives. Artillery support would come from timed concentrations moving ahead of each attack with the entire divisional artillery on hand, plus an additional two field and two medium regiments. The Valentines of 40th Royal Tanks were also available as was air support from Albacores and Wellingtons, which flew seventy-nine sorties, dropping 115 tons of bombs in the battle area.[5]

Such was the plan. And it worked well. Starting on time 2/48th quickly secured their first objective which was to be 2/24th's start line. C Company then passed through in their carriers and covered the 1,200 yards of desert in nine minutes to arrive on the spur as the artillery concentration lifted. The roar of the guns had drowned the sound of the carriers which, combined with the speedy advance, took by surprise the large number of German defenders on the spur, which was captured after a 'short fierce hand to hand encounter'.

The battalion then exploited to the north and west against stubborn opposition to accomplish its objectives by dawn. For the first half mile 2/24th Battalion's attack also went well but both attacking companies then ran into considerable resistance from enemy posts described as the strongest encountered by 26 Brigade during the battle; these included some deep shelters. This resistance delayed the attackers who, nevertheless, achieved their objectives only seventeen minutes late. Then the other two companies passed through and tried to catch up with the artillery but failed to do so. Although suffering heavy casualties they reached and captured the Fig Garden where they came under heavy fire, prompting the commanding officer to withdraw both companies. By 5.00am the battalion had consolidated and completed its re-organization, as had 2/48th.

During this action two soldiers of 2/48th had distinguished themselves to such an extent that one earned a posthumous Victoria Cross for his actions and another's actions contributed to the award of a further posthumous VC.

Private Percival Eric Gratwick, aged 40,* was serving in A Company which met determined opposition from strong German positions. As well as delaying the capture of the objective, this opposition caused severe casualties.

> Private Gratwick's Platoon was directed at these strong positions but its advance was stopped by intense enemy fire at short range. Withering fire of all kinds … reduced the total strength of the Platoon to seven. Private Gratwick grasped the seriousness of the situation and acting on his own initiative, with utter disregard for his own safety at a time when the remainder of the Platoon were pinned down, charged the nearest post and completely destroyed the enemy with hand grenades, killing amongst others a complete mortar crew.[6]

One of his comrades, Corporal Frank Dillon, described what Gratwick had done.

> Suddenly, without saying a word, Percy took out a grenade, climbed to his feet and galloped forward, holding his rifle in his left hand. It was so crazy and he was so quick, that the Jerries didn't realize what was happening. Percy gave them the grenade, dropped on to one knee, got out another one and let fly with that. Next instant he had scrambled forward and dropped into their pit.[7]

Having knocked out the first post, Gratwick charged a second from which the heaviest enemy fire had been directed. Against intense machine-gun fire he advanced with fixed bayonet. Dillon saw what happened.

> Another Jerry, about twenty yards down the slope, was trying to finish him off with a Tommy gun. There were two others in another post with a mortar. Percy must have seen them, but apparently he had no more grenades. Next time we looked he was up on his feet charging with fixed bayonet. It was all over in a few seconds. Percy had only twenty yards to go – and you don't miss much with a Tommy gun at that distance. But we saw him make it, and then disappear. He got the Jerry too, because we didn't hear that Tommy gun again, or the mortar.[8]

---

* Gratwick had turned 40 on 19 October and was old for a front-line infantryman.

Percy Gratwick had displayed the kind of courage under fire that is more often associated with young soldiers. In fact, in the British Army it is doubtful whether he would have been sent to Egypt with an infantry battalion, never mind being put into the front line. A gold prospector, he had volunteered in December 1940 and was described as a 'quiet and unaggressive man; a good soldier and a solid, reliable comrade'. The award of his Victoria Cross was announced in January 1943 and the Cross was presented to his mother, Mrs Eva Mary Gratwick, on 21 November 1943 by the Lieutenant Governor of Western Australia, Sir James Mitchell.[9]

The second VC to 2/48th was awarded to Sergeant William Henry Kibby, another 'old' soldier, born in County Durham in April 1903. Kibby had already distinguished himself on the first night of LIGHTFOOT by taking charge of 17 Platoon when his platoon commander was killed. On his own initiative, and alone, he charged an enemy post that was holding up his company's advance and, with his Tommy gun, silenced the post, killing three of its defenders and capturing twelve.

> After the capture of Trig 29 on 26th October, intense enemy artillery concentrations were directed on the battalion area which were invariably followed with counter-attacks by tanks and infantry. Throughout the attacks that culminated in the capture of Trig 29 and the re-organization which followed, Sergeant Kibby moved from section to section, personally directing their fire and cheering the men, despite the fact that the Platoon throughout was suffering heavy casualties. Several times, when under intense machine-gun fire, he went out and mended the platoon line communications, thus allowing mortar concentrations to be directed effectively against the attack on his Company's front. His whole demeanour during this difficult phase in the operations was an inspiration to his platoon.[10]

During the night of 30/31 October Kibby was killed in action, again inspiring his platoon. These three actions are included in the citation for his posthumous VC, announced in the *London Gazette* of 28 January 1943. (The citations for Gratwick and Kibby mistakenly refer to Point 29 being on Miteiriya Ridge and wrongly suggest they were serving in Libya.)

Although the Australians were successful that story was not repeated elsewhere. Kenchington's armour had been due to stay west of Miteiriya Ridge until first light when it was to move to join Fisher who would be advancing south of Kidney, which was to have been taken by the Green Jackets of 7 Motor Brigade. However, since 51st (Highland) Division was attacking again, with 1st Gordons directed on *Aberdeen*, 5th Black Watch on *Stirling* and 7th Argylls on *Nairn*, there was confusion arising from uncertainty about locations. *Aberdeen* was on the eastern edge of Kidney and thus it was not possible safely to provide artillery support; to prevent two formations attacking the same place simultaneously, the armour was restricted to following the infantry, mine clearing and helping Fisher get forward. Briggs did make efforts to get on to Kidney, engaging tanks of *Littorio*, and the Bays lost sixteen Shermans.

Confusion over a rendezvous point delayed a meeting between Kenchington and Briggs; they did not meet until 5.45pm when it was decided to move 24 Armoured Brigade during the night rather than wait until morning. That northward move took the brigade all night, their third without sleep. Tank crews were suffering from exhaustion and the supply of Benzedrine tablets, or pep pills, although useful at first, soon led to hallucinations. Major A.F. Flatow, commanding A Squadron, 45th (Leeds Rifles) Royal Tanks wrote that he saw a man on a bicycle coming straight towards him at night in the middle of the desert – perhaps during this night move? – and that the commanding officer was mistaking his officers for each other.[11] Flatow's testimony and that of Peter Ross provide further evidence of the degree of fatigue assailing soldiers during the campaign which is not considered to the degree it should be in many histories. Second Lieutenant Peter Ross, commanding Recce Troop, 3rd Royal Tanks, described how, as the battle progressed, he began to lose track of time and developed a feeling that all was unreal. At one point he noticed a line of what appeared to be small black cairns, which began to grow bigger; as he stared at them through his binoculars, wondering how this could be, it finally dawned on him that the 'cairns' were panzers and he reported them as such, hoping that no one would notice his inefficiency.[12]

We left Wimberley's Highlanders with 1st Gordons pinned down short of *Aberdeen* alongside men of the London Rifle Brigade. During the afternoon of the 25th, German and Italian tanks had attacked the riflemen near the junction with the Australians. They more than met their match as the anti-tank gunners allowed them to approach to within 800 yards, at which point the 6-pounders opened fire. Several tanks were hit, some bursting into flame. Although the tanks came on, with artillery support, the Green Jackets held their ground and continued pouring fire into their foes. At 250 yards' range, the tanks were stopped and withdrew with the loss of at least fourteen vehicles.

This was the first infantry versus armour action of Alamein and the first of several manifestations that were to follow (exemplified on both sides) of the helplessness of tanks in the face of stoutly manned anti-tank guns. It was a fine and highly significant little action that has hitherto remained in obscurity to nearly all but those who took part in it.[13]

In 1st Gordons' headquarters, plans were made to reinforce the men cut off in front of *Aberdeen*. The commanding officer, James Hay, was injured grievously by a mine while reconnoitring in a carrier and Major J.E.G. 'Scrappy' Hay took command. That night's attempt by B Company to reach the men before *Aberdeen* was a failure and the company commander ordered a withdrawal. The Middlesex machine gunners with the leading elements of the Gordons were in an especially bad situation as they had been told to leave their rations and water behind. Some water was drawn off the radiators of wrecked lorries for drinking while the cooling jackets of the Vickers guns were replenished by the traditional expedient. Later a subaltern with a small party of six managed to get forward with some water. No thought was given to withdrawal.

Elsewhere in the divisional sector 5th Black Watch attacked *Stirling* which was taken against much lighter opposition than expected while 7th Argylls pushed forward three companies in a 'silent' attack against *Nairn*.

When the three companies were forming up for the attack they came under considerable random shelling and machine-gun fire. The troops were physically exhausted after continual fighting and owing to lack of sleep, but the three companies crossed the start line on time, and eventually obtained a lodgement in the northern end of *Nairn* locality.[14]

But there were only some hundred men left of the three companies and neither A nor D Companies had any officers left. B Company's commander re-organized A and D Companies into a composite sub-unit and called for artillery support. Although there was the usual doubt about accurate locations, there was wireless communication with the gunner liaison officer of 126th (Highland) Field Regiment at battalion headquarters and arrangements were made for defensive fire to be called down to cover all approaches to the location. Accurate fire was brought down from 126th Regiment on an 88 close to the left of the captured position, knocking out the weapon. This increased faith in the gunners and the battalion's map-reading skills.

Although Wimberley suggested to Leese that Briggs might now switch his advance to the south, this idea was rejected and X Corps headquarters told both armoured brigades to contact 5th Black Watch to see if they could help the Highland Division. Although Lumsden instructed Briggs to move Fisher's brigade north-west to a locality where he could offer left flank protection to the Australians, this proved impossible and 2 Armoured Brigade maintained much the same positions as on the day before.

Down in XIII Corps' area plans had been made for 50th Division's attack. During the afternoon of the 25th the two dummy tank battalions, 118th and 124th Royal Tanks, moved forward to just behind 50th Division, under whose administrative control they passed, as a deception measure: their presence was intended to suggest to Axis air reconnaissance that armour would be supporting 50th Division's attack. There was a belief that enemy forces might attempt to withdraw from their foremost strongpoints in front of 50th Division, a belief based on the 'surprisingly feeble' Axis reaction to a sweep by carriers on the morning of the 25th and further reinforced by reports of westward movement of enemy transport. Additional probes by carriers of 69 Brigade strengthened the belief.

That evening 69 Brigade attacked Deir el Munassib from east and north. The assault by 6th Green Howards met with success, the battalion taking nearly all its objectives. However, their fellow Yorkshiremen of 5th East Yorkshires suffered horrendous casualties after becoming entangled in wire and running into S-mines. Some 150 men were killed or injured. The attack failed and a plan to renew it the following night was cancelled. Two battalions of Queen's were still isolated in forward positions and, on the night of 25/26 October, were ordered to withdraw, being relieved under shellfire by 132 Brigade.

However, the commanding officer of 1/6th Queen's, Lieutenant Colonel Gibbs, later wrote that the battalions were ordered to 'try again' on that night and described an advance under cover of a bombardment and casualties, including his batman, from mines. But he

> was lucky because my mind was on the matter of helping to keep people together and right up behind the firing, and encouraging them just to go on. That took one's mind off the general hubbub quite a lot.[15]

Gibbs was captured that night, which he attributed, in part, to his own inexperience; he had commanded his battalion since early 1942. His account, written in a prison camp some time later, describes this action as being on the third night of the battle but some of the detail that he provides, including his description of the advance, relate to the second night. Gibbs, subsequently awarded the DSO, believed that, had the armour managed to follow the infantry, the southern flank battle could have been highly successful.[16] In part, of course, it was successful since it pinned enemy armour in the southern area when the main body of British armour was in the north. But the third night brought operations in XIII Corps' area to a virtual end. Responsibility for the defence south of Munassib was assigned to 44th Division, the two brigades of which had suffered over 700 casualties, with the Fighting French Brigade under command, while 7th Armoured Division withdrew behind the minefields. The Desert Rats now had seventy Grants, twenty-seven Crusaders and fifty Stuarts.

Montgomery spent all day on the 26th in 'detailed consideration of the situation'. He realized that his plan needed to be revitalized but does not mention this day at all in his *Memoirs*, moving from consideration of the events of the 25th to Wednesday 28 October, when he

> began to realize from the casualty figures that I must be careful. I knew that the final blow must be put in on 30 Corps' front, but at the moment I was not clear exactly where. But I had to get ready for it. So I decided to turn my southern flank (13 Corps) over to the defensive except for patrol activities, to widen divisional fronts, and to pull into reserve the divisions I needed for the final blow. The N.Z. Division I had already got into reserve.[17]

But he had begun his reconsideration two days earlier when he knew that his casualties, until 6 o'clock that morning, numbered 6,135: of these 4,643 were from XXX Corps, 455 from X Corps and 1,037 from XIII Corps.[18] Although not excessive these figures counselled caution, especially as reinforcements for the New Zealand and South African Divisions were not available; the former had suffered over 800 casualties, some one-third of its fighting strength. The Australians were also due for repatriation after the battle. Another full-scale attack might cripple completely XXX Corps' infantry.

The momentum of X Corps' attack was much reduced and its armour had yet to break out into mine-free country. However, Eighth Army still had about 900 effective tanks with the armoured formations, with good administrative arrangements and plenty of fuel, water, food and ammunition. Montgomery's command maintained a distinct advantage over that of Rommel.

Rommel described the El Alamein battle as a 'battle without hope' and went on to write that '[t]he battle which began at El Alamein on the 23rd October 1942 turned the tide of war in Africa against us and, in fact, probably represented the turning point of the whole vast struggle'.[19] His letters to his wife during the battle are those of a man suffering from the greatest stress that the burden of command can impose and, furthermore, one who knew that he carried much of the responsibility for the suffering of his soldiers for, in spite of what he wrote in the quotation above, the real turning point of the campaign in Africa had been in July when he had failed to break through an exhausted Eighth Army to reach Cairo and Alexandria.

His assessment of the situation when he re-assumed command of *Panzerarmee* was true to his previous assessment of what the battle would be: a static battle of attrition, a *Materialschlacht*, in which Eighth Army would have the advantage. The dispositions of *Panzerarmee* had been intended to reduce that material advantage as much as possible – and to some extent they succeeded as Montgomery had not made the progress he had hoped against the deep defences Rommel had created. (At one stage Rommel had hoped that he might again send a right hook around the British southern flank[20] but a reconnaissance of the Qattara Depression had proved it impassable for armour. He did not know that British troops had crossed it in the retreat from Gazala, but these were light forces, although they did include some armoured cars.) However, Rommel was not despairing, even though the reports that he now received told him that 15th Panzer had but thirty-one tanks fit for action, that fuel supplies were reaching a critical state, and that British artillery and air superiority were having a detrimental effect on even the German soldiers of *Panzerarmee Afrika*. Most accounts state that Rommel found his command to have only three days' supply of petrol but this must be regarded with some cynicism: on 19 October the *Panzerarmee* daily report had noted eleven days' fuel and there had not been sufficient combat to use eight days in the meantime; the report of only three days' fuel is probably a case of Rommel exaggerating his problems, something he was apt to do. However, he had lost 127 German and Italian tanks.[21]

After a few hours' sleep Rommel was back in his command vehicle at 5 o'clock on the morning of the 26th. There he learned that British artillery had been hammering at his front during the night, covering assaults by infantry and armour; in some places Eighth Army's guns had fired as many as 500 rounds for every round fired by Axis forces. Bombers had also contributed to the onslaught. Rommel described graphically the British artillery bombardment throughout the battle: 'Such drum-fire had never before been seen on the African front, and it was to continue throughout the whole of the Alamein battle.'[22]

In the morning Rommel drove out to see the scene of the overnight Australian attack and noted that piecemeal counter-attacks had been beaten off by the Australians who were well dug-in with their heavy weapons already in position. He issued orders for 90th Light Division to move up to the line; his own *Kampfstaffel* was also brought up to help: a concerted counter-attack was to be launched at 3.00pm. But the storm of British artillery that met it was such that the attackers were forced to take cover, if they could find it; the fire reminded Rommel of the Western Front in France a generation before. As his men went to ground the artillery fire ceased, the bombers appeared overhead and 'party rally' attacks were maintained on an hourly basis. Axis aircraft attempting to support ground troops were themselves handled roughly by Allied aircraft, sixty of which caught Italian bombers and forced them to jettison their bombs; British anti-aircraft fire tore the attacking German formations to pieces over their targets.

Rommel was shaken by what had happened. This day's events had underlined the British superiority and caused him to decide to take what might be a major risk: having come to the conclusion that the main threat lay in the north, although his intelligence staff had considered otherwise, Rommel ordered 21st Panzer, about a third of *Ariete* and the bulk of his artillery in the south to move northwards to assist in stopping the British thrusts. The major risk lay in the effect this move would have on his fuel: if his assessment was wrong then he would have used precious petrol for nothing and there might not be enough for the armour to return south. But he had some reason for optimism: a tanker was due in Tobruk next day with 2,500 tons of petrol; this ship, *Proserpina*, would be followed by another, *Tergesta*, with another 1,000 tons of petrol and a similar weight of ammunition. Those 3,500 tons of fuel would provide six days' supply for his armoured divisions under battle conditions, allow him the luxury of manoeuvre and, perhaps, the opportunity to entice the British armour through the minefields and into a battle of movement south of El Daba. That would allow a greater chance of an Axis victory than the alternative of pushing his armour *en masse* into the present battle area where they would suffer from artillery and bombers. In a battle of manoeuvre Rommel was confident of success even now.

What we should really have done now was to assemble all our motorized units in the north in order to fling the British back to the main defensive line in a concentrated and planned counter-attack. But we had not the petrol to do it. So we were compelled to allow the armoured formations in the northern part of our line to assault the British salient piecemeal.

Since the enemy was operating with astonishing hesitancy and caution, a concentrated attack by the whole of our armour could have been successful, although such an assembly of armour would of course have been met by the heaviest possible British artillery fire and air bombardment. However, we could have made the action more fluid by withdrawing a few miles to the west and could then have attacked the British in an all-out charge and defeated them in open country. The British artillery and air force could not easily have intervened with the usual weight in a tank battle of this kind, for their own forces would have been endangered.[23]

It should be remembered that this was written after the event with the wisdom of hindsight although it reflects a scenario true to the Rommel spirit.

That night was broken by even more noise than Rommel's first night of the battle with British bombers active throughout and the 'drum-fire' of the artillery yet again brightening the northern sector sky. The bombers hit the coast road, dropped bombs in the battle area and caused serious delay to 21st Panzer Division on its northward march, although inflicting few casualties on the division. Dawn made clear that the Australians had improved their positions and brought the news that Eighth Army was attacking yet again around Kidney. With daylight Rommel made a reconnaissance along Telegraph track to behind the Aqqaqir ridge and observed the British bombardment and air attacks. As he awaited news of the arrival of 21st Panzer, and considered how best to deploy its tanks, he received the disastrous news that both *Proserpina* and *Tergesta* had been sunk. During that day he received seventy tons of petrol, courtesy of the Luftwaffe which flew it in. At 2.30pm he made another trip along Telegraph track, accompanied by Major Ziegler.

Three times within a quarter of an hour units of 90th Light Division, which had deployed and were standing in the open in preparation for the attack, were bombed by formations of eighteen aircraft. At 1500 our dive-bombers swooped down on the British lines. Every artillery and anti-aircraft gun which we had in the northern sector concentrated a violent fire on the point of the intended attack. Then the armour moved forward. A murderous British fire struck into our ranks and our attack was soon brought to a halt by an immensely powerful anti-tank defence, mainly from dug-in anti-tank guns and a large number of tanks. We suffered considerable losses and were obliged to withdraw. There is, in general, little chance of success in a tank attack over open country where the enemy has been able to take up defensive positions; but there was nothing else we could do.[24]

In the next chapter we shall look at these events from the perspective of 1st Armoured Division, the British formation that was attacking around Kidney.

That night Rommel wrote to his wife:

A very hard struggle. No one can conceive the burden that lies on me. Everything is at stake again and we're fighting under the greatest possible handicaps. However, I hope we'll pull through. You know I'll put all I've got into it.[25]

He also sent messages to Mussolini's and Hitler's HQs, asking for reinforcement and the necessary supplies of fuel. But he no longer held out

any hope of an improvement in the situation. It was obvious that from now on the British would destroy us bit by bit, since we were virtually unable to move on the battlefield. As yet, Montgomery had only thrown half his striking force into the battle.[26]

While 26 October was a day of unending battle for Rommel it was one of reflection and consideration for Montgomery. It was almost a quiet day, if such a description can be applied to a battle, for most of Eighth Army, although Rommel saw it otherwise. While Rommel could opine that his opponent had only thrown half his striking force into the battle, this may well have been because Montgomery had not yet been able to find a way of getting any more than half that force into action. That was what he was now considering, alongside the problem of maintaining the initiative while re-organizing his armour. Keeping the initiative was a task for the infantry and the Australian attack on and capture of Point 29 was an important part of this plan; activity would continue on the Australian front.

The re-organization of the armour was described as a regrouping of the 'army to create a reserve with which to restore [the impetus of the offensive]' and involved both X and XXX Corps redistributing their constituent formations to achieve that end. Freyberg's division, including 9 Armoured Brigade, was to be withdrawn into reserve alongside 10th Armoured Division, now minus 24 Armoured Brigade. Montgomery also had an eye on the veteran Desert Rats of 7th Armoured Division in XIII Corps for this reserve. The regrouping of

Eighth Army was to be complete, apart from minor changes, by dawn of the 28th.

While Montgomery was ruminating, Eighth Army's Intelligence staff produced figures for Axis casualties that must cause the thinking reader to doubt the intelligence of those very staff officers. The figures given to de Guingand suggested that Rommel had lost 61,000 men, 530 tanks and 340 field guns.[27] Had such been the case then Eighth Army had already won the battle and ought to have been well on the road to Tripoli; one wonders how those who produced the figures could consider them realistic, especially as the figure for the number of Axis tank losses exceeded *Panzerarmee*'s tank strength prior to the battle. The *Official History* notes a more realistic situation: German losses were 1,700 dead, wounded or missing while the Italian figure was 1,955; Axis tank losses, as already noted, totalled no more than 127.[28]

While Montgomery was refreshing his plan, there occurred two actions around Kidney which were part of X Corps' making ground. One was to achieve almost legendary status and produce the third Victoria Cross of the battle: the defence of the outpost known as *Snipe*. The second action, at the outpost known as *Woodcock*, was to see a fine British county battalion overrun.

Chapter Ten

A Change of Plan

We few, we happy few, we band of brothers

Told to make ground around Kidney, on the afternoon of the 26th Lumsden ordered 1st Armoured Division to capture the enemy strongpoints codenamed *Snipe* and *Woodcock*, beyond and about a mile south-west and north-west respectively of the feature. This was an initial stage of an attempted advance to the Rahman track to take up a position there to 'cut the enemy's main lateral communications [and] force him to attack us on ground of our own choosing'.[1] Lumsden's hurriedly issued orders coincided with Rommel's decision to concentrate forces on the same sector of front. Following the Desert Fox's order, *Afrikakorps*, with *Littorio*, 90th Light and various other elements began converging on the area.

The British assaults on *Woodcock* and *Snipe* were to be carried out by Green Jacket battalions: 2nd King's Royal Rifle Corps, still often referred to by their pre-1881 title of 60th Rifles, were to take *Woodcock* while their brothers of the rifle fraternity, 2nd Rifle Brigade, would take *Snipe*. Briggs' intention was that the positions would provide a secure base for 1st Armoured Division's forward move into the protective role demanded by Montgomery's orders. With *Woodcock* and *Snipe* held by 7 Motor Brigade, enemy anti-tank posts would be under British domination and safe passage created for 2 and 24 Armoured Brigades. At last Eighth Army's armour would be in the open and 7 Motor Brigade could follow, leaving 133 Lorried Infantry Brigade to hold *Snipe* and *Woodcock*.

Neither attacking battalion was certain where its objective was: when their commanding officers discussed the locations with the Highland Division, they found an incredible difference of 1,000 yards in the fixing of the positions between the Highlanders and 1st Armoured Division. As desert veterans 1st Armoured were confident that they were right but events proved that the Highlanders' map-reading was more accurate and their fixings closer to the truth. Young George Morrison's confidence in his map-reading skills and, by extension, those of his fellow navigating officers was thus vindicated. Clarification came as a result of Army Command's frustration at the arguments over map-reading: at a specified time that day flares were fired from advanced positions from which cross-bearings were taken. The armoured units were still not convinced that they had been mistaken.

There was little opportunity for reconnaissance by the two commanding officers and Lieutenant Colonel William Heathcoat-Amery of 2nd/60th Rifles, considered that the supporting bombardment for his battalion was not falling in the right direction. However, his carriers were obliged to follow it as they left their start line at 9.30pm. In motor battalion fashion the carriers preceded the foot soldiers who advanced into the dust clouds raised by the vehicles; the battalion was accompanied by guns of 310 Battery, 76th Anti-Tank Regiment, since part of their task was to provide an anti-tank screen to cover the divisional armour's push through to the open country beyond; there was also a section of No.3 Troop, 7 Field Squadron, Royal Engineers. En route the riflemen had an unexpected encounter with 1st Gordons and ran into some enemy anti-tank posts, which had not been expected either but from which they took almost 100 prisoners. When the noise of artillery and opposition stopped 2nd/60th Rifles also stopped and assumed defensive positions. However, dawn showed that they were on open ground south of *Woodcock* in positions that could not be held by day. Heathcoat-Amery therefore ordered his battalion to withdraw. They pulled back east of Kidney to a position not far from their starting point and were joined by the Deacons of ZZ Anti-Tank Battery which were to protect their southern flank.[2]

Snipe was the objective for 2nd Rifle Brigade, under Lieutenant Colonel Victor Turner, who had been commanding a minefield task force built around his battalion. Turner, also unconvinced of the accuracy of the Highlanders' navigation, was thus uncertain of the locations of both his start line and objective. He reported his worries to 7 Motor Brigade headquarters to be told that no change could be made at such a late hour. Turner's force included his own battalion, the 6-pounders of G and H Troops, 239 Battery, 76th Anti-Tank Regiment (one of many gunner regiments converted from infantry battalions, in this case 5th (Flintshire) Bn Royal Welch Fusiliers; 239 Battery served with 11 (HAC) RHA for much of 1942[3]) and sixteen sappers of 7 Field Squadron. In addition, the battalion anti-tank company had sixteen 6-pounders. Captain Noyes, 2 RHA, accompanied the force as the artillery Forward Observation Officer (FOO). Turner's force had twenty-two carriers, eleven short of a motor battalion's normal complement, a machine-gun platoon with Vickers MMGs and a mortar platoon with 3-inch weapons. Some carriers mounted weaponry that was not on the quartermaster's inventory – machine guns salvaged from crashed aircraft which added to the overall firepower. There were only seventy-six assault riflemen, against the normal ninety in such a battalion. Turner's total strength came to some 300 personnel.

> In his battalion there was a dash of Irish, but, otherwise, the rank and file were nearly all Londoners and very largely from the East End; the coming action, indeed, was to prove once more that in a tight corner there is no better fighter than your Cockney. It was characteristic of a Rifle battalion that most of the men, and several of the officers also, such as Turner himself and Tom Bird [commanding the anti-tank platoon; he held the MC with Bar],[4] were of small stature.[5]

An hour before midnight, the force moved off at its appointed time with the carriers leading the foot soldiers; the anti-tank guns on their portees remained on the start line with the lorries carrying water, rations and ammunition until called forward by the success signal. Turner's orders were to follow the artillery bombardment which, he was told, would be on a bearing of 233 degrees; if that were to change then he should still follow it. The actual bearing was 270 degrees and thus Turner's men moved off on that into the enemy-held territory beyond *Oxalic*.[6] Past the line of ridges on *Oxalic* the ground changed from hard rock to soft sand, almost dust, with some camelthorn. It was exposed and had virtually no recognizable features save the usual small folds in the desert and an oval mound shown on maps as a 35-metre ring contour; this was Hill 37, some three-quarters of a mile long, rising to thirty-seven metres in height.

The carriers raised a cloud of dust that turned the moon orange and made navigation difficult but Turner used the odometer of a 15-cwt wireless truck, hardly a precision instrument, to carry out dead-reckoning checks on progress.[7] When 3,000 yards had been covered he asked Captain Noyes to have a smoke shell fired on to the objective. This was done and the round burst within 300 yards. Satisfied that he had reached the objective, Turner occupied an oval-shaped depression measuring some 900 by 400 yards. Previously used as a German engineer depot, it contained a small dug-out which became battalion headquarters. Some previous occupants lay dead in the feature and the ground was also fouled by excreta, indicating that the unit's hygiene discipline had not been good.[8] At fifteen minutes past midnight Turner reported the objective secure. His men were digging in, a very difficult task in the soft sand, which slid back into any hole that was dug. However, he was not on the true objective but some 900 yards south of it, although the securing of the hollow feature proved fortunate as events developed. Nonetheless, we shall continue to refer to this location as *Snipe* since that has become the accepted description of 2nd Rifle Brigade's location.

The success signal received, the second-in-command, Major Tom Pearson, began bringing the portees and supply trucks forward through the treacherous sands. Enemy bombing and shelling had already caused casualties and the medical officer stayed behind to treat them. It was a difficult move, with frequent need to dig vehicles, especially those without four-wheel drive, out of the soft sand but, by 3.45am, nineteen 6-pounders (an official account, written shortly afterwards, puts the original complement at twenty-seven guns; other sources describe the two troops of 239 Battery as disposing only six weapons, giving a total of twenty-two), thirteen of them from 2nd Rifle Brigade, and the water, rations and ammunition were in place.[9] Turner deployed his battalion with A Company holding the north-east sector of the perimeter, B Company the south-east and C Company the west; the 6-pounders were divided between the companies with G and H Troops 239 Battery, commanded by Captain A.F. Baer and Lieutenant F.J. Wilmore MM respectively, supporting A Company.

As the motor companies consolidated, the scout platoons went forward to reconnoitre and cover the consolidation. That of C Company, under Lieutenant Dick Flower, found barbed wire after 250 yards but discovered a gap through which they drove and advanced for a mile in clear moonlight, causing some sixty enemy soldiers to run away; fourteen were made prisoner. Then Flower spotted the shapes of some three dozen enemy tanks and several soft-skinned vehicles, the leaguer of *Kampfgruppe* Stiffelmeyer, which included Germans and Italians. Normal procedure would have been to withdraw with this information but Flower did not follow procedure. Instead he opened fire on the enemy positions, even though his heaviest weapons were Brens. Three vehicles were set alight and the tank crews mounted up and engaged these brazen intruders, hitting a derelict close to Flower's carriers. The derelict burst into flames, the carriers were illuminated and one struck by a tank round. During the confusion the prisoners made a run for freedom but were shot down by fire from both sides. As the tanks advanced Flower withdrew his carriers and returned to Turner's position.[10]

By now Turner knew that his battalion was just inside the enemy front line. Camp fires were spotted to the west with many more 1,000 yards to the north where, in bright moonlight, could be discerned a large tank leaguer. This included elements of 15th Panzer Division. Then, at 3.45am, the roar of engines and the clank of tracks from the west indicated that *Kampfgruppe* Stiffelmeyer was leaving its leaguer. Soon it was spotted moving in two columns, one towards 15th Panzer and the other towards 2nd Rifle Brigade's positions.

The tank column heading for the hollow was led by a PzKw Mark IV Special, with a long-barrelled 75mm gun, the most powerful tank in the desert at the time. The Mark IV Special seemed unaware of the British presence in the hollow and C Company waited until it was under 100 yards away before opening fire; a single 6-pounder round from Sergeant Brown's gun wrote *finis* to the panzer, which burst into flames. Only one crewman, who proved extremely courageous, escaped. Running to the shelter of a trench, he sniped at the Rifle Brigade's positions throughout the remaining hours of darkness but, at first light, a Green Jacket located his trench, crept out and killed him with a grenade. At the same time A Company destroyed a 76.2mm self-propelled gun. Both detachments had waited until they were certain of a hit before firing since the sights of the 6-pounder were poor for night shooting. Their two kills made the rest of the enemy column veer to the west where they halted and waited for daylight. The first round in the defence of Outpost *Snipe* had taken place and 2nd Rifle Brigade had won it. Turner's gunners were decidedly pleased at their own performance but also at the quality of their new guns, so much more effective than the 2-pounders.[11]

Turner's riflemen had learned with delight of the exploits of the London Rifle Brigade two days earlier and were keen to follow in the steps of their fellows.

> From this moment the garrison was fired to a most astonishing degree with an eager and offensive confidence. As events disclosed themselves, this spirit swelled into something more impressive – the exultant spirit of the happy warrior.[12]

There was, however, one setback shortly after this encounter when Captain Noyes set out to reconnoitre the area and failed to return. Later it was learned that he had been captured by a German patrol. His loss left Turner with no proper means to control his supporting artillery; no replacement could get across the fire-swept ground.

At 5.45am, just before dawn, Pearson was sent back with the soft-skinned vehicles. Half an hour later the sky began to lighten as dawn crept over the horizon and, as the light improved, both enemy tank groups began moving westward, seemingly unaware that a force with strong anti-tank assets had infiltrated their own lines. The benefits of the hollow began to be felt while the cover afforded by the thorn scrub was also invaluable. Both columns obligingly presented their flanks to the 6-pounders, which fired from ranges of no more than 800 yards. Anti-tank rounds tore into the sides and rears of several targets and sixteen enemy vehicles were knocked out before both groups pulled back out of range. Turner's garrison at *Snipe* had now killed eighteen enemy armoured vehicles and taken about seventy prisoners but the element of surprise that had contributed so much to this success had gone: the enemy, aware that the hollow was manned by British troops, began subjecting it to heavy and sustained shellfire, causing many casualties. Daylight indicated that the gun positions chosen during the night were satisfactory: little change was needed other than moving one gun to avoid a mound in front of it.

> It was now possible to see what the ground looked like. There were no distinct features, with the exception of the 30 Ring Contour running NW from 867293 to 865295, and the 35 Ring Contour 864293. Even these alterations in height were difficult to distinguish owing to the undulating nature of the ground. There was a lot of sand and scrub which made easy the digging in and camouflaging of the A.Tk gun positions. On the other hand, this ground enabled enemy tanks to take up hull down positions almost anywhere except on the ground to the SW of the position, 865292, which was open and ran up to the 35 Ring Contour 864293.[13]

Turner was concerned that there was, as yet, no sign of 24 Armoured Brigade, who were to operate forward from his battalion base. There had been uncertainty about the parallel operation to take *Woodcock* as well as some internal problems within the brigade but, at about 7.30am, Kenchington's leading tanks moved westward, raising huge clouds of dust that signalled their imminent appearance to the garrison of *Snipe*. However, as the first tanks of 47th Royal Tanks reached the crest of the ridge on *Oxalic*, the sun rising behind them, they opened fire on *Snipe*. Some accounts suggest that this was because they mistook the strongpoint for an enemy one since it was surrounded by wrecked Axis vehicles but that, while true, is not the whole story: the tank crews had not slept since the beginning of the battle and the effect of that fatigue, combined with the pep pills intended to keep them alert, undoubtedly played its part in what might have been a catastrophe. The situation was saved when 2nd Rifle Brigade's intelligence officer, Lieutenant Jack Wintour, drove out in his carrier and asked the tankmen to desist from firing. He succeeded in silencing the leading squadron; however, it took some time for the message to be relayed to all tanks.[14]

As the fire from 47th Royal Tanks died away Turner spotted almost thirty enemy tanks, mostly German, and some SPGs approaching from the west to take up hulldown positions about 1,000 yards away. The tanks were engaged and one gun claimed to have set three on fire. As the leading tanks of 47th Royal Tanks moved up to the position they came under heavy fire from the enemy tanks, and from 88s, most of which were firing from Kidney. Axis artillery fire was also falling on the outpost into which 47th Royal Tanks had moved by about 8.30am. Seven Shermans were hit in little more than fifteen minutes and the decision was taken to withdraw 24 Armoured Brigade: 47th Royal Tanks returned behind the ridge, having been reduced to five Shermans and six Crusaders. As the brigade withdrew it came under fire from tanks around Kidney but one Mark IV among those latter was struck by a Rifle Brigade 6-pounder at a range of just over a mile. The damaged panzer was towed away by another German tank.[15]

As 47th Royal Tanks withdrew behind the ridge, 41st Royal Tanks did likewise to their left, having lost a dozen tanks. The armoured attack had been stopped; Turner's men were now alone. However, they were probably glad to see the armour depart since their presence had drawn too much attention to *Snipe*. As the armour withdrew a small party of 2nd Rifle Brigade left *Snipe* in three carriers to evacuate some of the more seriously wounded. They managed to reach the British front line, although one carrier took a direct hit en route. It had been hoped that this party could return with the medical officer but that proved impossible. Although a small convoy with ammunition under Major Pearson stood by all day, ready to dash across to *Snipe*, every attempt to move off was met with heavy shellfire through which no vehicle could pass.

The withdrawal of the British tanks opened the way for counter-attacks on Turner's position, the first being made almost immediately by Italian infantry who were beaten off by Flower's scout platoon carriers. Two enemy vehicles towing captured 6-pounders were destroyed and severe casualties inflicted on the Italians. There followed two attacks by enemy armour, the first by a baker's dozen Italian M13 tanks, which approached from the area of the 35-ring contour to the south-west. Turner redeployed two guns to meet this threat and the Italians were beaten off, with one tank destroyed, three more hit and a lorry destroyed. Moving the two 6-pounders had been no easy task in the soft sand and several men lost their lives in the process.[16]

The Italian attack appears to have been a diversionary move intended to draw off fire from *Snipe* while *Kampfgruppe* Stiffelmeyer attacked the retreating 24 Armoured Brigade. With the Italians faltering, about half the German tanks were deployed against *Snipe* when they moved forward at 10.00am. In the ensuing action the Germans came off worse as the tanks attacking 24 Armoured presented their flanks to *Snipe* and those attacking *Snipe* presented their flanks to 24 Armoured. At least eight enemy tanks were set ablaze and the Germans withdrew.

By 11 o'clock only thirteen of the nineteen 6-pounders at *Snipe* were still in action:

> those guns which had been shooting hard in the West and South-west sectors were running short of ammunition. The transporting of ammunition from one sector of the front to another was an extremely hazardous job owing to very heavy enemy shelling which was continually falling into the position.[17]

That shelling had also accounted for six carriers that were set on fire, even though they were in hulldown positions within *Snipe*.

A further attack was launched at about 1 o'clock when eight Italian M13s, supported by some Semovente SPGs, advanced from the direction of the 35-ring contour. Only one 6-pounder was able to engage due to the ammunition shortage. This gun was manned by Sergeant Charles Calistan, who acted as No.3, or layer, Colonel Turner, who loaded and observed, and Lieutenant Toms, the troop commander, who acted as No.1. Turner ordered that the tanks were not to be engaged until they were within 600 yards, at which point five M13s and one SPG were hit and set ablaze. By then only two or three rounds remained for the 6-pounder and the surviving three tanks were advancing, their machine guns engaging the defenders' position. Toms ran the 100 yards to his Bantam, loaded several boxes of ammunition from the neighbouring crippled 6-pounder and drove back to his own gun through a hail of fire. The Bantam was riddled and set on fire but Turner and Toms removed the ammunition to replenish their gun, which was reloaded to engage the last three tanks. Each tank was knocked out less than 200 yards from the gun position, Calistan taking his time with each shot. The lightly-armoured tanks brewed up immediately, becoming mobile crematoria for their crews. While carrying the ammunition to the gun, Turner received a head wound and was persuaded to rest.[18]

A spell of relative calm followed until about 4 o'clock when activity was spotted in 2 Armoured Brigade's area and a strong force of Axis tanks, mostly German, disposed in two groups was observed north of *Snipe*. In the *Woodcock* area and stretching southwards from there to *Snipe* were some forty tanks, of which ten were M13s and the remainder panzers. A second group of about thirty panzers was also spotted some distance off. At 5 o'clock the easterly group of enemy tanks moved rapidly east and south-east towards 2 Armoured Brigade to be heavily engaged. The southernmost element of this phalanx of tanks passed within 500 yards of *Snipe*'s north-east corner where several 239 Battery guns were located. Since these had not been presented with any targets since early morning, and had thus remained silent for most of the day, it seems that the Axis tankmen were unaware of their presence. They were soon shaken from their ignorance as the guns opened up on them, claiming nine set ablaze and several others hit.[19] Unfortunately, *Snipe* again came under attack from its friends at this time, the Priests of 11 (HAC) RHA shelling the position for a time in what Turner later described as 'the most unpleasant' thing of all in a very unpleasant day.[20]

To the left of 239 Battery's guns some Rifle Brigade weapons were also able to engage these tanks as well as some others farther north while the motor companies' machine guns harassed the crews as they abandoned their stricken vehicles. The northern group of tanks was also engaged by 2 Armoured Brigade and the Axis attack was finally brought to a halt just before 5.30pm, the tanks withdrawing to hulldown positions in the area of Kidney and *Woodcock*. This was the major counter-attack that Rommel watched from the Rahman track, the time difference between his account and the Rifle Brigade's being that between German time and Egyptian summer time.

Snipe came under attack again at about this time when the westerly group of enemy tanks, about fifteen Mark IIIs, moved slowly south-east towards it. Only three guns, with an average of ten rounds left, were in positions from which they could engage. Three panzers moved into hulldown positions in the 35-ring contour area from which they fired continuously at the Rifle Brigade's positions until well after dark. Of the tanks that carried on the attack, the leading Mark III was hit and destroyed at 200 yards and two tanks that followed the leader were also set on fire. Yet another was hit at about 100 yards but reversed away, although it burst into flames after moving some 500 yards. Another two panzers farther back were also hit and set alight. The remainder opted to back off to hulldown positions almost a half mile away, from which they continued to machine-gun *Snipe*. The 6-pounders in this sector of the perimeter had been reduced to an average of three rounds per gun and it was fortuitous that no further attacks developed, even though there were about twenty enemy tanks within 1,000 yards.[21]

Plans had already been made to evacuate Turner's force from *Snipe*: 133 Brigade was to relieve 7 Motor Brigade at both *Woodcock* and *Snipe* and, at

5.40pm, Turner learned that 2nd Rifle Brigade would be relieved that night. Some two hours later the twenty enemy tanks moved away to the north-west. The remaining rounds of 6-pounder ammunition were fired at their silhouettes; one hit was claimed. It was then decided that all the wounded should be evacuated immediately and that the battalion should withdraw to the area 869294 when the transport arrived in the wake of 133 Lorried Infantry Brigade. Since all codes had been destroyed little was known about the details of the latter brigade's operation.[22]

At about 8.30pm the three hulldown tanks behind the 35-ring contour started pouring machine-gun fire into the forward company's position. This was believed to be a prelude to an infantry attack but none developed and it is unlikely that any had been planned since very few infantry had been seen during the day. What was more likely was that the machine guns were putting down harassing fire on *Snipe* to protect recovery teams working on their own tanks and the medics and stretcher-bearers attending to and evacuating the wounded.

At 10.30pm the British artillery started bombarding the enemy positions, putting down fire in the leaguer some 1,200 yards north-west of *Snipe*. In turn the enemy took avoiding action which included moving eastwards towards 2nd Rifle Brigade. Forty-five minutes later, with no sign of 133 Brigade, the last elements of Turner's command slipped out of *Snipe*. All the wounded had been evacuated and all but one of the guns were destroyed as it was impossible to bring them back, although all other equipment was brought back.[23] The single gun that survived, one of 239 Battery's, was evacuated on a bullet-riddled portee.[24]

There had been many outstanding acts of gallantry among the garrison of *Snipe*. Not all could be recognized by the award of decorations but several deserve mention and exemplify the courage shown by Turner and his men. Not least was Lieutenant Colonel Victor Turner who received the Victoria Cross. Few would dispute that he deserved it for he had demonstrated leadership of the highest quality. The citation for his Victoria Cross noted that:

> After overcoming a German position, the battalion fought off desperate counter-attacks by 90 tanks, destroying or immobilizing more than 50 of them. During the action, one of the 6-pounder guns was left with only one officer and a sergeant, so Colonel Turner joined them as loader, and between them they destroyed another five tanks. Not until the last tank had been repulsed did he consent to having a wound in his head attended to.[25]

It was the second Victoria Cross for the Turner family: his brother Alexander had been awarded a posthumous VC during the First World War.

The gallant Sergeant Calistan, from Forest Gate in Essex, was also recommended for the Victoria Cross but received the Distinguished Conduct Medal, then the second-highest gallantry award for other ranks. One writer on the action at *Snipe* suggests that this may have been because of a change in 'the strict rules governing this award since it [had been] established'[26] but this presents no credible reason at all. Calistan plainly earned the Victoria Cross and was denied it, presumably by a bureaucrat who adjudicated in the calm of an office, and thus had to be content with the DCM. Later commissioned, Lieutenant Charles Vivian Calistan DCM did not survive the war; killed in action in Italy in July 1944 he is buried in Arezzo war cemetery.[27]

Two other awards deserve mention. Major Thomas Bird, commanding 2nd Rifle Brigade's anti-tank company, received the Distinguished Service Order, the second-highest gallantry award for an officer and one that suggests that he, too, was considered for the Victoria Cross. Bird, who already held the Military Cross and Bar, survived the war.[28]

One of Bird's troop commanders, Lieutenant James Benjamin Duncan Irwin, from Moyard, County Galway, was awarded the Military Cross for his gallant conduct during the action. Irwin's troop on the northern flank of *Snipe* was in action during the night and four times during the day. Each time it

> repelled the attacks with losses to the enemy. Lieutenant Irwin went from gun to gun encouraging his men and when one gun was knocked out supervised the removal of the wounded and the redistribution of ammunition under heavy fire. In the final attack by 50–60 German tanks at 1700 hours Lieutenant Irwin's troop had only 20 rounds left. He ordered his guns to hold their fire. When the nearest [tanks] were only 100–200 yards away he gave orders to fire, setting four tanks on fire and helping to turn the attack.[29]

His citation went on to note that his troop accounted for nineteen tanks burnt and other vehicles hit, stating that Irwin's courage was 'of the highest order'.

There could be no doubt of the gallantry shown by the men of 2nd Rifle Brigade and their gunner and sapper comrades at *Snipe* and the action has deservedly become one of the best-known elements of the battle. It became known throughout Eighth Army almost immediately and the defence of *Snipe* contributed significantly to weakening Rommel's tank strength, something the Desert Fox could not afford. He described the defence as 'a tremendously powerful anti-tank defence'. A month later a committee of inquiry visited the site to determine the results as accurately as possible and to record the facts. Some vehicles had been recovered by the Axis forces and others had been towed away by British recovery teams so that not all the destroyed machines remained; twenty-seven hulks were found. Even so, a careful and critical analysis of the performance of each gun led the committee to establish that twenty-one German and eleven Italian tanks had been destroyed, together with five SPGs, and that up to twenty more tanks or SPGs had been knocked out but subsequently recovered. The total of enemy armoured vehicles destroyed was fifty-seven, nineteen of which were attributable to 239 Battery. Turner's force, which initially had claimed to have knocked out seventy-six tanks or SPGs, had suffered fourteen dead, forty-four wounded and one man missing but Axis losses must have been much higher.[30]

There had been considerable confusion in 1st Armoured Division about the situation at both *Snipe* and *Woodcock*. Briggs believed initially that 2nd Rifle Brigade had been overpowered but later decided that they may have withdrawn, having exhausted their ammunition stocks. Not until next morning did he know the true situation. Renewed attempts to take *Woodcock* and *Snipe* using 133 Lorried Infantry Brigade led to the loss of 4th Royal Sussex. The battalion had a bad start when they clashed with 1st Gordons at *Aberdeen* and a company was all but wiped out when it advanced on what was probably a German tank leaguer. At 1.30am, having advanced some two miles, capturing 200 prisoners and five 88s en route, the commanding officer, Lieutenant Colonel Ronald Murphy, decided that he had reached his objective and ordered his men to dig. This proved very difficult as the ground was extremely hard and thus, shortly after dawn on the 28th, the battalion, still not dug in properly, came under attack in its extremely exposed position. German tanks concentrated on the anti-tank guns, which were knocked out one by one and then, at about 7.30am, the tanks closed on the battalion. Thirty minutes later, the 300 survivors of 4th Royal Sussex were marched off into captivity; they had suffered almost sixty dead, including Ronald Murphy.[31]

To the north a squadron of Yorkshire Dragoons was also overrun and the unit forced to withdraw while, to the south, 2nd Royal Sussex were pinned down about Kidney by heavy fire and their commanding officer killed. (Later that day the Yorkshire Dragoons managed to recover the anti-tank guns B Squadron had abandoned that morning as well as rescuing about half of 3rd Troop of that squadron who had been lying hidden in a wadi.[32]) Another battalion, 5th Royal Sussex, had moved towards the position vacated by 2nd Rifle Brigade but had not gone as far as the Green Jackets; they, too, lost their commanding officer, killed by a single bullet, ascribed by Carver to a sniper.[33]

Fisher's 2 Armoured Brigade had also been in action during 2nd Rifle Brigade's defence of *Snipe*. The brigade had moved forward at 6.00am but made slow progress, although the Bays resolved the problem of the location of Heathcoat-Amery's riflemen when they contacted 2nd/60th Rifles late in the morning. There was an initial belief that the enemy may have withdrawn, encouraged by 9th Lancers picking up about sixty German prisoners, but they soon found themselves disabused of this idea when they ran up against the usual doughty opposition. Then 10th Hussars reported heavy northward movement on the Rahman track and there were whispers of the arrival of 21st Panzer Division. Caution became the brigade watchword and by noon it was obvious that the Germans still held Point 33 in *Woodcock* and that Heathcoat-Amery's battalion had failed in its attack. By now the brigade was stretched out from a mile east of *Woodcock* to a point to the north of Kidney's east end, with 2nd/60th Rifles between the Bays and 9th Lancers.[34]

The Bays, with a troop of Churchills under command, were ordered to capture Point 33, 'a barely perceptible elevation in the desert floor which gave a commanding view of an extensive swathe of ground,'[35] at 1.30pm. When the attack began an hour later one Churchill was knocked out almost immediately by an 88 and the others withdrew with their guns out of action. The attack was then called off and the brigade assumed a defensive posture, expecting an enemy attack that never materialized. Although some tanks did attack 10th Hussars these were driven off, with the loss of three of their number.[36]

Fisher's brigade then took part in the battle with the panzers at 4.00pm, Rommel's counter-attack, although this appeared to them as little more than an attempt by two groups of tanks to advance south of *Woodcock*. An hour later a further attack against 10th Hussars was beaten off by the Hussars and 2nd Rifle Brigade, who engaged the attackers from the flank. It was at this time that the Priests of 11 (HAC) RHA fired on the Green Jackets in *Snipe*.

The following morning 2 Armoured Brigade moved forward again with 9th Lancers advancing to Point 33 at first light, to be joined there by the Bays. B and C Squadrons of the Bays were ordered to renew the attack on Point 33 but were repelled, again, by the fire of 88s.

Freddie Barnado and Stephen Christie-Miller, two of the best and bravest troop leaders, were killed. Those who had seen him before the attack said that they could read death in Freddy's face, so terrible was his premonition. In fact the advancing tanks had no chance against the dug-in 88, which was able to knock out any tank at ranges up to 3,000 yards.[37]

Then at 6.50am the brigade was told to stand fast; attempts to take Point 33 with unsupported tanks were abandoned.[38] As plans were being adjusted at X Corps and Gatehouse was to take over the front, the regiments withdrew slightly and settled down to breakfast. They did so at much the same time as 4th Royal Sussex and the Yorkshire Dragoons were being overrun. Needless to say, this did nothing for good relations between infantry and armour.

On the morning of 28 October Montgomery conferred with Leese and Lumsden and decreed that *Woodcock-Snipe* would now become a defensive front, to be held temporarily by 10th Armoured and then by XXX Corps. The attempt to break through in the Kidney area was abandoned. Briggs' 1st Armoured Division would withdraw to rest and re-organize while Lumsden was to be ready to exploit westwards from the flank of the attack to be launched by 9th Australian Division that night.[39]

Intelligence had now confirmed that 21st Panzer had moved to the north and the RAF was ordered to continue attacking targets in the Tel el Aqqaqir area, where it was believed that *Afrikakorps* was concentrated. Later that day Montgomery issued orders for Harding's 7th Armoured Division, less 4 Light Armoured Brigade, to move north and concentrate close to El Alamein station. The Eighth Army commander was now changing the point of his main thrust and had re-organized his command to do so. Freyberg's New Zealanders had been withdrawn and their positions taken over by the South Africans, who had side-stepped to the right and thinned out their line. Their vacated positions were taken over by 4th Indian Division, which had also side-stepped and thinned out. Since the divisional front included Ruweisat, it was decided that its artillery should be strengthened by the addition of two field regiments and two 6-pounder anti-tank batteries from XIII Corps.[40] The Australians, meanwhile, had been trying to straighten the line eastward from Point 29 to Tel el Eisa which had led to fierce fighting during the night of 26/27 October with 125th Regiment, from which the Australians emerged victorious. Morshead's division was to attack again on the night of the 28th in an ambitious plan that involved all three brigades with the support of 318 field guns and all forty-eight of Eighth Army's mediums; the divisional artillery was to be supported by the New Zealand, Highland and 10th Armoured Divisions' artillery. Armour support was to come from 23 Armoured Brigade while three additional anti-tank batteries were placed under Morshead's command.[41]

When 9th Australian Division received Montgomery's order to 'attack north' the initial plan considered was to do so on the night of 27/28 October but XXX Corps' Operation Instruction No.85 ordered 'a policy of mopping up and the completion of the capture of the final objective by all divisions on 27 October', which led to a decision to delay the planned attack until the following night – 28/29 October.[42]

Since all three Australian brigades were holding forward areas, it was important that one should be relieved to permit a further attack. This was achieved through a double relief on the night of 27/28 October in which Wimberley's 152 Brigade relieved 20 Australian Brigade which in turn relieved 26 Brigade so that the latter could move to a lying-up area east of Tel el Eisa station before daylight on the 28th. Thus would 26 Brigade have the opportunity of a brief respite to prepare for the attack. There were delays in the handovers and the final relief, of 2/24th Battalion, was not completed until 6.05am on the 28th.[43]

When Morshead outlined his plan it was with the information that the enemy appeared to have few positions south of the railway, save for the 'Switch Line' and the continuation thereof to the Thompson's Post strongpoint. However, it was realized from the sketches and information gained from the captured commander of 125th Panzergrenadier Regiment that 'an enemy line conforming to our new northern flank must exist'. As well as maintaining pressure on the enemy, the divisional attack was designed to clear the area south of the main road, thereby opening it for maintenance and ambulances to the forward troops. That would also remove the necessity to use the circuitous and exposed route along Diamond and the northbound tracks.[44]

In the initial phase 20 Brigade was to hold Point 29 with 2/17th Battalion while 2/15th would advance northwards about two miles to secure an area around enemy diggings after which 2/13th Battalion would extend their gains some 2,000 yards north-eastward; 40th Royal Tanks would face west between 2/17th and 2/15th Battalions to deter or fight off any counter-attacks. Upon the success of 2/15th and 2/13th Battalions depended the next phase, to be carried out by 26 Brigade. This formation's tasks were threefold: capture and hold the main road, with 2/23rd Battalion and 46th Royal Tanks; capture the enemy defended localities astride the main road, by 2/48th, opening that road;

and capture Thompson's Post. The end result of 26 Brigade's operation would be to clear the area between the division's most northerly positions and the salt marsh east of the road along the ridge, itself to the east of the Western Desert Railway. Once this had been achieved 24 Brigade would extend north-westward from its positions east of the railway and link up with 26 Brigade.

Although there was liberal artillery support the gunners had a problem: because of the different directions of attack the guns could not be sited as they would have wanted for their assigned tasks; thus it was decided that they would fire concentrations in enfilade while in the attack eastwards they would be firing in the face of the advancing infantry. However, the location of Composite Force's posts meant that their machine guns could also support the attack eastwards, firing enfilade concentrations lifting ahead of the infantry.

After a difficult forming up, in an area that 'became the bottleneck of the operation', the attack moved off on time at 10.00pm. The forming-up positions were shelled just after the battalions had moved off with the commanding officer and adjutant of 2/15th becoming casualties. Both battalion attacks went well with 2/15th reaching the final objective eight minutes before midnight against little opposition and with light casualties. They met no minefields but their comrades of 2/13th ran into a booby-trapped minefield after less than a mile. The battalion suffered more casualties from the mines than from enemy fire but reached the objective by five minutes past midnight and began mopping-up operations to the flank. This proved more difficult than the advance with some stubborn German outposts to be overcome but re-organization was complete by first light. Both battalions laid mines to protect their forward positions and 2/17th Battalion adjusted its positions northwards to link with 2/15th, thereby securing the extended divisional western flank.[45]

The next phase of the operation, by 26 Brigade, was led by 2/23rd and 46th Royal Tanks, units that had trained together as a semi-mobile reserve for both the Australian Division and XXX Corps; they were to capture the area on the main road. This entailed a long advance and, to reduce the time involved and gain surprise, the battalion used carriers – its own and those of 2/24th – to carry its soldiers, those for whom there was no room on carriers riding on the tanks of 46th Royal Tanks.

This phase was delayed by ten minutes, but the artillery plan was adjusted accordingly. There were problems almost immediately: the tanks were to move through marked gaps in the British minefields but some missed these in the prevailing dust cloud and were immobilized with smashed tracks. Others suffered in similar manner as they sought further gaps. Engineers widened the gaps and the advance finally resumed. Unfortunately, there were communication problems, including a breakdown in communications between infantry and tank commanding officers while 26 Australian and 23 Armoured Brigade headquarters were not in touch, although sited close together. Shortly before 2 o'clock in the morning the tanks were underway again but ran into anti-tank guns and dispersed. The attack was now losing cohesion and the commanding officer of 2/23rd Battalion decided to make an infantry assault on the German gun positions. Gathering as many of his men as possible – between sixty and seventy – he organized them for an attack which went in at 3.15am and took the German position with its six 50mm guns and 160 men. By 4 o'clock the Australian commanding officer, unable to collect any more soldiers, told brigade headquarters that he was re-organizing about 1,000 yards from the division's forward defended localities. He was still out of touch with 46th Royal Tanks and unaware of fifteen tanks of the regiment, with men of 2/23rd, advancing to the railway and coming under accurate fire that knocked out nine tanks and killed or wounded many infantrymen.[46]

The situation required a fresh plan but that produced by 26 Brigade involved 2/24th and 2/48th Battalions continuing the attack from 2/15th's area. As tank support could not be provided in time for the battalions to be on their objectives and re-organized before daylight, Morshead called off the operation. Headquarters 26 Brigade was ordered to ensure that 2/23rd was in secure positions and in touch with its neighbours, 2/13th and 2/15th, to right and left respectively. This was complete by last light on the 29th; most damaged tanks were also recovered.[47]

In the morning of 29 October the enemy were not certain where the Australians were and some Axis vehicles drove unwittingly into Australian positions. Soon, however, German artillery was harassing the Australians and several counter-attacks were launched, all of which were beaten off while dive-bombing by Ju87s caused little damage. The 30th passed quietly, probably due to a sandstorm that restricted visibility. Sappers created and marked two new northward tracks, Tent and Guillotine, from the western ends of Diamond and Boomerang, during the night of the 29th/30th and the following day; they also continued gap-marking in the minefields.[48]

To Rommel the weight of the Australian attack was 'something quite exceptional' and he believed that his artillery was responsible for bringing it to a halt. He had spent the night on the coast road, although he had moved his headquarters farther to the rear. On 29 October he wrote to his wife: 'At night I lie with my eyes wide open, unable to sleep, for the load that is on my shoulders.

In the day I am dead tired'. However, next day, the day of the sandstorm, he was able to write to Lu: 'Situation a little quieter. I've had some sleep, am in good spirits and hope to pull it off even yet.'[49] Rommel was ever the optimist.

In spite of the continuing action, Montgomery's rethink was causing consternation at home. Churchill saw only divisions being withdrawn during a major battle that Montgomery had guaranteed would be a success. In his diary for 29 October Brooke noted that Churchill was ready to send an unpleasant telegram to Alexander but managed to dissuade the prime minister from this course of action. Nonetheless, he found Churchill demanding to know why 'my Monty' was allowing the battle to peter out, why he had done nothing for three days and why he was withdrawing troops. The flow of abuse culminated in a favourite question from Churchill: did Britain not have a single general who could win even one single battle? It transpired that Anthony Eden was responsible for instilling these doubts into the premier and Brooke managed eventually, with the support of Field Marshal Smuts at a Chiefs of Staff meeting, to calm Churchill.[50] But Brooke harboured his own doubts, which he confined to his diary, and Churchill was not entirely satisfied. Casey, the minister of state in Cairo, was sent, with Alexander, to visit Montgomery. The latter explained his plans and told Casey that he was 'certain of success'. De Guingand was angry at this intervention and, with the innocence of a professional soldier protecting his master, threatened to have Casey drummed out of political life, although how a general could achieve that was not made clear and de Guingand seemed unaware that Casey was not really in political life. Nor was Montgomery aware of Brooke's doubts, writing in his *Memoirs* of his confidence that Brooke 'would know what I was up to'.[51]

Montgomery's rethink was shortly to be put into operation, although with some revision of his original plan.

Chapter Eleven

Monty Strikes Again: SUPERCHARGE

Once more unto the breach

Operation SUPERCHARGE was Montgomery's revised plan. To the military man 'supercharge' suggests an artillery shell with additional propellant, which may be what Montgomery intended. To the civilian mind the word is more likely to suggest engines: additional power can be obtained from an engine by forcing additional fuel or air into it. The dictionary defines 'supercharge' as 'charge to extreme or excess (*with* energy etc.)'. 'Supercharge' may indicate what Montgomery intended Eighth Army to do; whether Eighth Army had the energy to do so was another question; nor was there any additional fuel or propellant available. The army would have to do with what it already had in men and matériel; and the men were exhausted.

During the 29th it had become clear that Rommel had moved the bulk of the German formations into the northern sector where he expected the main British attack. (Only the Ramcke Brigade had not been pulled into the northern sector. It may be that Rommel had left Ramcke in his original positions because of tension between them. The brigade was a Luftwaffe formation strongly imbued with Nazism and its commander was a committed Nazi.) In that analysis the German commander had been correct: Montgomery's intention had been to launch his final breakout attack along the axis of the coast road.[1] However, the location of German forces in that area would make such a tactic extremely costly. On the other hand, the lamination of Axis forces, German units supporting Italian, had been torn apart and the Germans were now pulled against Eighth Army's right. This made it possible, and desirable, to direct the final blow in the area of the junction between German and Italian troops, overlapping on to the Italian front. At 11.00am on 29 October Montgomery took the decision that his final blow would be aimed at the Italian sector. The timing is significant: it places the decision during a conference at which Alexander and McCreery were present and it seems most likely that the change was made as a result of a suggestion by McCreery. Alexander notes that it was McCreery's recommendation 'as an experienced armoured commander, … that it should go in just north of the existing northern corridor'.[2] Montgomery's biographer, Nigel Hamilton, states that it was Freddie de Guingand who persuaded Montgomery to change his mind.[3] But change his mind he did. Montgomery later wrote that 'What ... I proposed to do was to deliver a hard blow with the right, and follow it the next night with a knock-out blow with the left'.[4]

Carver suggests that, while McCreery and Alexander could not initially deflect Montgomery from his intentions, the Army Commander changed his mind when de Guingand brought the information that all three regiments of 90th Light had been engaged against the Australians the previous night and that *Trieste*, Rommel's last reserve, had been committed to the line south of the Australians.[5]

The Royal Navy provided an interesting diversion that night. A force of three Hunt-class destroyers, HM Ships *Belvoir*, *Exmoor* and *Hurworth*, with eight MTBs and nine LCTs, carried out a feint landing near Ras el Kanayis, north-north-west of Fuka. After dark the destroyers turned back for Alexandria but the MTBs closed the beaches at about 12.45am on the 30th. A smoke cloud was laid and machine-gun fire opened on the beach to which the enemy replied with guns as the MTBs withdrew. Enemy aircraft also appeared and attempted to bomb the smoke cloud but by then the MTBs were well on their way back to Alexandria. No casualties or damage were suffered by the RN force.[6]

Montgomery wrote the directive for SUPERCHARGE on the morning of the 30th. Instead of attacking westwards along the coast with its right flank on the sea and its left protected by armour, 2nd New Zealand Division would strike farther south 'where there was every probability that only Italian opposition would be met'.[7] To keep Rommel's attention fixed on the coastal area, and to keep 90th Light Division in that sector, Montgomery decided that the Australians should attack once again northwards towards the sea on the night of 30/31 October. On the following night 2nd New Zealand Division would open SUPERCHARGE. Before looking in detail at the plans for this operation, let us turn to the Australian attack on the night of 30/31 October.

Twice already the tide of the Australian advance had swept towards the Axis defences but had failed to wash over the strongpoint of Thompson's Post. The latest attack, postponed until the night of 30/31 October, was preceded by aerial bombardment of the opposing forces with the 'main weight of the air effort on 29 October ... directed against German panzer divisions and 90th Light Division',[8] the latter then deployed about and south-east of Sidi Abd el

Rahman. It was also intended to save the bombing effort on the 30th so that the bombers could concentrate in support of the Australians.

The plan for this attack enlarged and altered the scope of the original laid down for two nights earlier but postponed. Two battalions, rather than one, would attack eastwards along the main road, and the line of the western forward defended localities was to be extended to the sea to cut off German defenders in the area. This elaborate plan, described by Lucas-Phillips as 'a strangling operation in three phases',[9] demanded great skill and courage on the part of the infantry and tremendous accuracy, and skill, on the part of the gunners, for the fire-plan would be a nightmare. In all, the plan constituted a situation that, had it been proffered as a solution to the problem by a Staff College student, would almost certainly have had him failed, as one senior officer commented to another.

Morshead, suffering a shortage of infantry, brought 2/3rd Pioneer Battalion into the line under command of 26 Brigade to strengthen his infantry, although one pioneer company would remain with Composite Force. The attack would be launched from the forward positions of 20 Brigade with 2/23rd Battalion holding the firm base while 24 Brigade's reserve battalion, 2/32nd, would also come under command of 26 Brigade. Although 23 Armoured Brigade would be held in reserve, its Valentines were allotted a specific role. Nonetheless, 40th Royal Tanks were placed under 26 Brigade's command for possible use by either attacking brigade. The battle would really be one of infantry and artillery, the former advancing with the support of the latter. A great volume of fire would be available with 360 guns under control of the CRA; machine-gun support was also on call.

As with the previous attack, tracks to the start line and space for forming-up areas were limited, although track extensions meant that Diamond-Guillotine and Boomerang-Tent tracks now led to 2/15th Battalion's forward positions and, since these were linked at their northern ends, a circuit was available to clear vehicles from the forming-up area, thus easing congestion. Engineers would create a gap in the railway embankment to assist the attack and an additional field company was placed under 26 Brigade to meet the demands of the operation. All three brigades were assigned tasks while 9th Australian Division Commando Platoon was to operate against the Axis headquarters in the area north of 2/15th Battalion to disrupt control of Axis defences during the attack. Both bomber and fighter support would be provided by the RAF.

There were to be three attacks in three directions in the course of the night, each with its own H Hour. The first attack, by 2/32nd Battalion, moved off ten minutes late, at 10.10pm, but went well against I/125 Panzergrenadiers: the Australians reached their objective on the coast road, although it was impossible to mop up all enemy outposts en route. However, the second phase did not achieve the same success. This was to be a right-handed pivot to sweep down the railway, executed by 2/24th and 2/48th Battalions. Both moved off under their supporting bombardment at 1.00am but were met by such intense frontal and enfilade fire that they suffered heavy losses and lost contact with each other. With too few soldiers, the attack ran out of energy and the attackers were withdrawn to a position in contact with 2/32nd. But, in the course of this action, County Durham-born Sergeant William Kibby of 2/48th Battalion lost his life while carrying out an action that was included in the citation for his posthumous Victoria Cross.

> when the battalion attacked 'ring contour' 25, behind the enemy lines, it was necessary for No.17 Platoon to move through the most withering enemy machine-gun fire … to reach its objective. These conditions did not deter Sergeant Kibby from pressing forward right to the objective, despite his platoon being mown down by machine-gun fire from point-blank range. One pocket of resistance still remained and Sergeant Kibby went forward alone, throwing grenades to destroy the enemy now only a few yards distant. Just as success appeared certain he was killed by a burst of machine-gun fire. Such outstanding courage, tenacity of purpose and devotion to duty was entirely responsible for the successful capture of the Company's objective. His work was an inspiration to all and he left behind him an example and memory of a soldier who fearlessly and unselfishly fought to the end to carry out his duty.[10]

Kibby was not the battalion's sole fatality: casualties were so heavy that the commanding officer, Lieutenant Colonel Hammer, discovered that his battalion was reduced to forty men, plus himself, less than half the strength of 2/24th which numbered eighty-four when it consolidated.

In the third phase of the attack, the men of 2/3rd Pioneer Battalion had their baptism of fire as infantry. They began their dash for the coast at 4.25am but met stiff resistance that stopped them halfway to their objective. Isolated in the positions in which they were pinned down the pioneers were withdrawn before daylight to tenable positions. The men of this battalion were generally older than those in the combat units – although some of the latter were older than their counterparts in a British battalion, as evidenced by the VCs – but were physically tough and strong-minded individuals; one company commander had been born in 1895.[11]

A deception attack by 24 Brigade in the coastal sector misled the enemy into believing that they had beaten off an attack of equal strength to the other Australian operation of the night. If anything, this stiffened the resolve of the Axis forces in the area who 'fought with a resolution … not experienced elsewhere'.[12] The enemy had been hammered hard by both artillery and aircraft. During the 30th 190,000 pounds of bombs had been dropped in the battle area, mostly by heavy bombers although 40,000 pounds came from fighter-bombers while enemy landing grounds had been hit by 77,000 pounds of bombs from heavies and a further 12,000 pounds from fighter-bombers.[13]

Thompson's Post, although hemmed in on three sides by Australians, remained in enemy hands. It had repelled a patrol from 2/24th and continued pouring fire into Morshead's men, striking at the flanks and rear of the Australian division. The Australians may not have taken all the ground intended but they had all but isolated Thompson's Post; and Rommel was devoting perhaps too much effort to its relief rather than withdrawing the garrison. It may be that the Desert Fox was preoccupied with his plans for a withdrawal to Fuka. He was certainly frustrated at the increasing inability of *Comando Supremo* to carry out its promises of resupply. Matters were not helped when news arrived of the loss of yet another tanker, *Louisano*, sunk by the British. Rommel was angry with the *Regia Marina* for failing to protect the tankers and also angry at a spurious report from *Comando Supremo* that two British divisions were some sixty miles south of Mersa Matruh, having crossed the Qattara Depression. There again, the degree of Rommel's reaction may have been a product of the surprise gained by the Australians who had attacked as *Trieste* was relieving 21st Panzer Division.

The first counter-attack, at 7.00am on the 31st, found Whitehead's 26 Brigade in a small area about a mile square, astride both road and railway, and two miles north-east of the nearest elements of 20 Brigade and a further mile north of the remainder of the division. The largest element of the brigade was 2/32nd Battalion; the survivors of 2/24th and 2/48th faced south and south-east respectively while the situation of 2/3rd Pioneer Battalion to the north was unclear. Artillery fire, including 'smoke which successfully blinded enemy OPs',[14] beat off that first counter-attack and it was some hours before the 'first serious counter attack developed'. This was thirty minutes before noon and it may have been precipitated by the move of 40th Royal Tanks, less A Squadron which remained with 20 Brigade, to try to join 26 Brigade, following the first attack. Although some Valentines were lost on mines, including the commanding officer's, two troops of 40th got north of the railway. Rommel hastened to set up a command post east of the mosque at Sidi Abd el Rahman when he heard this and summoned von Thoma, commanding *Afrikakorps*, and Bayerlein, *Afrikakorps'* chief of staff who had just returned from Europe, to join him there. Orders were then issued for the attack that began at 11.30am.

The new enemy attack included elements of 21st Panzer, identified by the Australians as fifteen Mark III and Mark IV tanks, and 90th Light, with air support from Ju87s plus artillery.

> They manoeuvred into a position whereby they attacked from the west, south of the main road, in support of the infantry attacking from the same direction just north of the railway. While the attack was held by artillery, infantry and anti-tank gun fire, 40 R.Tanks assisted through the minefields by 2/7 Fd Coy, moved forward along the track immediately west of Thompson's Post and took up hulldown positions just to the east of 2/48 Bn. From this position and assisted by [289] A.Tk Bty RA,[*] whose guns were in position in the north embankment of the railway, 40 R.Tanks succeeded in driving off the enemy. Several enemy tanks were knocked out.[15]

The air support Rommel was able to call upon was miniscule in face of the Allied air superiority and even German airmen were by now abandoning attacks, jettisoning their bombs whenever Allied fighters appeared. Morale was suffering among the Luftwaffe and the ground troops were also having their morale chipped away by the constant 'party rally' raids, which occurred almost hourly, and the intense artillery bombardments which met every attempt at counter-attack. As for the Italians, their morale was generally shattered, although formations such as *Folgore*, *Trieste* and *Ariete* still functioned well; but both *Trieste* and *Ariete* were now very weak and the latter was still in the south. (The battlegroup from *Ariete* that had moved north with 21st Panzer Division had returned to the southern sector on the 28th.[16])

Throughout the 31st a series of Axis counter-attacks was launched at the Australians, each meeting a storm of artillery fire, with much of the fighting

---

[*] The original narrative states 298 Anti-Tank Battery but the battery involved was the Rhodesian 289 Battery, D Battery of 102nd (Northumberland Hussars) Anti-Tank Regiment, RA, commanded by Lieutenant Colonel C.E. Lucas-Phillips.

in an area known as the 'Saucer'. The Australians fought ferociously, as did the Rhodesian anti-tank gunners and the crews of the Valentines with their puny 2-pounder guns that could only engage the panzers at less than 400 yards but could be knocked out by those panzers at ranges of more than 1,000 yards. And yet the Valentines fought on, trying to manoeuvre so that one troop might draw panzers into positions from which another troop could engage them in the flank. It seemed to be a battle that the Valentines were doomed to lose: several had been hit and burst into flames, incinerating their crews, while over twenty were knocked out. Then, to the surprise of the British tankers, the panzers began to withdraw, leaving behind five knocked-out tanks, one in flames, an 88 and several lighter vehicles. But the price to 40th Royal Tanks was heavy: forty-four men were dead; when the order to withdraw was given only ten tanks could comply. Not for nothing did the historian of 2/48th Battalion record a tribute to their courage, noting that the Valentines' action had been 'one of the most magnificent of the war'.[17]

At the end of the day General Morshead ordered the relief of 2/24th and 2/48th Battalions by two battalions of Brigadier Godfrey's 24 Brigade which had seen little action since the opening night of the battle. Dawn on 1 November saw the fresh battalions in position where they witnessed an air battle in which RAF and USAAF fighters shot down seven Ju87s and scattered the remainder of a force attempting to bomb Godfrey's positions. This morning also saw the first deployment of British heavy anti-aircraft guns in the battle area when Right Troop, 192 Battery, 69th HAA Regiment moved its four 3.7-inch guns into the forward area near El Alamein station to protect guns and B echelon transport from Stuka attack. With no aerial targets appearing, the 3.7s engaged a ground target instead, at a distance of 16,000 yards.[18]

In the Australian positions attention switched from the air to the ground as yet another enemy battlegroup approached just after midday in an attempt to relieve Thompson's Post. This group was at battalion strength with panzer and artillery support, the latter including a battery of 88s that fired airbursts over the Australians. Once again the attack was beaten off but twelve 6-pounders were lost, these having been targeted particularly by the Germans. Just over three hours later another attack 'developed into an almost continuous mêlée which showed no signs of flagging as the afternoon wore on.'[19] The attackers seemed impervious to the determined Australian defensive efforts and some panzers swept to the north and through the dunes to contact Thompson's Post, moving down on its north side. At much the same time Godfrey and three of his staff were killed by a shellburst in their headquarters in the 'Saucer'; two other officers were wounded seriously. Command devolved on the brigade major, Bernard Jackson, who could see that there were now no Australians across the road. Furthermore, with the loss of the anti-tank guns, the safest place for his infantry was south of the embankment and he ordered them to withdraw there. This improved Rommel's corridor to Tel el Eisa and opened up the opportunity to withdraw the embattled Axis troops in the salient threatened by the Australians.

Rommel had not been keen to evacuate Thompson's Post and had rejected suggestions to do so from von Thoma and Bayerlein on the grounds that the position could still cause problems for Eighth Army and that its evacuation would probably mean the loss of its heavy weapons. However, on 1 November, on his return from visiting other parts of the line, he was acquainted with the precarious situation of the defenders of Thompson's Post and rescinded his veto on evacuation, although he did not issue an evacuation order. There were other matters that held his concern, not least the impoverished state of his army in terms of fuel, ammunition and supplies. And there was more bad news that day: *Tripolino*, carrying fuel and ammunition, was sunk off Tobruk by a Wellington bomber while *Ostia*, in the same convoy, was torpedoed and sunk by a Beaufort. Attempts to fly in fuel from Crete were frustrated by bombing raids on Maleme airfield; these were renewed on 27 October. Rommel's humour could hardly have been improved by the receipt of a signal from Ugo Cavallero in Rome.

> The Duce authorizes me to convey to you his deep appreciation of the successful counter-attack led personally by you. The Duce also conveys to you his complete confidence that the battle now in progress will be brought to a successful conclusion under your command.[20]

By contrast with this surreal optimism, Rommel's letter to Lu that evening was coldly realistic: 'It's a week since I left home. A week of very, very hard fighting. It was often doubtful whether we'd be able to hold out.'[21]

His own realism was matched by that of his staff who were reporting that another major British offensive was about to begin. Montgomery was massing troops to the south of the Australian positions and his own front was but a shadow of the defences before the 23rd. The last phase of this battle seemed about to be unleashed.

Montgomery was finalizing his preparations. He had intended to launch SUPERCHARGE on the night of 31 October/1 November but had been persuaded by Freyberg that a delay of twenty-four hours was essential to ensure that everything was in place for the attack and to remove from the area units not involved in the operation. Montgomery, of course, made no mention of Freyberg's part in this delay, claiming that it was clear to him (Montgomery) that 'the stage management problems' of the operation might lead to its failure if it were to be launched on the 31st. Among those problems was the difficulty encountered by 151 Brigade of 50th Division which was moved northwards to reinforce 2nd New Zealand Division for the assault. En route from south of Ruweisat Ridge the Geordies had to traverse desert that was almost unmapped but still congested with traffic and units in position, many of which seemed reluctant to permit the passage of the three battalions of Durhams – 6th, 8th and 9th.

For the new operation Montgomery was using only XXX Corps and X Corps; there would be no role for XIII Corps which would continue holding in the south, although 7th Armoured Division and several other elements would be brought northwards. Horrocks' corps had failed to provoke an enemy reaction to a dummy attack on the night of 29/30 October which it was felt might

indicate enemy's correct appreciation of XIII Corps' weakness and inability to attack in strength or it might reflect the enemy's own passive attitude in defence, though so far *Folgore* Division had fought well and had shown high morale.[22]

Thus it seems that XIII Corps, now reduced to three weak infantry divisions and a light armoured brigade, failed to create the impression of a major attack in the south. Rommel's eyes remained fixed on the northern front where he believed that Montgomery would attack from the Australian sector 'without pause towards Sidi Abd el Rahman'.[23] To meet such an attack he had withdrawn 21st Panzer Division north of Tel el Aqqaqir as a mobile reserve but Montgomery's change of direction would catch him wrong-footed.

XXX Corps' infantry for SUPERCHARGE would be provided by the New Zealand Division, which had been given a short spell to rest and re-organize. However, the divisional casualties thus far, 1,578 to 30 October, meant that Freyberg simply did not have enough foot soldiers: his division was already reduced to two infantry brigades and was to be reinforced for the operation. (The heaviest casualties had been suffered by the Highland Division which had lost 1,728 dead, wounded or missing by this date. Australian casualties matched exactly those of the New Zealanders, although there were three Australian infantry brigades, while the South Africans had lost 734 and the Indians eighty-one. Proportionately, therefore, the highest casualty rate had been sustained by the New Zealanders.[24])

Freyberg had told Montgomery that he was not prepared to send his soldiers into another assault and thus Montgomery, who wanted him to command the infantry assault, offered to reinforce 2nd New Zealand Division with brigades from other divisions. We have already noted that 151 Brigade, the Durham Brigade, under Brigadier Percy, was to be detached from 50th Division to Freyberg's command. Montgomery's rule that divisions should fight only as divisions and not be broken up was proving extremely flexible in definition. In addition, one of Wimberley's brigades, 152, including 2nd and 5th Seaforth and 5th Cameron Highlanders and sometimes known as the Seaforth and Cameron Brigade (presaging the 1961 amalgamation of the regiments as the Queen's Own Highlanders (Seaforth and Camerons), which amalgamated with the Gordons to form The Highlanders (Seaforth, Gordons and Camerons) in 1994), would also come under command of 2nd New Zealand Division, as would the Royal Sussex Brigade of 44th Division. Currie's faithful 9 Armoured Brigade would remain part of the division. In the event, the Sussex Brigade was placed under command of 51st (Highland) Division. The Greek Brigade was also available should Freyberg want it. For artillery support there would be thirteen field and three medium regiments.

The final order of battle of 2nd New Zealand Division included 5 New Zealand Brigade, 133 Royal Sussex Brigade, 151 Durham Brigade, 152 Highland Brigade and 9 Armoured Brigade, with anti-tank, engineer and machine-gun support; 28th (Maori) Battalion was attached to 151 Brigade. Also included was 23 Armoured Brigade, less 40th and 46th Royal Tank Regiments, C Troop 168 LAA Battery and a detachment of 295 Army Field Company RE. Freyberg's other brigade, 6 New Zealand, was temporarily under command of 51st (Highland) Division and holding part of the line on the Highlanders' right in touch with the left of 20 Australian Brigade, but would revert to Freyberg's command when the operation began.

The artillery for SUPERCHARGE was three field or RHA regiments from 1st Armoured Division, four field or RHA regiments from 10th Armoured, three field regiments from 2nd New Zealand, one field regiment from 9th Australian, two field regiments from 51st (Highland) and three medium regiments from XXX Corps' artillery.

In the days prior to SUPERCHARGE Montgomery authorized the re-equipment of 9 Armoured Brigade's three regiments, bringing the brigade up to seventy-nine heavies – Shermans and Grants – and fifty-three Crusaders. This was achieved, partially, by passing some of 24 Armoured Brigade's surviving tanks to Currie's regiments, although most went to 2 Armoured Brigade. Thus 24 Armoured Brigade was broken up. Although the title was later revived it had fought its first and only battle; the new 24 would be a formation of dummy tank regiments.

As the days ticked down to D Day for SUPERCHARGE concern arose over security when 10th Armoured Division headquarters informed XXX Corps that abandoned tanks of 24 Armoured Brigade that were now in enemy hands had contained 'certain secret codes'. These included map reference codes, Aldis lamp ground/air recognition signals and details of the divisional order of battle. When Eighth Army headquarters learned of this, on 29 October at 4.10pm, a fuller report was demanded, as was an explanation as to why the matter had only come to light three days after the event. Although the operative date of the lost map reference codes was not known and the Aldis codes were obsolete by the 29th, security had still been compromised; orders were issued to change codes.[25] Another complication was the change from summertime, due to happen that weekend. The change, moving the clocks back an hour, should have been effected at midnight on 31 October/1 November. Montgomery decided that Eighth Army would retain Egyptian Summer Time as 'Eighth Army Time' until further notice, although everywhere else the clocks would change as usual.

The confusion which would inevitably ensue from a change of time while active operations were in progress was so serious that it was considered preferable to accept the disadvantage of keeping a separate time for 8 Army. These disadvantages were indeed serious. The Western Desert Railway, for example, was to use Egyptian Standard Time, as did the Royal Navy and the Royal Air Force. To avoid confusion therefore it became necessary to time all messages from 8 Army addressed to formations and units outside the Army's area by Greenwich Mean Time which was 3 hours behind 8 Army Time after 31 October. Furthermore it had to be remembered that incoming messages would be timed by Egyptian Standard Time and would require conversion to 8 Army Time. In the event, the difference of time between 8 Army and the Royal Air Force caused many difficulties, but no disaster.[26]

The basic plan for SUPERCHARGE was a variation on that used for LIGHTFOOT with XXX Corps' infantry making a night attack with heavy artillery support and clearing the way for the armour of X Corps, which would follow when gaps had been cleared in any minefields that were encountered. However, this attack was to be on a much smaller frontage of 4,000 yards, would be made by two infantry brigades and would penetrate to a depth of 4,000 yards, bringing the infantry to within some 800 yards of the Rahman track, north of Tel el Aqqaqir. To obtain maximum light from the now waning moon, the attack would begin at five minutes past one o'clock on the morning of 2 November, when the moon would have risen; thus there were only some four and a half hours for the infantry to gain their objectives, the sappers to create gaps, and the armour to pass through. Information on enemy dispositions forward of the Rahman track was sparse and called for a further artillery bombardment to cover the armour as it made its way forward through the infantry's objectives, through the enemy gun line along the track and beyond that line. The respective roles of infantry and armour in this operation were described by Lucas-Phillips:

> The infantry … were only a means to an end. Theirs was the task to storm the approaches to the citadel. It was for the armour to break in the gates and to destroy the enemy within. The most critical of all tasks was that designed for 9 Armoured Brigade, who were to break open the gate so long locked by the enemy's anti-tank guns, now ranged in strength along and before the Rahman Track.[27]

The artillery for the assault was under the operational control of the New Zealand CRA, Brigadier C.E. 'Steve' Weir and would fire over 50,000 shells during the four and a half hours of the attack. That weight of shells would make but a small dent in the stockpile available to Eighth Army: 110,631 rounds for 25-pounders were drawn from the railheads at El Imayid and Burg el Arab on 31 October and a further 81,044 next day.[28] The guns were to open fire at H Hour and a shell would drop every twelve yards along the opening line. Then, as the infantry closed up to that line, the bombardment would move forward in steps of 100 yards every two-and-a-half minutes. It would take the infantry onto their objectives and then do likewise for the armour. Bofors guns firing tracer rounds would mark brigade boundaries.

The assaulting infantry brigades were to be 151 and 152 Brigades, the Durham and Seaforth and Camerons respectively, with the former on the right of the attack where enemy defences were thickest. On the Durhams' sector were some of the Axis pre-LIGHTFOOT defences while his counter-attack forces were also close. To assist in right-flank protection Freyberg placed the Maoris of his 28th Battalion under Brigadier Percy's command with the specific task of eliminating a known enemy strongpoint at the junction with 9th Australian Division, close to Point 29. Left-flank protection was the role of 133 Royal Sussex Brigade, disposing only two battalions. This brigade's peregrinations during the battle and the preparation period were interesting: originally part of 44th (Home Counties) Division, the brigade had been transferred as lorried infantry to 10th Armoured, from whom it was borrowed to assist the New Zealanders' attack but under command of 51st (Highland) Division. Its role on the opening night of SUPERCHARGE was to neutralize *Woodcock*, where it had suffered heavy losses some nights before. Valentines from 8th and 50th Royal Tanks were assigned as close support for the assaulting brigades whose final objectives were somewhat whimsically named *Neat* for the Highlanders and *Brandy* for the Durhams.

Once the assaulting brigades had taken *Neat* and *Brandy*, 9 Armoured Brigade would advance, pass through the infantry and attack the enemy guns dug in along the line of the Rahman track. The objective for Currie's regiments was the Aqqaqir ridge, which had the mound, or Tel, as its highest point. This beautifully-named knoll, the 'mound of the acacias,' was not to see the tanks of 9 Armoured Brigade that night as most of Currie's tanks would be knocked out along the gun line on the Rahman track. Their crews would die in a charge every bit as hopeless as that of the Light Brigade at Balaclava. But, in this case, their army commander was prepared to risk their lives. It will be remembered that the brigade was an integral part of 2nd New Zealand Division and when Freyberg was giving out his orders to his commanders in his headquarters, he emphasized that the assault had to be carried through at all costs, leading Currie to comment that the task assigned to his brigade could result in losses of some 50 per cent. Freyberg responded by telling Currie that Montgomery was prepared to accept 100 per cent losses. It was a grim prospect for Currie and one that was to be a very accurate prophecy. Peter Willett, of the Bays, wrote that Monty's comment that he was prepared to accept 100 per cent casualties in the brigade was 'not a very sensible thing to say, because if you have 100 per cent casualties you have lost the battle'.[29]

The minefield task force of 1st Armoured Division, now X Corps' sole division as 10th Armoured had been withdrawn, was re-formed under Major T.C.H. Pearson DSO and included 2nd Rifle Brigade, 7 and 9 Field Squadrons and 572 Army Field Company RE, together with Troops of A Squadron Bays,

A Squadron 9th Lancers and B Squadron 10th Hussars with detachments of 1st Armoured Division Signals and 1st Armoured Division Provost Company. 'Particular care was taken to ensure that, so far as was possible, the same personnel were detached to form part of the Minefield Task Force as had served with it during Operation Lightfoot.'[30] Since it was not expected that there would be mines in the same concentrations as had been met during LIGHTFOOT, but that there would probably be more scattered groupings, it was decided that Scorpions would operate as part of the mine-clearing operation.

Briggs' 1st Armoured Division included 2 and 8 Armoured Brigades, the latter from 10th Armoured Division, and 7 Motor Brigade; their final conference was marked by a confident prediction from Lumsden that they were 'on a winner'.[31] Following the minefield taskforce through, the division was to deploy with 2 Armoured Brigade on the right flank advancing to a ring contour some two miles north-west of Tel el Aqqaqir while 8 Armoured Brigade, on the left, would make for Tel el Aqqaqir itself. Having reached those objectives the armour would prepare to meet any counter-attacks that Rommel might launch. Briggs considered that attacks from the north would be most likely and most dangerous. The Motor Brigade was to follow through by battalion groups and deploy in a central area, ready to meet counter-attack from north-west or north and the divisional artillery, once released from support of the New Zealand attack, would join 7 Motor Brigade. The armoured cars of 12th Lancers were to advance behind 2 Armoured Brigade ready to slip through the front to penetrate the enemy positions. Two other armoured-car regiments, the Royal Dragoons and 4th/6th South African Armoured Car Regiment, were also ready to break out. Briggs was adamant that 1st Armoured Division would fight to reach the objectives even if the New Zealanders failed.

Freyberg's timings for the assault were for the infantry to move forward from their tapes at 12.55am, the guns to open fire ten minutes later, H Hour, the infantry objectives to be taken at 3.45am and the tanks of 9 Armoured Brigade to begin their advance at 5.45am. X Corps was to take over at 6.45am and pass 1st Armoured Division through 9 Armoured Brigade.

Air operations were planned on a massive scale. Once again Wellingtons would be out in force with Fleet Air Arm Albacores marking their targets. The Wellingtons were to attack the Axis armour in the northern area while medium bombers dropped some 413,000 pounds of bombs in the battle area. Night-flying Hurricanes would patrol the area and raid the Stuka base at Sidi Haneish. The Royal Navy was also making a contribution with another feint landing, this time between Ras Gibeisa, north of Sidi Abd el Rahman, and Ras el Daba, north of El Daba, carried out with four MTBs from Alexandria that fired flares and dropped rafts. As before, the aim of the naval operation was to make the enemy reluctant to move reserves until the tactical situation was clear, lest he come under attack from the rear.

On the evening of 1 November Axis forces were still counter-attacking the Australians who, in spite of hard fighting, had the situation well under control. There were no indications that Rommel expected a major attack south of the Australians: his dispositions, as known to Eighth Army headquarters, suggested that he expected any further attack to be made along the main road in the north; 21st Panzer Division seemed to be located with a view to countering such an attack. During that day Eighth Army believed that there had been no significant change in Axis dispositions. It was believed that 361st Panzergrenadier Regiment, supported by *Kiel* Group, was in the area of the northern battalion of Morshead's 20 Brigade and north of the railway in the area of 24 Brigade, while information from an Italian prisoner suggested that 21st Panzer Division had been withdrawn to act as a mobile reserve for counter-attack. It was known that 90th Light was counter-attacking on the Australian front in an effort to rescue the remnants of 125th Panzergrenadier Regiment about Thompson's Post.

All information available to Montgomery suggested that German forces were concentrated in the northern sector and that Italian troops held the front the New Zealand Division was to attack. Since Rommel had failed to use the opportunity for counter-attack presented by Eighth Army's re-organization and seemed focused on the operations against the Australians to relieve Thompson's Post, it appeared safe to assume that he had no idea of either the strength or direction of the attack about to fall on his forces.

On the night of 1 November, as the infantry moved up to their start lines, the Albacores and Wellingtons began their operations. The sound of their bombs could be heard by the waiting infantry who could see the glow from fires started by the bombing which also wrecked the signal system at *Afrikakorps* headquarters. It was a cold night and the infantry shivered as they awaited the order to advance. The Durhams, having marched seven miles from Tel el Eisa, felt the cold more than the Highlanders as they cooled after their exertions, the dust of that march caked about their bodies. Even the cardigans the soldiers wore did not prevent the shivering. Last-minute preparations were made, checks were completed. The Jocks had, again, adopted a night identification sign, strips of rifle-cleaning flannel fixed to the braces of their web equipment on their backs in the form of Saint Andrew's cross.

The minutes ticked by. In the gun lines the order 'Fire' was given. Hundreds of guns fired as one huge battery. Infantrymen moved forward from the line of cairns marking their start line. At 1.05am on 2 November Operation SUPERCHARGE began. Surprise had been achieved.

Chapter Twelve

The Final Blows

Steed threatens steed

In his *Memoirs* Montgomery devotes almost four pages to the plan and preparation for SUPERCHARGE but summarizes the battle in a few paragraphs. He describes how the attack went in on a front of 4,000 yards to a depth of 6,000 yards. 'It was a success and we were all but out into the open desert' is how he recounts the events of Monday 2 November.[1] The following day was one with 'indications that the enemy was about to withdraw; he was almost finished' while for Wednesday he wrote that he 'directed two hard punches at the "hinges" of the final break-out area where the enemy was trying to stop us widening the gap which we had blown. That finished the battle'.[2]

For the soldier on the ground the story was not so simple. The New Zealand Division's attack began on time under cover of a heavy artillery bombardment and the assaulting brigades, 151 Durham and 152 Highland, advanced through dust and smoke, each on a 2,000–yard frontage. From the ranks of the attacking Highlanders, 5th Seaforth and 5th Camerons, came the savage but inspiring strains of highland pipes; the Jocks were moving to battle once again. A hunting horn sounded from the ranks of 9th Durhams, answering the call of the Scottish pipes.

On the extreme right flank the Maoris assaulted the strongpoint just west of Point 29. Opposition was fierce from the start and one company was all but wiped out as the Maoris strove for their objective. Fortunately the company to the left of the stricken soldiers reached its objective on time and dug in, forming a base to support their comrades. After taking several enemy posts at bayonet point or with grenades, the Maoris captured their objective and linked up with 9th Australian Division. The battalion had suffered 100 casualties in so doing, including their commanding officer, Fred Baker, whose tongue was ripped out by a bullet.[3]

On the left flank the Royal Sussex Brigade captured *Woodcock* with 2nd Royal Sussex, reinforced by C Company, 4th Royal Sussex, reduced to two weak platoons and its anti-tank platoon. The advancing Sussex met only minor opposition although they lost contact with 5th Camerons on the right. *Woodcock* was reached by the forward companies at 2.45am and the battalion was consolidating on its objective just over an hour later. Sixty prisoners were taken, a number that increased considerably after dawn, for relatively light casualties of one dead and sixteen wounded. By dawn the battalion was in contact with 5th Seaforth to the right and 5th Royal Sussex to the left who continued the line back to *Oxalic*, now held by 5th/7th Gordon Highlanders.

The Durham Brigade was led by 8th Durhams on the right and 9th Durhams on the left, with 6th Durhams following up some 500 yards behind 8th. Although about 100 casualties were suffered 8th Durhams' two assault companies reached their objective on schedule, having broken through a line of Axis medical posts, a German tank recovery park and a medical dressing station. The reserve company then passed through and made the final objective, near the Rahman track, by 4.00am, taking almost fifty prisoners. With their wireless link knocked out they were out of contact temporarily but, gradually, the remains of the other companies arrived, as did the New Zealand anti-tank and machine-gun platoons. By dawn 8th Durham LI were established firmly on their objectives.

Their sister battalion, the 9th, met little opposition until the second half of their advance when they ran into dug-in tanks and guns. But the cumulative effects of battle fatigue and the shock and effectiveness of the artillery bombardment meant that those manning these weapons showed no great spirit for fighting and 9th Durhams reached their objective by 4.00am. Joined by their heavy weapons and supporting anti-tank guns, they had consolidated well before dawn. The third Durham battalion, 6th, although following in the tracks of 8th Durhams, ran into opposition on drawing level with the area where the Maoris were fighting. Heavy machine-gun fire raked them and an entire company was deployed to suppress that fire. The other companies then swung right to create a north-facing battalion front between the salient's corner and the Maoris' intended positions, although a gap still existed. Heavy machine guns and anti-tank guns arrived soon afterwards and the battalion had secured its sector by dawn. Thus had the Durham Brigade achieved its objectives at a cost of 350 killed, wounded or missing. About that number of prisoners had been taken, mostly Italians from *Littorio* or *Trento* Divisions but including some Germans from 115th Panzergrenadier Regiment.

The attack achieved an unexpected degree of surprise due to confusion at *Panzerarmee* headquarters. On this night *Panzerarmee* had chosen to switch from German Summer Time to Central European Time, which alone could have caused confusion but, taken with the effects of a bombing raid on von Thoma's advanced headquarters of *Afrikakorps*, was guaranteed to confuse the situation. The bombing destroyed telephone communications and wounded von Thoma. One result of the lack of communication was that Rommel was led to believe that the British attack was being made westward from the Australian positions to south-east of Sidi Abd el Rahman. Not until first light was the true situation appreciated which meant that it took longer to launch counter-attacks.

The Highlanders' advance went 'like a drill' as Freyberg later described it. On the right were 5th Seaforth, with 5th Camerons to their left and 2nd Seaforth following to 'mop up'. Brigadier George Murray was in constant wireless contact with his battalions and with Freyberg. Their objective, *Neat*, was reached by 4.17am where both leading battalions engaged enemy tanks. D Company of the Camerons, however, had lost all their officers, except the company commander at which point Company Sergeant Major James Ahern took command of one platoon and company headquarters and 'led them in a most aggressive manner against seven enemy tanks which he found on the company's objective. He then proceeded to organize these platoons in a defensive position and got them dug in'. Ahern, an Irishman, born in Queenstown (now Cobh), County Cork, was subsequently awarded the Military Medal for his inspiring leadership and example.[4]

Artillery support was called for and, by 5.25am, the tanks were retreating and the battalion heavy weapons and supporting anti-tank guns arriving. Re-organization was soon completed with casualties for the attack not more than forty per battalion. How different it all was from D Day for LIGHTFOOT. The operation had been carried out in the full heat of battle but with more smoothness than in many an exercise. The New Zealand Division had achieved its objectives but Rommel considered that he had stopped the British advance. 'After some heavy fighting we succeeded in halting this advance by throwing in the 90th Light Division's reserves. The enemy steadily strengthened his forces in the wedge he had driven into our line.'[5] But that wedge was the planned limit of XXX Corps' penetration; the battle was now to be handed over to X Corps' armour.

Montgomery's plan called for X Corps to break out into the open through the gap made by XXX Corps, securing the area around Point 46 and Tel el Aqqaqir before developing operations to destroy the enemy armour and 'bring about the complete disintegration of the enemy's rear areas'.[6] X Corps was to secure its first objective before daylight and thereafter develop its operations.

However, the first armoured strike was to be by 9 Armoured Brigade which was to breach the Axis gun line along the Rahman track, clearing the way for 1st Armoured Division. Although Montgomery had given the brigade priority for replacement tanks, so that it mustered almost eighty Shermans and Grants and over fifty Crusaders on the evening of 1 November, few of the replacements were new. Most of the brigade's tanks were decidedly war-weary: the Crusaders issued to the Wiltshires were in a sorry state with equipment missing or not working: guns, compasses and radios all displayed faults. However, the men of 9 Armoured were in good spirits, few being aware of Montgomery's willingness to accept the loss of the complete brigade; Currie had informed his regimental commanders who, in turn, had told most of their squadron leaders but the message had percolated down no further. Perhaps it was as well the soldiers did not know what faced them.

The brigade's approach to its start line was difficult enough, with only the leading vehicles of each regimental group enjoying anything other than a jolting journey through clouds of choking dust and fog. Each column included not only tanks but also supply vehicles, numbering about 300 vehicles for 3rd Hussars and some 120 in the Warwickshire Yeomanry column. The Hussars suffered shelling from the Axis forces harassing the Durhams and lost six tanks as well as losing contact with their anti-tank guns; all the officers of their supporting Sherwood Foresters' company were killed or wounded. Many soft-skinned vehicles were lost through collisions and tanks lost tracks to mines since many of the lights marking the cleared routes had disappeared. Of the 123 tanks of the brigade that had left their rest area near El Alamein station, only ninety-four were fit for action on reaching their start line; and the Warwicks did not make the start line on time.

With the Warwicks falling behind schedule Currie asked for a delay in his H Hour. Although the commanding officers of the Hussars and Wiltshires wanted to go ahead on schedule, Currie was concerned about the security of the Wiltshires' left flank. Since he also wanted to make the gap as wide as possible, he asked Freyberg for a thirty-minute delay in the bombardment. Freyberg agreed and 9 Brigade made its final preparations. Aware of the sacrifice being demanded of his soldiers, Currie placed himself in the van rather than in one of the accepted positions for command, thereby causing some to wonder what was ahead. This was the modern equivalent of Balaclava and the charge of the Light Brigade.

Clearing the minefields, the tanks shook out into attacking formation, line-abreast by squadrons in the irregular pattern known as artillery formation. On the right were 3rd Hussars with Wiltshires in the centre and Warwicks on the left; the New Zealand Divisional Cavalry light tanks followed. Both yeomanry regiments were accompanied by companies of Sherwood Foresters, either on foot or in carriers. Now awaiting the final order to advance, the regiments waited, tank engines ticked over and the dust began to settle as officers walked about, issuing final orders. Then, at 6.15am, came the sound everyone was waiting for: the guns roared again, tank drivers heard the order 'advance', gears were engaged and 9 Armoured Brigade moved forward to battle, once again raising a storm of dust, with the Crusaders leading the Grant and Sherman squadrons of the three regiments.

At Balaclava the gallant 600 rode into a valley of death with cannon to right of them, cannon to left of them, cannon in front of them. Now a gallant 400 rode 'Into the jaws of Death/Into the mouth of Hell' and, as with the Light Brigade of Balaclava, they, too, were 'Stormed at with shot and shell'. Their charge is not so well known as that of their predecessors in the Crimea but is equally deserving of recognition. This was one of the most courageous actions fought by British tankmen during the Second World War and their losses were horrendous: of 400 who rode into battle some 230 were killed or wounded; of the ninety-four tanks that were their steeds seventy-five were lost.

All seemed to go well initially as the tanks advanced behind their artillery cover. Battle-shocked Axis infantry emerged to surrender, in which case they were signalled to begin moving to the rear, or to continue the fight in which case the tanks' machine guns dealt with them. The Hussars and Wiltshires moved on past the line of telegraph poles marking the Rahman track, which ran diagonally across their axis of advance. As they did so, one tank commander noticed the top third of the closest telegraph pole already being lightened by dawn's approach and felt a jab of concern at what that augured. Then the tanks were amid the enemy anti-tank guns, some of which had already been destroyed by the artillery bombardment. Others, however, were intact: their gunners, resolute in their determination to resist the British tanks, opened fire at close range. Among their first victims was the squadron leader's tank of the Hussars' Crusader squadron. With its loss the squadron also lost contact with the heavy squadrons. The Wiltshires' Crusaders had remarkable initial success against the anti-tank guns; at one point they crushed an entire line of guns while others, both German 50mms and Italian 47mms, were knocked over. It seemed as if 9 Armoured Brigade's efforts were to be crowned with success. Then a quartet of German officers decided to make a rapid departure in a staff car. It was an injudicious move: the Wiltshires' Crusader squadron leader shot at the car with his revolver with surprising results; the bullet struck the petrol tank and the car exploded.

But the tide of battle was about to turn. The sky was turning to that pale grey of dawn and light soon painted the crest of the Aqqaqir ridge. Behind that ridge lay the main weight of the enemy anti-tank defence, the redoubtable 88s and 75s, well dug in and camouflaged, while the British tanks were silhouetted against the brightening eastern skyline. (The German soldier was a master of camouflage and concealment with his discipline in this respect much greater than his British counterpart. Heinz Werner Schmidt recounted an incident near Agedabia, as *Panzerarmee* retreated before Montgomery's forces, when he ordered his guns to be camouflaged with camel-thorn. 'Taking a leaf from Rommel's book, I inspected my positions from the front.'[7] Only one gun failed to satisfy him. A similar camouflage discipline would have been observed by the guns at Tel el Aqqaqir.)

One survivor described this as the time when the 'whole world seemed to blow up' as the heavy anti-tank guns spewed forth fire at British tanks.[8] With the western horizon resembling the special effects of a Hollywood film, 75mm and 88m rounds began smashing into the Crusaders and then Grants and Shermans. As the high-velocity rounds struck, the tanks' carapaces glowed bright red at the points of penetration. Crippled tanks slewed out of control before erupting into flames. Crewmen tried to escape. Some, unable to do so, died horribly as their tanks became crematoria. Others managed to get out and many displayed the utmost courage in going back to blazing tanks to rescue trapped comrades.

In the midst of this horror the Wiltshires had advanced farther than the other regiments with John Currie in their heart at the forefront of battle. The Wiltshires seemed determined to maintain their habit of being in the van of any advance, although they believed the Warwicks to be on their left flank. In that belief they were mistaken: the 'Warwick' tanks were, in fact, panzers of 15th Panzer Division and the truth was brought home to the Wiltshires when the latter opened fire on them. The Wiltshires' last Crusaders were struck and set alight. Their crews tried to make their way to safety, covered by smoke laid down by their own heavy squadrons and those of 3rd Hussars. That smoke would cover them from the Axis machine gunners behind and the Durhams in front, who might believe they were enemy infantry.

If the tanks on the left flank were not those of the Warwicks, then where was 9 Armoured's third regiment? A navigational error had taken the Warwicks too far south, allowing the panzers to slip in between two British regiments. The

Warwicks' advance had met with similar results as that of the remainder of the brigade, initial success giving way to the fearfully accurate fire of anti-tank guns hidden on the ridge. Then the panzers in the gap on the regiment's right took up the quarrel. Rounds hammered into the Crusaders, tearing many of the lighter tanks apart, and bringing the heavy Shermans and Grants to a halt.

Currie's brigade had crashed into the enemy defences along Aqqaqir ridge but failed to punch the hole needed for 1st Armoured Division to pass. The timetable called for 2 Armoured Brigade to come up behind 9 Armoured, in which case the former should be able to crack through the dent made by Currie's men, expand it, pass through, followed by 8 Armoured Brigade, and bring the enemy armour to battle, destroying Rommel's panzers in the process. But of 2 Armoured Brigade there was no sign. However, Freyberg believed that 9 Armoured had achieved a pivotal success.

> Although 9th Brigade did not reach its objective and had heavy casualties, the action was a success in Freyberg's opinion as the enemy gun line was smashed. It may be argued, he went on, that it was a costly and incorrect method of using armour; but if one is to believe General von Thoma ... it may well prove to have been the deciding factor in breaking the German line, though advantage was not taken of the breach until later.[9]

Of course, there was no real breach, although there was a dent in the enemy gun line. Lucas-Phillips argues that it was 'beyond question that 3rd Hussars and the Royal Wiltshire Yeomanry made a definite breach in the Rahman Track'.[10] Against that is the evidence of Lieutenant Colonel Gerald Grosvenor, commanding 9th Lancers, who was told by Currie that 9 Brigade had made a gap and that Grosvenor's brigade – 2 Armoured – had to pass through, 'and pass through bloody quick'. Grosvenor, the future 4th Duke of Westminster, told Currie that he had never seen anything less like a gap.

Within fifteen minutes Freyberg made three calls to Leese, asking him to contact Lumsden 'to order Briggs, to press Fisher' to get 2 Armoured Brigade forward as quickly as possible. The battle still suffered from the fundamental flaw of Montgomery's 'master plan' – the imposition of one corps on another. Fisher's regiments had departed their assembly area at 2.30am on a frustratingly slow move forward through clouds of dust and the congestion caused by many other units using the tracks: supply trucks bumped forward to the Durham and Highland Brigades, engineers worked on mine-clearing, ambulances went about their work of mercy and the tail of 2 Armoured Brigade was still trying to move forward. In Pitt's words, 'The wonder was not so much that 2nd Armoured Brigade were late, but that they got through at all.'[11]

Shortly after Freyberg made his third call to Leese, Fisher's tanks, Bays, 9th Lancers and 10th Hussars, were moving into action. At 4.00am brigade headquarters reported that 10th Hussars had taken a wrong turning on Moon track and lost an hour before finding the correct track. The regiment was forced to retrace its steps; the error was attributed to the track being 'very inadequately marked'.[12] Both the Bays and 9th Lancers had passed Eighth Army's front infantry positions with the Bays closing up to the Rahman track. Peter Willett's troop, leading the Bays, 'was the leading troop of the leading squadron of the leading regiment of 1st Armoured Division'. As his tank cleared the sand fog of the lane through the minefield, Lieutenant Willett could see,

> far ahead, the chaotic evidence of 9 Armoured Brigade's battle. Tracer trails criss-crossed the sky, guns flashed and tanks exploded in smoke and flame. Tom Toller's troop, the next through the minefield, was to come up level with me on my right, but it seemed to take ages to appear. My left flank was clear; the 9th Lancers took care of that.[13]

Fisher believed that both the Bays and 9th Lancers were across the track but this was not so. However, both were forward of the Durhams and in hulldown positions, having been engaged by enemy tanks. All three regiments had a good idea of what lay ahead: as they advanced they endured heavy enemy shelling, saw German and Italian prisoners make their way back and, not least, witnessed the bursts of enemy armour-piercing and high-explosive shells that had been fired at Currie's tanks without hitting. Some rounds travelled remarkable distances: one gunner reported that some of his battery HQ were gathered around a table in the lee of a lorry well to the rear when an 88 shell passed between them and pierced the side of the lorry. Before long they had dug in their headquarters.

X Corps' battle plan was predicated on an enemy reaction by counter-attack to the New Zealand attack. It was believed that such counter-attack would come from either north or west; 1st Armoured Division was to deploy to positions that offered the British armour the best chance of destroying the Axis tanks. Thus 2 Armoured Brigade's deployment area was to be some two miles north-west of Tel el Aqqaqir while 8 Armoured was to deploy at Tel el Aqqaqir itself with 7 Motor Brigade positioned between the armoured formations. At 6.50am 10th Hussars reported 'contact with 7 enemy tanks'. Further reports of contact with tanks and anti-tank guns were made by both 9th Lancers and Bays. However, shortly after 9.00am, 2 Armoured Brigade, although engaged with both panzers and anti-tank guns, was still just forward of the Durhams. At 9.10am all armour passed under command of X Corps.

Fisher had asked Briggs whether he should push on or stay in his positions. To this the divisional commander responded with the message that, since Fisher's mission was to destroy tanks, he should take up positions from which that could be achieved. Soon after Fisher responded with news that his brigade was positioned where it could meet attacks from either north or west and being engaged by tanks and anti-tank guns. To this Briggs replied with an order to destroy the opposition and advance, quickly following with an exhortation that Fisher should get on as the division needed room. However, 2 Armoured Brigade could not move forward for the time being, nor could it disengage easily. Little did the tankmen know that they were now about to fight one of the fiercest armour-versus-armour clashes of the campaign.

The Bays and the survivors of 3rd Hussars, with some Valentines from 8th Royal Tanks, were developing good north-facing defensive positions, while 9th Lancers and the Wiltshires had married, facing west in the Durham and Seaforth forward positions. Another loose group of 10th Hussars, Warwicks and 50th Royal Tanks was also in action, trading blows with panzers to the south-west on the Rahman track. The broken ground forward of the British infantry positions allowed deployment into hulldown positions from which the tanks of X Corps now hoped to destroy the enemy armour, drawing Rommel's tanks into attacks on the British tanks and anti-tank guns. No one thought of advancing further: the evidence of 9 Armoured Brigade's attack was plain to see and the rising sun exposed fresh enemy preparations: a new anti-tank gun line was seen to the north with a group of panzers forming up behind it.

At 10.05am Briggs told Fisher that there were indications that a strong counter-attack might come in from the north; 8 Armoured Brigade was ordered to link up with Fisher's command to meet the threat. A report from 9th Lancers suggested that enemy tanks to the west were sheltering behind an anti-tank screen which the Lancers were 'trying to destroy … to get at the tanks'. Ten minutes later the Bays reported being engaged with thirty to forty tanks approaching from the north-west while 10th Hussars were 'fully engaged to [the] south'. In fact 2 Armoured Brigade's advance had been brought to a halt by 88s on Tel el Aqqaqir 'and for the next two days there was little movement'.[14]

That first counter-attack was beaten off quickly but the enemy was not to be browbeaten in any clash of armour; he had spent too much time delivering master classes in armoured warfare to his British opponents to have anything other than a proper conceit of his own abilities, even when outnumbered. Further attacks followed but Rommel was now doing exactly what Montgomery had wanted him to do: sending his armour against British armour in strong defensive positions backed by anti-tank guns. Moreover, a massive concentration of artillery could be called upon, the effectiveness of which Rommel knew only too well. And then there was the air arm: British, South African and US aircraft played an invaluable role in the day's battle with fighters chasing off Axis dive-bombers and their escorts while 'party rally' formations of bombers continued their work with seven attacks in two hours.

The next enemy counter-attack was more dangerous with a small panzer formation threatening the salient's northern edge. Custance's 8 Armoured Brigade had begun debouching onto the battlefield some time earlier with the Staffordshire Yeomanry leading. The Staffords' commanding officer, Lieutenant Colonel James Eadie, noticed that a group of over two dozen panzers had slipped into the northern edge of the British salient, on the Durham Brigade's flank, having found a gap between 6th Durhams and the Maoris. Eadie ordered his Crusader squadron to engage them. The heavy squadrons were then despatched as they arrived to support their lighter brothers. In the ensuing encounter three panzers and several anti-tank guns were destroyed. The Germans turned back.

But the main battle, the engagement between X Corps' armour and that of *Panzerarmee*, was underway. It lasted some hours, being at its most intense for the two hours around midday, the desert heat haze adding to a surreal vision that not even Dante could have dreamed of in his worst visions of hell. The surviving tanks of 15th and 21st Panzer and *Littorio* Divisions dashed themselves against British armour and anti-tank guns and, forced to attack across open ground in daylight, suffered as they had made British armour suffer so often before. At times some 120 German and Italian tanks – the latter much lighter, much more vulnerable and the courage of their crews admirable almost beyond belief – were making co-ordinated attacks on the British salient, assaulting the western face of the salient as well as the northern and north-western faces. Although Rommel tried to provide as much support as possible, the Ju87s, the once-feared Stukas, were being torn out of the sky by Allied fighters, while the artillery support, including two dozen 88s, could not swing the balance in favour of *Panzerarmee*.

Enemy attempts to mount air attacks on Eighth Army's echelons were also thwarted by aircraft and anti-aircraft fire. On 2 November additional AA assets were removed to El Alamein railhead. These included B and C Troops of the Irish 6 LAA Battery, whose D Troop was providing protection for Montgomery's tactical headquarters, and Right Troop 192 HAA Battery. The latter engaged enemy aircraft on three occasions, firing forty-seven rounds and claiming one machine destroyed while Left Troop also engaged enemy aircraft, claiming one destroyed, as well as two ground targets at ranges of 15,000 and 17,000 yards. 'The appearance of HAA guns in the forward area clearly surprised the enemy.'[15]

Montgomery had gone to Leese's tactical headquarters near Tel el Eisa during the morning and received an encouraging progress report. He learned that XXX Corps' right flank was secure but that X Corps was meeting strong opposition as it tried to push west. On the southern flank the Royals already had two armoured-car squadrons out into open desert and it seemed that opposition there was weaker. Montgomery decided to exploit that weakness and Custance was instructed to move around 2 Armoured Brigade's southern flank rather than wait to follow Fisher. In this move 8 Armoured Brigade was blocked by an enemy anti-tank gun screen.

XXX Corps was also ordered to attack Point 38, codenamed *Skinflint*, that afternoon, an operation carried out by 2nd Seaforth Highlanders and 50th Royal Tanks with the usual heavy artillery support. The attack was delayed several times from its scheduled time of 4.00pm but it also went like a drill and the Seaforth suffered no casualties in the assault, although four Valentines of 50th Royal Tanks were lost. *Skinflint* fell with 100 prisoners from *Trieste*. The Italian division was so knocked about that it also surrendered *Snipe* before 5th Royal Sussex had time to attack it. These successes aside, the British armour was still not across the Rahman track, although Fisher believed it to be.

In all respects, however, the enemy was suffering: Montgomery's crumbling was finally paying off. Rommel was losing tanks at a rate he could not afford and more depressing news of the loss of tankers was coming in, while Eighth Army could afford a much higher rate of attrition. At the end of the day Rommel's tank strength was down to thirty-five panzers in *Afrikakorps* and about twenty Italian tanks. The evidence of the sacrifice of the Axis tankmen was seen clearly on the battlefield: over 100 wrecked tanks were littered about; even the efficiency of the German recovery crews could not achieve the retrieval of more than a few.

That night Rommel wrote to his wife: 'Very heavy fighting again, not going well for us. The enemy, with his superior strength, is slowly levering us out of our position. That will mean the end. You can imagine how I feel. Air raid after air raid after air raid!'.[16]

The end was indeed near. Rommel wrote that *Panzerarmee* had counter-attacked 'with some success but at the cost of severe losses' while his supply situation was worsening: his army had fired off 450 tons of ammunition but only 190 tons had arrived, brought into Tobruk by three destroyers.[17] The uneven struggle could not last much longer. On that evening Rommel decided to withdraw to Fuka, some sixty miles away. During the night the soldiers in the southern sector would pull back to the line Qaret el Abd–Gebel Kalakh while those mobile forces in the north, *Afrikakorps*, XX Italian Corps and 90th Light Division, would continue resisting Montgomery's advance while withdrawing slowly on the 3rd to a line running south from El Daba, some twenty miles back. That would allow the infantry to escape on foot or on whatever vehicles they could use. Rommel reported his decision, and his reasons for it, to Hitler's headquarters.

> Montgomery's 'Operation Supercharge' … was the end at El Alamein. The 21st Panzers had put up their last effective struggle, and, although at one time they almost mastered their old enemies, the British 1st Armoured, they were beaten. Rommel decided to withdraw on the night of November 2–3.[18]

But Hitler had other ideas. Obsessed, as he would continue to be, with holding ground at all costs, he ordered Rommel to stand where he was, telling him that 'it would not be the first time in history that a strong will has triumphed over the bigger battalions. As to your troops, you can show them no other road than that to victory or death'.[19] Orders to withdraw were countermanded, although Rommel sent his aide, Leutnant Berndt, off to Germany on a mission to persuade the Führer to change his mind; since Berndt was a committed Nazi, Rommel felt that he might succeed.

As darkness fell over the battlefield on the 2nd, Briggs' two brigades still mustered 186 tanks, having lost only ten during the day, eight of them from the Bays. Close behind 1st Armoured Division was John Harding's 7th Armoured, ready for its role in the breakout. However, X Corps was no further on and Lumsden planned a fresh night attack in which 2 and 8 Armoured Brigades would advance about five miles to the west while 7 Motor Brigade moved southwards across the Rahman track. At first light 7th Armoured Division would move forward. This plan was later changed to a simpler one: 7 Motor Brigade would attack and capture the area north of Tel el Aqqaqir, after which both armoured brigades would pass through, followed by 7th Armoured

Division; the Royals and 4th/6th South African Armoured Car Regiment were also to slip out of the salient.

The change of plan, probably instigated by Montgomery, was made so late that 7 Motor Brigade had little time to work out a solid plan and the riflemen advanced with scant artillery support to objectives a mile beyond the Rahman track (2nd Rifle Brigade), Tel el Aqqaqir (2nd/60th Rifles), and the track itself (7th Rifle Brigade). Both Rifle Brigade battalions were forced to withdraw to their start lines while 2nd/60th, moving off late, dug in just over quarter of a mile short of the track where, when dawn broke, they found themselves overlooked by Tel el Aqqaqir itself. However, as the result of a message that became corrupted as it passed up the chain of command, Briggs believed that the battalion had captured the tel. That belief lasted for twelve hours and influenced planning for the next day. On the morrow Lumsden ordered 8 Armoured Brigade to probe forward and around the south of where he thought 2nd/60th Rifles were dug in. He also ordered 4th/6th South African Armoured Car Regiment to slip out and join the Royals but, two hours later, the South Africans were back with news of strong opposition all along the ridge, as well as minefields. Although the reports were confirmed by infantry observers they were not believed at the headquarters of 7 Motor Brigade, 1st Armoured Division or X Corps. The attempt to probe forward by 8 Armoured Brigade, in which 2 Armoured Brigade later joined, achieved nothing other than the destruction of a few enemy anti-tank guns. The armour lost three tanks in an attempt to charge the Aqqaqir ridge and ease the pressure on the Green Jackets who remained in place all day, with X Corps and Eighth Army command believing that they were on the ridge, and that 8 Armoured Brigade was moving towards them, having crossed the Rahman track.

While Montgomery was receiving unduly optimistic reports from this sector, other reports were also optimistic but true. In the south XIII Corps' reports of fires and explosions unrelated to any obvious action were confirmed by air reconnaissance as part of an enemy withdrawal; columns of men and vehicles were seen heading north-west. And the Australians were also able to report an enemy that had vanished; radio intercepts had earlier told Eighth Army headquarters that 90th Light Division had ordered a battalion to send vehicles to extract the heavy weapons at Thompson's Post. Australian patrols confirmed that the enemy had gone.

As the day wore on there were more and more reports from aircraft of Axis withdrawal in both south and north. Rommel was pulling back but Montgomery was anxious that *Panzerarmee* should be pinned in its positions long enough for his armour to push out from its salient, move around *Panzerarmee*'s southern flank, and cut off its withdrawal. Lumsden was told to keep his armoured formations pounding away all day while being ready to move with speed when darkness fell. Wimberley was to send troops forward during the late afternoon to position themselves south of 2nd/60th Rifles on the ridge, thereby giving Eighth Army control of the Rahman track to the south. Briggs' division would drive through the area thus secured, pushing south-west and west before swinging north to trap *Panzerarmee* against the coast. Harding's 7th Armoured Division, who had played but a small part in the battle thus far, would follow 1st Armoured but make a wider swing towards Ghazal station. In turn they would be followed by Freyberg's New Zealand Division, with 4 Light Armoured Brigade (which was still coming up from the south) under command in place of 9 Armoured, who would strike towards Sidi Ibeid and then Fuka or perhaps Matruh, depending on circumstances.

Rommel's letter of the 3rd to his wife is a missive of despair. He wrote that the battle was going very 'heavily against us' and that his command was being crushed by the enemy weight. He told Lu that he had made an attempt to salvage part of the army and wondered if that would be successful. And he told her that 'At night I lie open-eyed, racking my brains for a way out of this plight for my poor troops'.[20]

Plans were formulated quickly for Eighth Army's long-awaited breakthrough into open country and the pursuit and destruction of *Panzerarmee Afrika*. But those plans continued to assume that 2nd/60th Rifles were on Aqqaqir ridge and that 8 Armoured Brigade was across the Rahman track. This assumption had a devastating effect on Wimberley's Jocks. Wimberley was asked to launch three attacks in twelve hours, one using 5 Indian Brigade, the others by his own battalions. He was shocked to learn from Leese that Briggs was protesting at plans to provide artillery support for Wimberley's first attack, by 5th/7th Gordon Highlanders from *Skinflint* to just south of Tel el Aqqaqir, on the grounds that the shells would fall first on 8 Armoured Brigade and then on the Green Jackets on the ridge. As a result the Gordons went forward under cover of smoke, supported by 8th Royal Tanks.

The advance went well until the leading Valentines emerged from the final smokescreen to face into a setting sun that blinded both drivers and commanders and a tornado of machine-gun and anti-tank fire from a ridge supposedly in friendly hands. Twenty tanks were wrecked almost immediately; 125 Gordons and tankmen were killed, wounded or missing. Then came a message from 1st

Armoured Division headquarters to 51st (Highland) headquarters: artillery support *could* be given since 1st Armoured had learned that their infantry and tanks were not so far forward as had been thought.

The next two attacks were launched by 11 Indian Brigade, under Wimberley's command, and 7th Argylls. In the first attack there were problems arranging start lines and finding one of the brigade's battalions but, although 1/4th Essex only received their orders at 7.15pm and 3/10th Baluchs could not be found, the attack went ahead at 2.30am on the 4th with the Essex on the right and 6th Rajputana Rifles on the left. The attack was a complete success with the Essex taking 100 German prisoners, followed by a further eighty on their objective on the Rahman track about three miles south of Tel el Aqqaqir. There they were joined by the Rajputs and the Baluchs, who had been found and had followed up without opposition.

The Argylls took their objective, Tel el Aqqaqir itself, with no casualties. They were on the tel by dawn and found the enemy gone. Rommel had decided to ignore Hitler's order to stand and die, arguing that he could save his command. And so *Panzerarmee* had begun withdrawing during the night, leaving only stragglers, wrecked equipment, mines and booby-traps. The battle of El Alamein was over. Eighth Army had now to exploit its success and reap the full harvest of victory by destroying *Panzerarmee Afrika*.

Plans for exploitation were in hand. On the evening of the 3rd Montgomery had issued his orders for the final breakout. While the Australians cleared up east of Sidi Abd el Rahman, 2nd New Zealand Division, with 4 Light Armoured Brigade, was to break out, as we have seen, for Sidi Ibeid and be ready to move on to Fuka to block Rommel's retreat. We have also seen the plans for X Corps, including Harding's Desert Rats, but another element had been created for the pursuit. This was 8th Armoured Division's headquarters with a force of almost seventy Valentines of 23 Armoured Brigade on light tank transporters, 5 RHA, a battalion of lorried infantry, a machine-gun battalion, sappers, light AA and anti-tank gunners, and an RAF contingent of some 160 vehicles. The force was also to take over command of the two armoured-car regiments operating in Rommel's rear areas. This was Operation GRAPESHOT, designed to race for and seize Tobruk before Axis forces could organize its defence, while securing a landing ground en route in the vicinity of Sidi Barrani.[21] But the operation was to come to naught. A Rommel or a Patton might have implemented it. Montgomery did not.

Dawn on 4 November found elements of *Panzerarmee* well back from the El Alamein line while Eighth Army realized that it had won the long, weary struggle. *Afrikakorps* and 90th Light were in rearguard positions: 90th Light at Ghazal, 15th Panzer some six miles west of the Aqqaqir ridge with their left flank on the bump known as Tel el Mampsra, joining 21st Panzer who continued the line to the railway. Survivors of *Ariete* and *Trieste* were also in the region, although very weak. Eighth Army's armour spent the morning trying to move out into the open through the exit that was most likely to be free of mines, the salient made in SUPERCHARGE. As a result that salient was choked with traffic in congestion that was worse than anything seen earlier in the battle.

Carver, who was present, commented that

> Little if any attempt seems to have been made on a higher level to co-ordinate the confusion that was bound to arise from so many divisions struggling to push out through the bottleneck .... It would have been hard enough if all had been under the command of the same corps; with two different corps, who were not on the best of terms anyway, both trying to carry out the same task in the same area, it was chaotic. There is no other word to describe the incredible confusion of that dark night in a sea of dust. Vehicles of every formation were travelling in every direction on every conceivable track, looming up in front of each other from unexpected directions out of the thick, stifling pall of dust.[22]

Such chaos did not bode well for a successful pursuit. While Montgomery could urge his commanders to 'get on' there was little they could do to extricate formations from such congestion. The first tanks to get away were Fisher's since 2 Armoured Brigade had been on the western face of the salient. Led by the armoured cars of 12th Lancers, they probed forward across the Rahman track – at last – across the northern extremity of the Aqqaqir ridge and down to ground in front of Tel el Mampsra. There they met what was left of *Afrikakorps*, its panzers and anti-tank guns ready, once again, to take on the British tanks, its commander, von Thoma, determined to fight with his men this one last time, for he had decided that he would no longer soldier for the madman in Berlin and his regime of 'unparalleled madness'.

One of *Afrikakorps'* first shells hit General Briggs' tank and soon several more were alight. Briggs ordered the tanks into cover and called on artillery to deal with *Afrikakorps*. Steadily the German tanks and guns were pounded to destruction, although several escaped to fight another day. Thoma surrendered to Eighth Army. Some miles south 7th Armoured Division met, first, a line of 88s and, then, *Ariete* Division. The Italians, although poorly equipped with their mobile coffins, as their light tanks were described, fought tenaciously and did so for the rest of that day. As light faded 1st Armoured Division was still at Tel el Mampsra, 7th Armoured Division was no more than three miles west of the Rahman track and 10th Armoured Division was still east of that track. X Corps had made little progress in pursuit of Rommel who had finally decided that retreat was the only sensible option and was closing down the rearguard actions of *Afrikakorps* and *Ariete*.

Freyberg seemed more prepared than anyone else for the pursuit. Since 3 November he had sensed that *Panzerarmee* was on the point of cracking and when he learned that the Argylls were on Tel el Aqqaqir he set off to reconnoitre south of the tel to seek out a passage for his division to pursue Rommel's forces. For that pursuit 2nd New Zealand Division would include the two infantry brigades with the addition of 4 Light Armoured Brigade, from 7th Armoured Division, in lieu of the shattered 9 Armoured. He then waited while 5 and 6 NZ Brigades came forward to join his headquarters and 4 Light Armoured made its way forward from Alamein station. His intention was that the armoured brigade would lead the divisional breakout and the race to Fuka, almost sixty miles westward.

Both 2nd Derbyshire Yeomanry, with their armoured cars, and the Royal Scots Greys, with Grant and Stuart tanks, made good time in reaching Freyberg's headquarters. Perhaps the prospect of action at last, after seeing little in XIII Corps' sector, was a spur. The brigade was with Freyberg by 10.00am on the 4th and the armoured cars were probing down the Rahman track a half hour later. There they came on 7th Armoured Division, engaged with the Italian XX Corps. Rommel was learning of a British breakthrough in the centre, that of Roddick's 4 Light Armoured, and of XX Corps coming under pressure from a mass of British heavy tanks that had come around its southern flank. Rommel's decision not to obey Hitler's 'last stand' order meant that he was now trying to extricate his armour from a possible encirclement by an armoured force that outnumbered him by twenty tanks to one.

Freyberg wanted a quick pursuit, free from the problems of being caught up in the logistical problems of others, and was determined to clear the battlefield by nightfall. His tactical headquarters went ahead with the rest of the division to follow as soon as it had petrol sufficient for 200 miles, water and rations for eight days and ammunition on a scale of 360 rounds per field gun. That evening the head of the New Zealand column had passed through Sidi Ibeid and reached the old Barrel track. When he believed he was south of El Daba, Freyberg halted to allow the remainder of the division to catch up, since he had learned that the Axis armour was also making for Fuka. When Kippenberger's 5 Brigade arrived at about midnight there was a brief skirmish at the tail of the column with some stragglers, believed to be from the Ramcke Brigade, which left some New Zealand dead but more enemy dead and saw the enemy make their getaway with some captured vehicles and eight prisoners. A blazing vehicle acted as a guide for Gentry's 6 Brigade to join the column.

Freyberg had shown initiative and dash in his pursuit. That was not repeated throughout Eighth Army. Montgomery's orders to X Corps were relayed to Briggs as an order to advance 'to outflank the enemy', hardly the clearest of orders. Custance, with 8 Armoured Brigade, had refuelled and replenished at last light and set off in the darkness on the evening of the 4th; he was to make for Galal, between El Daba and Fuka. However, 8 Armoured Brigade had little experience in moving over unfamiliar desert at night and so Custance called a halt after an hour; the brigade would not move again until it was light. As with so many other decisions and events on the ground, this appears not to have become known to higher authority for some time.[23]

Thus it was 5 November before the pursuit proper got underway. Then, the following day, the heavens opened. Desert tracks became quagmires and even tanks had difficulty in moving while wheeled vehicles bogged down. The torrential rain lasted into the 7th, giving Rommel a new and unexpected ally. Horrocks wrote that 2nd New Zealand, 1st and 10th Armoured Divisions 'might have been stuck in glue' and that their supply vehicles could not reach them. He added that 1st Armoured 'was almost in sight of the vital desert road' but that, by 9 November, the enemy had slipped away.[24] Montgomery had ordered elements of X Corps on a short thrust to the coast but only Custance's brigade had any success. B Squadron, 11th Hussars, the desert veteran Cherrypickers, led 8 Armoured Brigade to Galal where a block was established on the coast road and railway. Before long an enemy column was being engaged by 3rd Royal Tanks. Then followed a substantial Axis convoy of transport, artillery and tanks which, not anticipating the presence of Custance's armour, suffered a serious defeat, losing some fifty tanks, over 100 lorries, several guns and about 1,000 prisoners. Carver suggests that this was probably the remnant of de Stefanis' Italian XX Corps.[25]

Rommel, meanwhile, was making good his retreat, showing the same skill in withdrawing that he had so often shown in attack. Although the coast road was packed with transport, the Desert Air Force did not trouble him as much as it might have done since its aircraft were concentrating on close support of the ground forces rather than interdiction of the transport columns. The air commanders were keen that the ground troops should seize from the enemy the landing grounds at Sidi Haneish and El Daba before striking farther west.

Ignoring the advice of the desert veterans, who counselled a pursuit striking deeply westwards through the desert, parallel to Rommel's line of retreat, before swinging to the coast and cutting off *Panzerarmee*, Montgomery initiated a series of short jabs to the coast that achieved little and dissipated effort. He planned to spring his trap at Ma'aten Baggush, east of Mersa Matruh, on the 6th but this caught only thin air: Rommel had already gone. However, some elements of 21st Panzer Division, stopped by lack of fuel, engaged 22 Armoured Brigade, holding off the British armour until darkness fell, fuel supplies arrived and the panzers could top up their tanks and make off. With the soft sand south of Matruh now a morass, X Corps was bogged down and Rommel was able to slip away. Although the rain fell equally on British and Axis forces, Montgomery offered it as the reason for his failure to destroy *Panzerarmee*, claiming that it had saved his foe from complete encirclement at Matruh.

Clausewitz argued that the fruits of victory are won in the pursuit. By that measurement, Montgomery failed to obtain the full fruits of victory at El Alamein. But there could be no doubt that Rommel had been defeated and the threat to Egypt and the entire Middle East was over. The war in Africa would continue until May 1943 and the final Axis surrender in Tunisia, far to the west. As Eighth Army began its pursuit, Allied ships were approaching the ports of French north-west Africa with the leading elements of the force that would execute Operation TORCH. Another British army was coming to fight in North Africa.

Chapter Thirteen

The Battle in Retrospect

There is some soul of goodness in things evil

T he battle of El Alamein was over. No more would Eighth Army reel back across the desert towards the Egyptian frontier. On 8 November, as Allied troops came ashore far to the west in Operation TORCH, Tobruk changed hands for the last time, passing to the Allies. Although the newspapers lauded Eighth Army's great pursuit, that chase continued to be ponderous, and much slower than might have been the case had roles been reversed and Rommel been the hunter rather than the hunted.

Was Montgomery in thrall to the Rommel legend, and was this the root cause of his caution? Although Montgomery knew Rommel's situation very well, through ULTRA intercepts, he still seems to have been unable to press his undoubted advantage. Rommel was allowed to slip out of Egypt, a virtually non-existent battle at El Agheila became a significant clash in Montgomery's *Memoirs*,[1] and Rommel was then allowed to slip out of Libya so that the next major battle between *Panzerarmee Afrika* and Eighth Army occurred in Tunisia. Correlli Barnett suggests that *Panzerarmee's*

> shield during that epic retreat was its commander's reputation. And this interpretation is corroborated by a senior officer close to Montgomery at the time, who agrees that 'Rommel's reputation did make an impression on Monty's mind'.[2]

Certainly the man dubbed 'master of the battlefield' by Nigel Hamilton was no master of the pursuit. His strange reluctance to chase down Rommel can only be attributed to a fear of Rommel that he never acknowledged publicly. In that respect Montgomery was a lesser commander than Auchinleck. That Auchinleck had the measure of Rommel without Montgomery's advantages in October may also explain Montgomery's antipathy towards the Auk and his vindictive campaign against him.

The battle of El Alamein had wrought serious harm to *Panzerarmee Afrika*, destroying much equipment and removing several divisions from its order of battle. Montgomery suggested that the enemy was 'completely crippled',[3] which makes his reluctance to seek the full fruits of victory all the stranger. He noted that many divisions had ceased to exist as effective fighting formations and that some 30,000 prisoners had been taken, including nine generals.[4] The official figure for prisoners was over 30,000, including 10,000 Germans, while enemy fatal casualties were estimated at 10,000 with another 15,000 wounded. Fewer than one in three Axis soldiers escaped from El Alamein. Of 600 tanks, some two-thirds were abandoned as casualties of battle or through lack of fuel while about 1,000 guns of all calibres had been destroyed or captured. On 5 November it was estimated that some 150 enemy tanks remained but about seventy of these were Italian, and in *Ariete*, and most were abandoned during the retreat, either through mechanical breakdown or lack of fuel. (Lack of fuel was probably Rommel's greatest handicap; he was unaware that British Intelligence, through ULTRA decrypts, knew the details of his supply convoys and could ensure interdiction by air or submarine.) The remaining elements of 15th and 21st Panzer Divisions mustered no more than eighty tanks while 90th Light and 164th Divisions were reduced to the strength of regimental groups. Italian divisions had all but disintegrated. Two Italian divisions in reserve, *Pistoia* and *Spezia*, were on the frontier and in Tripolitania respectively but were not believed to be of good quality.[5]

British casualties totalled some 13,500 dead, wounded or missing, slightly under 8 per cent of the forces engaged. Some 500 tanks had been damaged by enemy action or breakdown, 150 being beyond repair. The artillery had lost about 100 guns to enemy action or premature shellbursts.[6] Eighth Army's field artillery had fired constantly throughout the battle, with X Corps' guns firing 1,043 rounds per gun, an average of eighty-seven rounds per gun per day, those of XIII Corps a total of 578 rounds per gun, forty-eight per gun per day, and XXX Corps' guns 1,909 per gun, with a daily gun average of 159 rounds.[7] A typical field regiment was 2/7th Australian which fired 65,594 rounds and lost five 25-pounders, three to enemy bombing and two through prematures.[8] Not for nothing did Rommel note that the British artillery 'once again demonstrated its well-known excellence'. A particular feature of that excellence, in his view, was 'its great mobility and tremendous speed of reaction to the needs of the assault troops'.[9]

Rommel was otherwise not so complimentary to the British command. He was especially critical of Montgomery for using his armoured formations separately instead of sending in 900 tanks on the northern flank to obtain a quick decision with minimum casualties and maximum effect. He noted that the usual 'rigid adherence to system' was still the principal feature of British tactics but that, on this occasion, this had favoured Eighth Army because of the tactical situation with no open desert flank to allow manoeuvre in the open.[10]

Victory had been decisive but it could have been overwhelming. Had Montgomery adopted a different plan an overwhelming decision might have been obtained. We have seen how General Sir Richard McCreery believed that LIGHTFOOT was flawed from the beginning, since it was impossible to achieve what Montgomery wanted in the first night due to the depth of enemy defences. McCreery's view was that Montgomery should have taken two bites at the break-in battle, with the second following either on the night of D+1, or D+2 if moving the guns proved necessary. He suggested that this would have been much simpler and less costly in infantry than Montgomery's 'master plan'.[11] Since Eighth Army was short of infantry it would also have made much more sense. That shortage of infantry also meant that the battle could have ended in stalemate; in some respects it was close-run.

Perhaps LIGHTFOOT's greatest flaw was the superimposing of one corps upon another. That X Corps had to advance over the same ground as XXX Corps, contending with the logistical tails of the latter's formations, proved a nightmare. Congestion caused horrendous problems, not least in getting the armour through the infantry on time. The additional twenty-four hours needed for 'stage management' before SUPERCHARGE was almost entirely due to congestion caused by this ponderous superimposition of corps commands. Looking at the delay in launching the pursuit one must also consider that this basic flaw in the plan also played a part. Even Ronald Lewin, an admirer of Montgomery, who averred that the latter's Second World War battles were 'always prefabricated down to the smallest detail', concedes that Eighth Army's commander 'notably failed' in his planning for the pursuit, which contrasted 'strangely with the far-sighted and meticulous preparations which led to the success of the twelve-day battle'.[12]

It would have been more sensible to have had two balanced corps, each including infantry and armoured divisions, as with XIII Corps, operating in discrete areas with the front divided into three corps' sectors of responsibility. The so-called *'corps de chasse'*, which did not exist when it was needed, might have been held in reserve, ready to move through the most appropriate gap to chase down, bring to battle and destroy the fleeing *Panzerarmee*. Montgomery's lack of understanding of the limitations of armour must have had much to do with his flawed plan. (That lack of understanding is all the more surprising when it is remembered that Montgomery's brother-in-law was that pioneer of armoured warfare, Major General Sir Percy Hobart.) Certainly Rommel had expected the full mass of British armour – 900 tanks – to pour through the northern gap in an 'expanding torrent' that would destroy *Panzerarmee* with minimum casualties to the attackers. This, after all, was a British concept – from the brain of Liddell Hart – but, instead, Rommel was faced with a trickle of British armour, against which his anti-tank screen proved formidable.

The untidiness that Montgomery's plan led to is illustrated by the uncertainty in Eighth Army about when, exactly, the battle was over and pursuit should have begun. War diary after war diary suggests that units and formations were unaware that the enemy had begun withdrawing until 5 November, although that of 69 Brigade notes that there 'was every indication of his hurried withdrawal'[13] on the 4th, a day on which 7 Motor Brigade's diary also comments that it was becoming 'obvious that the enemy was withdrawing N.W. to the line of the main road'.[14] Even allowing for the fact that most war diaries were written retrospectively, this is surprising and indicates that Montgomery's famous 'grip' might not have been as firm as he would have had history believe. Thus there is considerable evidence to support Barnett's contention that the failure to trap Rommel immediately after the battle was due 'to the chaotic state of the Eighth Army' rather than the rain that began late on 6 November. But that rain fell principally in the coastal area and a pursuit deep in the desert, parallel to the coast, as suggested by Gatehouse on 8 November, would have been unimpeded and could have pulled ahead of Rommel before swinging for the coast to block the Axis retreat.

Similarly, Barnett's argument that the pursuit was 'needlessly and incomprehensively slow and cautious' is validated.[15] (Some indication of the slowness of that pursuit can be gained by looking at the experience of 9th (Londonderry) Heavy Anti-Aircraft Regiment. In Palestine at the time of the battle, at the request of the Royal Navy the regiment was ordered to follow Eighth Army to lead the defence of Tripoli when that port fell. That order was received on 25 November and the regiment began its move on the 27th, reaching Tobruk by 8 December. In early January 1943 it came under command of 51st (Highland) Division and remained with it for the advance on Tripoli, putting it in the van of Eighth Army. Regimental reconnaissance parties of the entered Tripoli early on 23 January and later watched the 'first' elements of Eighth Army enter the city.) One is led to wonder at what a Rommel or a Patton at the head of Eighth Army would have done. What, indeed, would Auchinleck have done? Or the first British victor in the desert, Richard O'Connor? Any of them would have produced a much clearer victory than did Montgomery, and would have harvested the full fruits of victory in the pursuit.

However, the greatest criticism levelled about the battle is that it was unnecessary, that Allied landings at the other end of the Mediterranean made it redundant. This criticism, made by Barnett in his book *The Desert Generals*, deserves to be considered. He argues that the TORCH landings made Montgomery's battle at El Alamein redundant and 'therefore, in my view, [it must] go down in history as an unnecessary battle'.[16] Quoting Rommel's statement that the landings in French north-west Africa spelt the end of the German-Italian army in Africa, Barnett averred that TORCH would have forced Rommel to withdraw from the El Alamein line: 'it is certain that, even if Montgomery had not fought his battle, Rommel would have been out of Egypt within a month and in Tunisia within three'.[17] How this can be *certain* is not explained. Rommel was in Tunisia by the end of January 1943, his last units crossing the frontier from Libya on 12 February, a little over Barnett's three months. Barnett moves on to suggest that history's ultimate verdict on Alamein 'may well be to record it as a political victory'.[18]

However, following the Clausewitzian principle that war is a continuation of politics by other means, all battles are political: Alamein was no exception. In describing Alamein as a 'political' battle, Barnett was expressing his view that there was a political imperative for a British victory *before* the arrival of Allied forces at the other end of the Mediterranean; that defeat of *Panzerarmee* at Alamein after TORCH would have been attributed to those landings, at least in part. Such an argument ignores the fact that the Operation TORCH forces were weak and failed to defeat quickly the Axis in Tunisia, in the face of German – or rather Hitler's – determination not to give up ground; this led to massive reinforcement of that theatre. Had Rommel been able to take *Panzerarmee* back to Tunisia in strength comparable to that deployed before LIGHTFOOT, an Allied victory might have been long delayed and could not have been guaranteed. This is the essential weakness of Barnett's argument.

In his book *The Montgomery Legend* R.W. Thompson further develops this argument, stating that there was no need to fight the battle at all. In contrast, Carver expressed his opinion in the foreword to the third edition of his book *El Alamein* that such was not the view that Churchill and the Chiefs of Staff took. They still pressed for a major victory over Rommel before the Operation Torch landings, primarily to influence Spain not to intervene and to divert Axis effort and attention from them, but also to show both the Americans and the Russians that Britain could gain a victory on her own.[19]

Carver, therefore, accepted the political expedient inherent in the battle but points out the moral as well as the military-political imperative in British minds for fighting the battle. British national pride was at stake, as well as the self-esteem of Eighth Army: the need to lay the ghost of the Rommel legend exercised many minds, not least Churchill's. Arthur Bryant commented that it was this legend that caused Churchill to pace up and down in the embassy in Cairo crying, 'Rommel, Rommel, Rommel! What else matters but beating him!' Barnett is undoubtedly correct in stating that Montgomery was under the influence of the Rommel legend; for him the ghost was not laid.

El Alamein gave Churchill his much-needed victory. Not only did it have the immediate effects of removing the threat to Egypt, of destroying much of the strength and manpower of *Panzerarmee Afrika* and forcing the Axis to begin the long retreat to Tunisia but it must be remembered that it led to the final Axis surrender in Africa in May 1943 when some 200,000 Axis personnel were made prisoner. (Some writers estimate the figure of Axis prisoners taken as high as 275,000. If accurate, this would include Arab auxiliaries as well as regular German and Italian personnel.) When other Axis casualties between 23 October 1942 and May 1943 are considered the Alamein 'effect' on Axis manpower was equivalent to that of Stalingrad, and it has never been suggested that Stalingrad, from an Allied view, was a redundant battle. It also brought about the long-awaited relief of Malta: airfields around Martuba were in Eighth Army hands by mid-November, although unusable immediately due to rain; from there air cover could be provided for Malta convoys. The STONEAGE convoy put into Malta on 20 November, the day Benghazi fell, for the last time, to Eighth Army. El Alamein was not unnecessary.

Moreover, the controversial Italian campaign was a by-product of the presence of such large Allied forces in the Mediterranean and, in turn, tied down large numbers of German troops who might otherwise have been fighting the Soviets on the Eastern Front or waiting for the Allies in France. Had Rommel, the defender of Normandy, had such additional troops, the outcome of OVERLORD, close-run as it was, would have been very much in the balance. Nor could the additional Allied troops have been inserted easily into France to make a difference; the advantage of internal lines of communications lay with the Germans. Flawed plan and flawed victory though it may have been, El Alamein was decisive and was, as Rommel put it, the turning point of the war. (However, let us not forget that Rommel attributed the *real* victory in North Africa to Auchinleck's doughty stand at El Alamein in July.) Montgomery was the final victor of El Alamein, who never acknowledged his debt to those who went before and built up the machine he refined, and impressed his personality on Eighth Army to the extent that today few, other than military historians and veterans of subsequent campaigns, would be able to name later commanders of that army.

What should never be forgotten or debated is the courage of those who fought at Alamein; Eighth Army lost 2,350 dead, 8,950 wounded and 2,260 missing.[20] The tank crews of John Currie's 9 Armoured Brigade who suffered so much at Tel el Aqqaqir, that purgatory of British armour that bore such a beautiful name; the infantrymen, George Morrison and his comrades from so many lands across the globe, Commonwealth, Empire and home nations of the United Kingdom; the sappers who cleared the way for the tanks; the military policemen who carried out their traffic control duties; the drivers, doctors and chaplains who performed their duties in dreadful conditions, were all contributors to this signal victory. They fought their own fears and physical exhaustion and went forward to battle, believing that they were serving a just cause, 'the good and the right'. The 'butcher's bill' in Eighth Army was paid principally by soldiers from the United Kingdom, who represented 58 per cent of those casualties, followed by Australia with 22 per cent, New Zealand with 10 per cent, South Africa with 6 per cent, India with 1 per cent and other Allies with 3 per cent.[21]

Their courage was demonstrated in so many ways and marked by many awards, chief among them the Victoria Crosses seen in this narrative. Many other awards and decorations included DSOs to the commanding officers of 9th Lancers, Warwickshire Yeomanry and Royal Wiltshire Yeomanry, Lieutenant Colonels Gerald Grosvenor, Guy Jackson and Martin Valentine respectively, while Major General Allen Francis 'John' Harding of 7th Armoured Division received a second Bar to the DSO and Bars to the DSO were awarded to Brigadiers Philip 'Pip' Roberts, 22 Armoured Brigade, John Currie, 9 Armoured Brigade, James Bosvile, 7 Motor Brigade, and Cyril Weir, CRA, 2nd New Zealand Division.[22]

In the wake of El Alamein, the men of Eighth Army became a legend, claiming a place for themselves in British history equal to that of those who fought at Agincourt and Waterloo. Their immediate reward was the ringing of church bells at home on the orders of Winston Churchill, who had been asked to ring those bells by General Alexander. Their long-term reward was the knowledge that they had played a significant part in the final Allied victory that brought peace, however uncertain, to Europe and the world.

So they rang the bells for us and Alamein.

Notes

Chapter 1

1. Pitt, *The Crucible of War. Wavell's Command*, p.xv.
2. Neillands, *The Desert Rats*, p.37.
3. Verney, *The Desert Rats*, p.19.
4. Doherty, *A Noble Crusade*, p.4.
5. Barnett, *The Desert Generals*, p.23.
6. Doherty, op. cit., p.13.
7. Kesselring, *Memoirs*, pp.129–30.
8. Barnett, op. cit., p.69.
9. NA Kew, CAB44/97 p.23.
10. Playfair, *The Mediterranean and the Middle East*, Vol.III, p.286.
11. NA Kew, CAB44/98, op. cit.
12. Kesselring, op. cit., p.129.
13. Smyth, *The Victoria Cross*, pp.367–8.
14. Playfair, op. cit., p.295.
15. Verney, op. cit., p.116.
16. Hamilton, *Armoured Odyssey*, p.66.
17. Carver, *Out of Step*, p.119.
18. NA Kew, CAB44/98, op. cit.
19. Tedder, *With Prejudice*, p.304.
20. Schmidt, *With Rommel in the Desert*, p.162.
21. Author: interview with Sister Mary Richard OSF, October 1997.
22. von Mellenthin, *Panzer Battles*, p.125.
23. Ibid.
24. NA Kew, CAB44/98, p.340.
25. Lewin, *Rommel as Military Commander*, p.135.
26. Ibid.

Chapter 2

1. Playfair, Vol.iii, pp.335–7.
2. Ibid, pp.341–2.
3. Ibid, p.342.
4. Pitt, *The Crucible of War. Montgomery and Alamein*, p.28.
5. Playfair, op. cit., p.341.

6. H.G. Harris, IWM 84/44/1.
7. Ibid.
8. Playfair, op. cit., p.343.
9. Ibid.
10. Ibid.
11. Ibid., p.344.
12. Ibid., p.331n.
13. Liddell Hart, *The Rommel Papers*, p.248.
14. Kesselring, *Memoirs*, p.129.
15. Lewin, *Rommel as Military Commander*, p.136.
16. Ibid.
17. von Mellenthin, op. cit., p.127.
18. Playfair, op. cit., pp.345–6.
19. McKee, *Alamein*, p.73.
20. Playfair, op. cit., p.346.
21. von Mellenthin, op cit, p.127.
22. Ibid.
23. Playfair, op. cit., p.336.
24. Ibid., pp.335–6.
25. Ibid., p.335.
26. Ibid.
27. Ibid., p.336.
28. Ibid.
29. Waldau, quoted in ibid.
30. Parkinson, *The Auk*, pp.208–9.
31. Ibid., p.210.
32. NA Kew, CAB44/97, p.10.
33. Kippenberger, *Infantry Brigadier*, p.180.
34. Ibid.
35. Playfair, op. cit., pp.351–2.
36. Ibid., p.349.
37. *London Gazette*, 26 Sep 1945.
38. *London Gazette*, 24 Sep 1942.
39. von Mellenthin, op. cit., p.129.
40. Playfair, op. cit., p.352.
41. Ibid., p.353.
42. Ibid., p.354.
43. Ibid., p.355.
44. Ibid., pp.355–6.
45. *London Gazette*, 14 Sep 1942.
46. NA Kew, CAB44/97.
47. Liddell Hart, op. cit., p.257.

48. Ibid.
49. Warner, *Auchinleck. The Lonely Soldier*, p.157.
50. Liddell Hart, op. cit., p.262.

Chapter 3
1. Warner, op. cit., p.158.
2. Ibid.
3. De Guingand, *Generals at War*, p.66.
4. The appreciation is reproduced in full, except for appendices, in Greacen's book.
5. Hogg, *British and American Artillery of World War 2*, p.30.
6. Pitt, *The Crucible of War. Auchinleck's Command*, p.273.
7. NA Kew, CAB44/97, p.10.
8. Lucas, *Panzer Army Africa*, pp.18–20.
9. Horrocks, *A Full Life*, p.112.
10. Brooke, *War Diaries, 1939–1945*, p.287.
11. Ibid., p. 289.
12. Pitt, op. cit., p.335.
13. Ibid., p.339.
14. Warner, op. cit., p.166.
15. Montgomery, *Memoirs*, p.99.
16. Ibid., p.100.
17. Hamilton, *Montgomery. The Making of a General*, p.605.
18. Warner, op. cit., p.166.
19. Brian Montgomery, *A Field Marshal in the Family*, p.269.
20. NA Kew, WO169/4171, war diary 1942, 51 (H) Recce Regt.
21. NA Kew, CAB44/99.
22. Lucas-Phillips, *Alamein*, p.66n.
23. Montgomery, *Memoirs*, p.92.
24. NA Kew, WO201/2699, C-in-C Eighth Army's Despatch, 1 Aug 42–31 May 43.
25. Greacen, *Chink*, p.95.
26. Lucas-Phillips, op. cit., p.71.
27. Schmidt, op. cit., p.169.
28. Playfair, op. cit., p.383n.
29. von Mellenthin, op. cit., p.132.
30. Jack McIlmoyle, 24 HAA Battery to author, October 1986.
31. von Mellenthin, op. cit., p.132.
32. Playfair, op. cit., p.380.
33. von Mellenthin, op. cit., p.133.
34. Schmidt, op. cit., p.169, title of Chapter 32.
35. NA Kew, WO201, Defensive Planning in the Western Desert, 24 Aug-6 Nov '42.
36. Ibid.

37. NA Kew, WO201/2699, op. cit.
38. Lucas, *War in the Desert*, p.43.
39. Roberts, *From the Desert to the Baltic*, p.91.
40. Ibid., p.95.
41. Liddell Hart, op. cit., p.280.
42. Quoted in CAB44/99, p.135.
43. Montgomery, *Memoirs*, p.113.
44. NA Kew, CAB44/99.
45. Montgomery, op. cit., pp.112–13.
46. Liddell Hart, op. cit., p.262.

Chapter 4
 1. Playfair, *The Mediterranean and the Middle East*, Vol.iv, p.8.
 2. Ibid., p.8n.
 3. Ibid., p.10.
 4. NA Kew, CAB44/99.
 5. Montgomery, *Memoirs*, p.117.
 6. Ibid.
 7. Ibid., p.118.
 8. NA Kew, WO201/433, Op LIGHTFOOT, memorandum by army commander.
 9. Montgomery, op. cit., pp.119–20.
10. Ibid., p.120.
11. Pitt, *The Crucible of War. Montgomery and Alamein*, pp.71–2.
12. Carver, *El Alamein*, p.86.
13. Fraser, *And We Shall Shock Them*, pp.242–4.
14. Montgomery, op. cit., p.120.
15. Ibid., p.123.
16. Ibid., p.119.
17. This was *Infanterie greift an*, or *Infantry Attacks*.
18. Playfair, op. cit., p.29.
19. NA Kew, WO201/551, XIII Corps operations: reports, 1 Sep–31 Oct 42.
20. Ibid.
21. NA Kew, WO169/3942, war diary, Chief Engineer, HQ Eighth Army, 1942.
22. This description of the mine marshes is based upon Barrie Pitt's in *Montgomery and Alamein*, pp.63–7, Lucas-Phillips' in *Alamein*, pp. 90–102, and contemporary official documents, especially from the Royal Engineers, in NA Kew.
23. Lucas-Phillips, op. cit., p.95.
24. Pitt, op. cit., p.65.
25. Ibid.
26. NA Kew, WO169/3942, op. cit..
27. Ibid.

28. Pitt, op. cit., p.65.
29. This description is also based on those in Pitt and Lucas-Phillips, as well as contemporary documents.
30. NA Kew, CAB44/101.
31. Pitt, op. cit., p.67.
32. NA Kew, WO169/3942, op. cit.
33. NA Kew, WO169/3940, war diary, BRA HQ Eighth Army, 1942.
34. NA Kew, WO169/3993 & 4010, war diaries, HQ RA X Corps and XIII Corps, 1942.
35. Doherty, *Irish Volunteers in the Second World War*, pp.119–20.
36. NA Kew, XIII Corps RA Inst. No.26, in WO169/4010, war diary HQ RA XIII Corps, 1942.
37. Ibid.
38. Lucas-Phillips, op. cit., p.85.
39. Fraser, op. cit., p.246.
40. NA Kew, CAB44/103, p.94.
41. NA Kew, WO201/555, HQ RA Eighth Army, 'Operations Report El Alamein'.
42. Cruickshank, *Deception in World War II*, pp. 26–7.
43. Strawson, *Alamein. Desert Victory*, p.91.
44. Doherty, op. cit., pp.199–200.
45. Playfair, op. cit., p.15n.
46. Ibid., p.15.
47. Lucas-Phillips, op. cit., p.41.
48. NA Kew, WO201/538, Eighth Army: lessons from operations, 1 Sep 41–31 Aug 42.
49. NA Kew, WO201/449, Lessons on operations, 1 Oct 42–30 Nov 43.
50. Doherty, *Irish Men and Women in the Second World War*, p.169.
51. NA Kew, WO201/449, op. cit.
52. Ibid.
53. Ibid.
54. Ibid.
55. IWM 85/34/1, A.Vincent, Middlesex Yeomanry.
56. NA Kew, CAB44/104, p.462.
57. NA Kew, WO201/603 'Points for conference on lessons from recent ops: Sep 42–May 43'.
58. NA Kew, WO201/2699, Eighth Army CinC's Despatch, 1 Aug 42–31 May 43.
59. NA Kew, WO201/551 BGS XIII Corps, Ops BERTRAM and MELTINGPOT.
60. Pitt, op. cit., p.75.
61. Cruickshank, op. cit., p.27.
62. Ibid., p.30.
63. Ibid., pp.26–7.
64. Pitt, op. cit., p.76.

65. Ibid., p.75.
66. Cruickshank, op. cit., pp.26–7, p. 30.
67. Horrocks, *A Full Life*, p.125.
68. NA Kew, WO201/551 BGS XIII Corps, Ops BERTRAM and MELTINGPOT, op. cit.
69. Ibid.
70. NA Kew, CAB44/99, passim.

Chapter 5
1. Pitt, op. cit., p.61.
2. Salmond, *The History of the 51st Highland Division*, p.23.
3. Ibid., p.31.
4. Ibid., p.32n.
5. Pitt, op. cit., p.62.
6. IWM DS/MISC/63, Lt George F. Morrison.
7. Montgomery, op. cit., p.136.
8. Pitt, op. cit., p.70.
9. IWM P470, Lt Col D.L.A. Gibbs DSO.
10. Pitt, op. cit., p.72.
11. NA Kew, CAB44/101, p.8.
12. NA Kew, CAB44/97, p.11.
13. NA Kew, WO201/2605, AFV situation, Jul 42–Jul 43.
14. NA Kew, WO201/573: X Corps training instruction.
15. NA Kew, WO169/4478, war diary 1942, 1 RB.
16. NA Kew, WO169/4251, war diary 1942, 22 Armd Bde.
17. NA Kew, WO169/4054, war diary 1942, 1st Armd Div.
18. NA Kew, WO169/4210, war diary 1942, 2 Armd Bde.
19. Ibid.
20. Merewood, *To War with The Bays*, p.66.
21. NA Kew, WO169/5068, war diary 1942, 4 R. Sussex.
22. NA Kew, WO169/4230, war diary 1942, 8 Armd Bde.
23. NA Kew, WO169/4985, war diary 1942, 7 A&S Hldrs.
24. NA Kew, WO169/5060, war diary 1942, 5 Seaforth (Account: '5th Bn The Seaforth Highlanders in the Battle of El Alamein').
25. Ibid.
26. Ibid.
27. Ibid.
28. NA Kew, WO201/2495: Report on Operations; 9th Aus Div.
29. NA Kew, WO201/2813: 9th Aus Div. Report on LIGHTFOOT.
30. Horrocks, op. cit., pp.134–5.
31. Lucas-Phillips, op. cit., p.101.
32. Doherty, *Only the Enemy in Front*, p.23.

33. NA Kew, WO169/4138, war diary 1942, 44 Recce Regt.
34. NA Kew, WO169/3942 war diary, CE, Eighth Army, op. cit.
35. Pitt, op. cit., p.82.
36. NA Kew, WO169/3942, op. cit.
37. Ibid.
38. NA Kew, WO169/5068, war diary 1942, HQ 133 Bde.
39. NA Kew, WO201/2495, Report on Operations, 9th Aus Div, op. cit.
40. Ibid.
41. NA Kew, WO169/4230, war diary 1942, 8 Armd Bde.
42. NA Kew, WO169/4210, war diary 1942, 2 Armd Bde.
43. IWM, Morrison, op. cit.
44. Mr Roy Stewart: Information to author.
45. Pitt, op. cit., p.82.
46. NA Kew, WO201/605, Battle of Egypt, narrative by Lt Col Oswald.
47. Lucas-Phillips, op. cit., p.113.
48. Playfair, op. cit., p.32.
49. NA Kew, WO201/555, op. cit.
50. NA Kew, WO201/2494, Tactical reconnaissance reports, Egypt and Western Desert.
51. Ibid.
52. Ibid.
53. Ibid.
54. NA Kew, WO201/553, Libya, weekly reviews of military situation, 1 Jan-30 Jun 1942.
55. McKee, *Alamein*, p.67.
56. NA Kew, WO201/553, op. cit..
57. Playfair, op. cit., p.30; Pitt, op. cit., p.81.
58. Pitt, op. cit., p.89.
59. Hunt, *A Don at War*, pp.134–5.
60. NA Kew, WO106/1741, Bartholomew Committee Report.
61. NA Kew, WO169/4054, war diary, 1st Armd Div (G. Br.).
62. Strawson, op. cit., p.97.
63. Ibid., p.98.
64. Salmond, op. cit., p.30n.
65. NA Kew, WO 169/5060, war diary 1942, op. cit.

Chapter 6

1. Wingfield, Brigadier A.D.R., letter to his father, 19 Nov 42, in 'Memoirs 1930–1948', IWM: PP/MCR/353.
2. Playfair, op. cit., p.36.
3. NA Kew, WO169/4295, war diary 1942, 153 Bde.
4. Mead, *Gunners at War*, p.55.

5. Playfair, op. cit., p.37.
6. Mead, op. cit., p.55.
7. NA Kew, WO201/605, op. cit..
8. Ibid.
9. Ibid.
10. NA Kew, CAB44/101, p.43.
11. Salmond, op. cit., p.39.
12. Lucas-Phillips, op. cit., p.160.
13. Kippenberger, op. cit., p.233.
14. Ibid.
15. NA Kew, WO201/425, Battle for Egypt: Report.
16. Ibid.
17. Pitt, op. cit., p.106.
18. NA Kew, CAB44/101, p.10.
19. Army Order (AO) 167 of 1946.

Chapter 7
1. Quoted in Hunt, *Hard Fighting*, p.181.
2. Ibid.
3. Lucas-Phillips, op. cit., p.189.
4. Hunt, op. cit., pp.181–2.
5. Carver, *Alamein*, pp.110–11.
6. NA Kew, CAB44/101.
7. Horrocks, op. cit., p.131.
8. Ibid., p.137.
9. Neillands, op. cit., p.152.
10. Montgomery, op. cit., p.129.
11. Ibid.
12. NA Kew, CAB44/102.
13. Playfair, op. cit., p. 44.
14. Fraser, op. cit., pp.243–4.
15. Doherty, *Irish Volunteers in the Second World War*, pp.240–1.
16. Strawson, op. cit., p.172.

Chapter 8
1. Playfair, op. cit., pp.43–4.
2. Ibid., p. 43.
3. NA Kew, CAB44/102, p.299.
4. Ibid., p.301.
5. NA Kew, WO169/4210, war diary 1942, 2 Armd Bde.
6. Ibid.
7. NA Kew, WO201/2495, op. cit.

8. Ibid.
9. Montgomery, op. cit., p.129.
10. Freyberg, *Freyberg,* p.401.
11. Ibid.
12. Montgomery, op. cit., p.130.
13. NA Kew, WO201/2495, op. cit..
14. Majdalany, *Alamein,* p.95.
15. Freyberg, op. cit., p.402.
16. Montgomery, op. cit., p.131.
17. Liddell Hart, op. cit., pp.305–6.

Chapter 9
1. Pitt, op. cit., p.145.
2. NA Kew, WO201/2495, op. cit.
3. Ibid.
4. Ibid.
5. Playfair, op. cit., p.49.
6. *London Gazette,* 28 Jan 43.
7. Lummis Files, Military Historical Society.
8. Ibid.
9. Ibid.
10. *London Gazette,* 28 Jan 43.
11. IWM 99/16/1, Major A.F. Flatow TD.
12. Ross, *All Valiant Dust,* p.68.
13. Lucas-Phillips, op. cit., p.214.
14. NA Kew, CAB44/102, p.486.
15. IWM Gibbs, op. cit..
16. Ibid.
17. Montgomery, op. cit., p.131.
18. NA Kew, CAB44/102, p.533.
19. Liddell Hart, op. cit., p.302.
20. Ibid., p.297.
21. Playfair, op. cit., p.51n.
22. Liddell Hart, op. cit., p.302.
23. Ibid., pp.307–8.
24. Ibid., pp.309–10.
25. Ibid., p.309.
26. Ibid., p.310.
27. Pitt, op. cit., p.151.
28. Playfair, op. cit., p.51n.

Chapter 10
1. NA Kew, WO169/3990, war diary 1942, HQ X Corps.
2. Lucas-Phillips, op. cit., p.267; Pitt, op. cit., p.153.
3. Frederick, *Lineage Book of British Land Forces*, p.922.
4. Lucas-Phillips, op. cit., p.270.
5. Ibid., p.269.
6. NA Kew, WO201/547 Account of the action by 2RB at 'SNIPE' on 26/27 Oct 42.
7. Lucas-Phillips, op. cit., p.273.
8. Perrett, *Last Stand*, p.119.
9. NA Kew, WO201/547, op. cit.
10. Perrett, op. cit., p.119.
11. Ibid., pp.119–21.
12. Lucas-Phillips, op. cit., p.277.
13. NA Kew, WO201/547, op. cit.
14. Pitt, op. cit., p.156.
15. Ibid.; NA Kew, WO201/547, op. cit.; Perrett, op. cit., p.122.
16. Perrett, op. cit., p.122.
17. NA Kew, WO201/547, op. cit.
18. Pitt, op. cit., p.160; NA Kew, WO201/547, op. cit.
19. Lucas-Phillips, op. cit., pp.290–1.
20. Ibid., p.289.
21. NA Kew, WO201/547, op. cit.
22. Ibid.
23. Ibid.
24. Lucas-Phillips, op. cit., p.296.
25. *London Gazette*, 20 Nov 42.
26. Perrett, op. cit., p.125.
27. www.cwgc,org/find-war-dead CWGC website.
28. Lucas-Phillips, op. cit., p.297.
29. Doherty, *Irish Men and Women in the Second World War*, p.233.
30. NA Kew, WO201/547, op. cit.
31. Pitt, op. cit., p.165; NA Kew, WO169/5068, war diary 1942, 4 R. Sussex.
32. NA Kew, CAB44/104, p.175.
33. Carver, op. cit., p.137.
34. NA Kew, WO169/4210, war diary 1942, 2 Armd Bde.
35. Willett, *Armoured Horseman*, p.78.
36. NA Kew, WO169/4210, op. cit.
37. Willett, op. cit., p.80.
38. Ibid.
39. NA Kew, WO169/4210, op. cit.
40. Ibid.

41. Montgomery, op. cit., p.131.
42. Pitt, op. cit., pp.151–2.
43. NA Kew, WO201/2495, Report by 9 Aus Div, operations El Alamein, op. cit.
44. Ibid.
45. Ibid.
46. Ibid.
47. Ibid.
48. Ibid.
49. Liddell Hart, op. cit., p.312.
50. Brooke, op. cit., pp.335–6.
51. Montgomery, op. cit., p.133.

Chapter 11
 1. Montgomery, op. cit., p.131.
 2. Alexander, *Memoirs*, p.28.
 3. Hamilton, op. cit., p.828.
 4. Montgomery, op. cit., p.132.
 5. Carver, op. cit., pp.141–2; see also Mead, *The Last Great Cavalryman*, p.108.
 6. NA Kew, CAB44/104, p.335.
 7. Ibid., p.279.
 8. NA Kew, WO201/2495, op. cit.
 9. Lucas-Phillips, op. cit., p.311.
10. *London Gazette*, 28 Jan 43.
11. Pitt, op. cit., pp.176–7.
12. NA Kew, WO201/2495, op. cit.
13. NA Kew, CAB44/104, op. cit., p.357.
14. Ibid., p.473.
15. NA Kew, WO201/2495, op. cit.
16. Playfair, op. cit., p.55n.
17. Quoted in Pitt, op. cit., p.184.
18. NA Kew, CAB44/104, p.532.
19. NA Kew, WO201/2495, op. cit.
20. Liddell Hart, op. cit., p.316.
21. Ibid.
22. NA Kew, CAB44/104, p.354.
23. Playfair, op. cit., p.59.
24. NA Kew, CAB44/104, p.367.
25. Ibid., pp.284–5.
26. Ibid., p.356.
27. Lucas-Phillips, op. cit., p.331.
28. NA Kew, CAB44/104, p.461.
29. Willett, op. cit., p.82.

30. NA Kew, CAB44/104, pp.387–8.
31. Lucas-Phillips, op. cit., p.337.

Chapter 12

 1. Montgomery, op. cit., p.136.
 2. Ibid., p.137.
 3. Lucas-Phillips, op. cit., p.343.
 4. Doherty, *Irish Men and Women in the Second World War*, p.233.
 5. Liddell-Hart, op. cit., p.317.
 6. Quoted in Montgomery, op. cit., p.134.
 7. Schmidt, op. cit., p.187.
 8. Quoted in Pitt, op. cit., p.198.
 9. Freyberg, op. cit., p.406.
10. Lucas-Phillips, op. cit., p.360.
11. Pitt, op. cit., p.200.
12. NA Kew, WO169/4210, war diary 1942, HQ 2 Armd Bde.
13. Ibid.
14. Willett, op. cit., p.83.
15. NA Kew, CAB44/105, p.699.
16. Liddell-Hart, op. cit., p.317.
17. Ibid., p.318.
18. Schmidt, op. cit., p.177.
19. Liddell-Hart, op. cit., p.319.
20. Ibid., p.320.
21. Carver, op. cit., p.162.
22. Ibid., p.164.
23. Ibid., p.166.
24. Horrocks, op. cit., p.141.
25. Carver, op. cit., p.167.

Chapter 13

 1. Montgomery, op. cit., p.147.
 2. Barnett, *The Desert Generals*, p.291.
 3. Montgomery, op. cit., p.144.
 4. Ibid.
 5. NA Kew, CAB44/106, p.975.
 6. Ibid.
 7. NA Kew, WO201/555, Eighth Army report on Battle of El Alamein.
 8. NA Kew, CAB44/106, p.975.
 9. Liddell Hart, op. cit., p.330.
10. Ibid., p.329.
11. Strawson, op. cit., p.172.

12. Lewin, *Montgomery as Military Commander*, p.94.
13. NA Kew, WO169/4271, war diary 69 Bde.
14. NA Kew, WO169/4226, war diary 7 Motor Bde.
15. Barnett, op. cit., p.300.
16. Ibid., p.272.
17. Ibid.
18. Ibid.
19. Carver, op. cit., p.11.
20. NA Kew, WO201/580, Eighth Army Ops 23 Oct 42–23 Jan 43: Brief Summary.
21. Ibid.
22. *London Gazette*, 26 Jan 43.

Bibliography

Alanbrooke, Field Marshal Lord, *War Diaries 1939–1945*, ed. by Alex Danchev and Daniel Todman (Weidenfeld & Nicolson, London, 2001)

Barnett, Correlli, *The Desert Generals* (George Allen and Unwin, London, 1960)

——, *The Battle of El Alamein: Decision in the Desert* (Macmillan, London, 1964)

Bates, Peter, *Dance of War – The Story of the Battle of Egypt* (Leo Cooper, Pen & Sword Books, London, 1992)

Blaxland, Gregory, *The Plain Cook and the Great Showman – The First and Eighth Armies in North Africa* (William Kimber, London, 1977)

Borthwick, Capt. James, *The 51st Highland Division in Africa and Sicily* (51st Highland Division Trust, Glasgow, 1943)

Brookes, Stephen (ed.), *Montgomery and the Eighth Army* (Army Records Society, London, 1991)

Bryant, Arthur, *The Turn of the Tide* (Collins, London, 1977)

Carell, Paul, *The Foxes of the Desert. The story of the Afrika Korps* (Macdonald, London, 1960)

Carver, Michael, *El Alamein* (Batsford, London, 1962)

——, *The Apostles of Mobility* (Weidenfeld & Nicolson, London, 1979)

Churchill, Sir Winston, *The Second World War* (Collins, London, 1951)

Clarke, Rupert, *With Alex at War from the Irrawaddy to the Po 1941–1945* (Pen & Sword Books, Barnsley, 2000)

Connell, John, *Auchinleck – A Critical Biography* (Cassell, London, 1959)

Cooper, Matthew, *The German Army 1933–1945 Its Political and Military Failure* (Macdonald and Jane's, London, 1978)

Crew, F.A.E., FRS, *The Army Medical Services, Campaigns Vol II* (HMSO, London, 1957)

Cruickshank, Charles, *Deception in World War II* (Oxford Paperbacks, Oxford, 1979)

De Butts, Freddie, *Now the Dust has Settled. Memories of War and Peace 1939–1994* (Tabb House, Padstow, 1995)

De Guingand, Francis, *Operation Victory* (Hodder & Stoughton, London, 1947)

——, *Generals at War* (Hodder & Stoughton, London, 1964)

——, *From Brass Hat to Bowler Hat* (Hamish Hamilton, London, 1979)

Delaforce, Patrick, *Monty's Marauders. Black Rat and Red Fox: 4th and 8th Independent Armoured Brigades in WWII* (Tom Donovan, Brighton, 1997)

——, *Taming the Panzers. Monty's Tank Battalions, 3 RTR at War* (Sutton, Stroud, 2000)

Doherty, Richard, *Only the Enemy in Front: The Recce Corps at War 1940–1946* (Tom Donovan Publishing, London, 1994)

——, *A Noble Crusade: A history of the Eighth Army 1941–45* (Spellmount Publishers, Staplehurst, 1999)

——, *Irish Men and Women in the Second World War* (Four Courts Press, Dublin, 1999)

——, *Irish Volunteers in the Second World War* (Four Courts Press, Dublin, 2002)

——, *Ireland's Generals in the Second World War* (Four Courts Press, Dublin, 2004)

——, *Ubique: The Royal Artillery in the Second World War* (The History Press, Stroud, 2008)

——, *In the Ranks of Death: The Irish in the Second World War* (Pen & Sword, Barnsley, 2010)

——, *British Armoured Divisions and their Commanders*, 1939–1945 (Pen & Sword, Barnsley, 2013)

Douglas, Keith, *Alamein to Zem Zem* (Faber & Faber, London, 1966)

Duncan, W.E., H.F. Ellis, R.L. Banks & Norman Scarfe (Eds), *The Royal Artillery Commemoration Book 1939–1945* (G. Bell & Sons, London, 1950)

Farrar-Hockley, Anthony, *The War in the Desert* (Faber and Faber, London, 1969)

Forty, George, *Afrika Korps at War* (Arms & Armour, London, 1978)

——, *The Armies of Rommel* (Weidenfeld and Nicolson, London, 1997)

Fraser, David, *Alanbrooke* (HarperCollins, London, 1982)

——, *And We Shall Shock Them: The British Army in the Second World War* (Hodder & Stoughton, London, 1983)

——, *Knight's Cross: A Life of Field Marshal Erwin Rommel* (HarperCollins, London, 1993)

Frederick, J.B.M., *Lineage Book of British Land Forces 1660–1978* (Microform Academic Publishers, Wakefield, 1984)

Greacen, Lavinia, *Chink: A Biography* (Macmillan, London, 1989)

Greene, Jack & Massignani, Alessandro, *Rommel's North Africa Campaign September 1940–November 1942* (Combined Publishing, Conshohocken, PA, 1994)

Greenwood, Alexander, *Field Marshal Auchinleck* (Pentland Press, Brockerscliffe, 1991)

Hamilton, Nigel, *Monty: The Making of a General 1887–1942* (Hamish Hamilton, London, 1981)

——, *Monty: Master of the Battlefield* (Hamish Hamilton, London, 1983)

——, *The Full Monty: Montgomery of Alamein* (Hamish Hamilton, London, 2001)

Hinsley, F. H., *British Intelligence in the Second World War* (HMSO, London, 1993)

Holmes, Richard, *Battlefields of the Second World War* (BBC Books, London, 2001)

Horrocks, Brian, *A Full Life* (Collins, London, 1960)

Howard, Michael, *British Intelligence in the Second World War, Vol V: Strategic Deception* (HMSO, London, 1990)

Howarth, P., *My God, Soldiers: From Alamein to Vienna* (Hutchinson, London, 1989)

Hunt, David, *A Don at War* (Routledge, London, 1966)

Hunt, Jonathan, *Hard Fighting: A History of the Sherwood Rangers Yeomanry, 1900–1946* (Pen & Sword, Barnsley, 2016)

Ireland, B., *The War in the Mediterranean 1940–1943* (Seaforth Publishing, London, 1993)

Jackson, W.G.F., *The North African Campaign 1940–1943* (Batsford, London, 1971)

Jarymowycz, Roman Johann, *Tank Tactics from Normandy to Lorraine* (Boulder, CO., & London, 2001)

Johnstone, Tom & Hagerty, James, *The Cross on the Sword*, (Geoffrey Chapman, London, 1996)

Joslen, Lt Col H.F., *Orders of Battle Second World War* (HMSO, London, 1960)

Keegan, John (ed.), *Churchill's Generals* (Weidenfeld & Nicolson, London, 1991)

——, *The Second World War* (Weidenfeld & Nicolson, London, 1989)

Kesselring, Field Marshal Albert, *Memoirs* (William Kimber, London, 1953; Greenhill Books/Lionel Leventhal Ltd, London, 2007)

Kippenberger, Maj Gen Sir Howard, KBE CB DSO, *Infantry Brigadier* (Oxford University Press, London, 1949)

Latimer, Jon, *Deception in War* (John Murray, London, 2001)

Lewin, Ronald, *Rommel as Military Commander* (Batsford, London, 1968)

——, *Montgomery as Military Commander* (Batsford, London, 1971)

Liddell Hart, Basil H. (ed.), *The Rommel Papers* (London, 1953)

Lucas, James, *Panzer Army Africa* (Arms & Armour, London, 1977)

——, *War in the Desert: Eighth Army at El Alamein* (Arms & Armour, London, 1982)

——, *Storming Eagles: German Airborne Forces in World War Two* (Arms & Armour, London, 1988)

Lucas Phillips, C.E., *Alamein* (Heinemann, London, 1962)

Macksey, Kenneth, *Rommel: Battles and Campaigns* (Arms & Armour, London, 1979)

——, *Military Errors of World War Two*, (Arms & Armour, London, 1987)

Majdalany, Fred, *The Battle of El Alamein: Fortress in the Sand* (Weidenfeld and Nicolson, London, 1965)

Marrinan, Patrick, *Churchill and the Irish Marshals* (Pretani Press, Belfast, 1986)

McKee, Alexander, *El Alamein: Ultra and the Three Battles* (Souvenir Press, London, 1991)

Mead, Peter, *Gunners at War* (Ian Allan, Shepperton, 1982)

Mead, Richard, *The Last Great Cavalryman: The Life of General Sir Richard McCreery, Commander Eighth Army* (Pen & Sword, Barnsley, 2012)

Mellenthin, Maj Gen F.W. von, *Panzer Battles* (Cassell, London, 1955)

Merewood, Jack, *To War with The Bays* (Queen's Dragoon Guards, Cardiff, 1996)

Montgomery, Viscount of Alamein, *El Alamein to the River Sangro* (Hutchinson, London, 1948)

——, *Memoirs* (Collins, London, 1958)

Montgomery, Brian, *A Field Marshal in the Family* (Cassell, London, 1973; Pen & Sword, Barnsley, 2010)

Moorehead, Alan, *The Desert War: the North African Campaign 1940–1943* (Hamish Hamilton, London, 1965)

Neillands, Robin, *The Desert Rats: 7th Armoured Division 1940–1945* (Weidenfeld and Nicolson, London, 1991)

Nicolson, Nigel, *Alex* (Weidenfeld and Nicolson, London, 1973)

North, John (ed.), *The Memoirs of Field Marshal the Earl Alexander of Tunis 1940–1945* (Cassell, London, 1962)

O'Brien, G., & Roebuck, P. (eds), *Nine Ulster Lives*, (Ulster Historical Foundation, Belfast, 1992)

Parkinson, C. Northcote, *Always a Fusilier: The War History of the Royal Fusiliers (City of London Regiment) 1939–1945* (Sampson Low, London, 1949)

Parkinson, Roger, *The War in the Desert* (Hart-Davis, London, 1976)

——, *The Auk: Auchinleck, Victor at El Alamein* (Hart-Davis, London, 1977)

Perrett, Bryan, *Last Stand! Famous Battles Against the Odds* (Arms & Armour, London, 1991)

——, *Iron Fist. Classic Armoured Warfare Case Studies* (Weidenfeld Military, London, 1995)

Pitt, Barrie (ed), *The Military History of World War Two* (Hamlyn, London, 1986)

——, *The Crucible of War. Vol. I, Wavell's Command* (Cassell, London, 1980)

——, *The Crucible of War. Vol. II, Auchinleck's Command* (Cassell, London, 1980)

——, *The Crucible of War. Vol. III, Montgomery and Alamein* (Cassell, London, 1982)

Playfair, I.S.O., et al., *The Mediterranean and the Middle East, Vol III: British fortunes reach their lowest ebb* (HMSO, London, 1960)

——, *The Mediterranean and the Middle East, Vol IV: The destruction of the Axis forces in Africa* (HMSO, London, 1966)

Powell, Geoffrey, *The History of the Green Howards: Three Hundred Years of Service* (Weidenfeld Military, London, 1992)

Roberts, G.P.B., *From the Desert to the Baltic* (William Kimber, London, 1995)

Rommel, Erwin, *The Rommel Papers* Ed. by B.H. Liddell Hart (Collins, London, 1953)

Ross, Peter, *All Valiant Dust: An Irishman Abroad* (The Lilliput Press, Dublin, 1992)

Routledge, N.W., *History of the Royal Regiment of Artillery: Anti-Aircraft Artillery, 1914–1955* (Brassey's, London, 1994)

Salmond, J.B., *The History of the 51st Highland Division* (Blackwood, London, 1953)

Schmidt, Heinz Werner, *With Rommel in the Desert* (Collins, London, 1951)

Stevens, G.R., *Fourth Indian Division* (McLaren & Son, Toronto, 1948)

Stewart, Adrian, *Eighth Army's Greatest Victories: Alam Halfa to Tunis, 1942–1943* (Leo Cooper, Barnsley, 1999)

——, *The Early Battles of Eighth Army: 'CRUSADER' to the Alamein Line 1941–1942* (Leo Cooper, Barnsley, 2002)

Strawson, John, *El Alamein: Desert Victory* (Weidenfeld and Nicolson, London, 1981)

Strawson, John, et al., *Irish Hussar* (The Queen's Royal Irish Hussars Association, London, 1986)

Tedder, Lord, *With Prejudice: The War Memoirs of Marshal of The Royal Air Force Lord Tedder* (Cassell, London, 1966)

Thompson, R.W., *The Montgomery Legend* (Allen & Unwin, London, 1967)

Tuker, Sir Francis, KCIE CB DSO OBE, *The Pattern of War* (Cassell, London, 1948)

——, *Approach to Battle* (Cassell, London, 1963)

Verney, Maj Gen G.L., *The Desert Rats – The 7th Armoured Division in World War II* (Hutchinson, London, 1954)

Warner, Philip, *Alamein* (William Kimber, London, 1979)

——, *Auchinleck: The Lonely Soldier* (Buchan & Enright, London, 1981)

Willett, Peter, *Armoured Horseman: With The Bays and Eighth Army in North Africa and Italy* (Pen & Sword, Barnsley, 2015)

Young, Desmond, *Rommel* (Collins, London, 1950)

Newspapers
London Gazette

Unpublished
Department of Documents, Imperial War Museum

Bassam, F.J., 51st (Highland) Reconnaissance Regt.	94/41/1
Briggs, Maj Gen Raymond, CB OBE, GOC 1st Armoured Division.	99/1/2
Challoner, L., 2nd Regiment, Royal Horse Artillery.	P479
Collins, A.C. (Mick), R. Wiltshire Yeomanry.	92/1/1
Crimp, R.L., 2nd Rifle Brigade (Prince Consort's Own).	96/50/1
Drew, J.E., 18th Durham Light Infantry.	Misc. 93 (1410)
Flatow, Maj A.F., TD, 45th (Leeds Rifles) Bn Royal Tank Regiment.	99/16/1
Gibbs, Lt Col D.L.A., DSO, 1/6th Queen's Royal Regiment.	P470
Green, J.K., Corps of Military Police.	98/35/1
Harris, A.S., 299 Battery, 149th (Lancashire Yeomanry) Anti-Tank Regiment RA.	96/35/1
Harris, H.G., 75th Heavy Anti-Aircraft Regiment RA	84/44/1

Holworthy, Maj Gen A.W.W., DSO MC, 7 Brigade, 4th (Indian) Division.	91/40/2
Main, Lt D.A., MC DCM EM, 7th Rifle Brigade (Prince Consort's Own) (1st London Rifle Brigade)	87/35/1
McClure, Lt Col W.D., MC, 64th Medium Regiment RA.	94/47/1
Morrison, Lt G.F., 7th Black Watch (Royal Highland Regiment).	DS/MISC/63
O'Brien, Sir Richard, DSO MC, 14th Sherwood Foresters.	98/3/1
Parker, Lt Col M.E., 65th (Norfolk Yeomanry) Anti-Tank Regiment RA.	88/4/1
Vincent, A., Middlesex Yeomanry/10th Armoured Division Signals.	85/34/1
White, H.L., 2nd Derbyshire Yeomanry.	01/4/1
Wingfield, Brigadier A.D.R., DSO MC, 10th R. Hussars.	PP/MCR/353

National Army Museum, Chelsea
Lummis Files on Victoria Cross winners: Adam Wakenshaw, 9th Bn The Durham Light Infantry; Charles Hazlitt Upham, 20th (The Canterbury Regiment) Bn 2nd NZEF; Keith Elliott, 22nd Bn 2nd NZEF; Arthur Stanley Gurney, 2/48th Bn (South Australia) AIF; Percival Eric Gratwick, 2/48th Bn (South Australia) AIF; William Henry Kibby, 2/48th Bn (South Australia) AIF; Victor Buller Turner 2nd Bn The Rifle Brigade

National Archives, Kew
Many files relating to Eighth Army and Middle East Forces during 1942 were consulted during research for this book, among which were included the following.

AIR27/1245	Operational Record Book No.208 Sqn RAF
CAB44/100–106	Official History series
WO169/3911	Tactical HQ Eighth Army logs, Oct-Dec 1942
WO169/3918	Main HQ Eighth Army messages, Oct 1942
WO169/3919	Main HQ Eighth Army messages Nov 1942
WO169/3940	War Diary, BRA Eighth Army 1942
WO169/3942	War Diary, CE Eighth Army 1942
WO169/3990	War Diary, HQ X Corps, Oct-Dec 1942
WO169/3993	War Diary, HQ RA X Corps
WO169/4010	War Diary, HQ RA XIII Corps 1942
WO169/4039	War Diary, XXX Corps RA – Counter Battery Sect
WO169/4054	War Diary, HQ 1st Armoured Division, Aug-Dec 1942
WO169/4056	War Diary, 1st Armoured Division RA
WO169/4057	War Diary, 1st Armoured Division RE
WO169/4089	War Diary, 7th Armoured Division RA

WO169/4091	War Diary, 7th Armoured Division CRE
WO169/4104	War Diary, 8th Armoured Division RA
WO169/4105	War Diary, 8th Armoured Division RE
WO169/4117	War Diary, HQ 10th Armoured Division, Aug-Dec 1942
WO169/4118	War Diary, 10th Armoured Division CRA
WO169/4119	War Diary, 10th Armoured Division CRE
WO169/4133	War Diary, HQ 44th Division
WO169/4145	War Diary, HQ 50th Division
WO169/4164	War Diary, HQ 51st Division
WO169/4210	War Diary, HQ 2 Armd Bde
WO169/4216	War Diary, HQ 4 Armd Bde
WO169/4226	War Diary, HQ 7 Motor Bde
WO169/4230	War Diary, HQ 8 Armd Bde
WO169/4233	War Diary, HQ 9 Armd Bde
WO169/4251	War Diary, HQ 22 Armd Bde
WO169/4260	War Diary, HQ 23 Armd Bde (Corps Reserve XXX Corps)
WO169/4266	War Diary, HQ 24 Armd Bde
WO169/4271	War Diary, HQ 69 Bde
WO169/4276	War Diary, HQ 131 Bde
WO169/4279	War Diary, HQ 132 Bde
WO169/4283	War Diary, HQ 133 Bde
WO169/4288	War Diary, HQ 151 Bde
WO169/4292	War Diary, HQ 152 Bde
WO169/4295	War Diary, HQ 153 Bde
WO169/4298	War Diary, HQ 154 Bde
WO169/4476	War Diary, H'hld Cav. Regt
WO169/4478	War Diary, R. Dgns
WO169/4479	War Diary, Queen's Bays
WO169/4481	War Diary, 9 L.
WO169/4482	War Diary, 12 L.
WO169/4483	War Diary, 3 H.
WO169/4484	War Diary, 4 H.
WO169/4487	War Diary, 8 H., Oct/Nov
WO169/4489	War Diary, 10 H.
WO169/4490	War Diary, 11 H.
WO169/4493	War Diary, 2 Derby Yeo
WO169/4496	War Diary, 4 County of London Yeo
WO169/4497	War Diary, Notts Yeo
WO169/4499	War Diary, Staffs Yeo
WO169/4500	War Diary , Warwicks Yeo
WO169/4501	War Diary , R. Wilts Yeo
WO169/4502	War Diary, Y'shire Dgns

WO169/4504	War Diary, 1 RTR
WO169/4506	War Diary, 3 RTR
WO169/4508	War Diary, 5 RTR
WO169/4518	War Diary, 40 RTR
WO169/4519	War Diary, 41 RTR
WO169/4522	War Diary, 45 RTR
WO169/4524	War Diary, 47 RTR
WO169/4555	War Diary, 1 RHA
WO169/4556	War Diary, 2 RHA
WO169/4557	War Diary, 4 RHA
WO169/4558	War Diary, 4 RHA
WO169/4559	War Diary, 5 RHA
WO169/4560	War Diary, 11 (HAC) RHA
WO169/4562	War Diary, 104 RHA
WO169/4567	War Diary, B Bty 1 RHA
WO169/4570	War Diary, Mercer's Tp G Bty RHA
WO169/4575	War Diary, 74 Fd Regt RA
WO169/4587	War Diary, 57 Fd Regt RA
WO169/4591	War Diary, 65 Fd Regt RA
WO169/4601	War Diary, 98 Fd Regt RA
WO169/4602	War Diary, 111 Fd Regt RA
WO169/4606	War Diary, 126 Fd Regt RA
WO169/4607	War Diary, 127 Fd Regt RA
WO169/4608	War Diary, 128 Fd Regt RA
WO169/4610	War Diary, 146 Fd Regt RA
WO169/4724	War Diary, 73 A/Tk Regt RA
WO169/4725	War Diary, 76 A/Tk Regt RA
WO169/4728	War Diary, 84 A/Tk Regt RA
WO169/4730	War Diary, 102 A/Tk Regt RA
WO169/4732	War Diary, 149 A/Tk Regt RA
WO169/4886	War Diary, 34 A/Tk Regt RA
WO169/4894	War Diary, 53 LAA Regt RA
WO169/4895	War Diary, 56 LAA Regt RA
WO169/4986	War Diary, 7 A. & S. Hldrs
WO169/4988	War Diary, 1 Black Watch
WO169/4990	War Diary, 5 Black Watch
WO169/4991	War Diary, 7 Black Watch
WO169/4995	War Diary, 2 Buffs
WO169/4997	War Diary, 5 Camerons
WO169/5002	War Diary, 6 Cheshire
WO169/5007	War Diary, 6 Durham LI
WO169/5008	War Diary, 8 Durham LI

WO169/5009	War Diary, 9 Durham LI
WO169/5011	War Diary, 1/4 Essex
WO169/5017	War Diary, 1 Gordons
WO169/5018	War Diary, 5/7 Gordons
WO169/5022	War Diary, 6 Green Howards
WO169/5023	War Diary, 7 Green Howards
WO169/5027	War Diary, 4 R. W. Kents
WO169/5028	War Diary, 5 R. W. Kents
WO169/5032	War Diary, 1 KRRC
WO169/5033	War Diary, 2 KRRC
WO169/5035	War Diary, 11 KRRC
WO169/5043	War Diary, 1 R. N'ld Fus
WO169/5048	War Diary, 1/5 Queen's
WO169/5050	War Diary, 1/6 Queen's
WO169/5052	War Diary, 1/7 Queen's
WO169/5054	War Diary, 1 Rifle Brigade
WO169/5055	War Diary, 2 Rifle Brigade
WO169/5056	War Diary, 7 Rifle Brigade
WO169/5059	War Diary, 2 Seaforth
WO169/5060	War Diary, 5 Seaforth
WO169/5061	War Diary, 6 Seaforth
WO169/5067	War Diary, 2 R. Sussex
WO169/5068	War Diary, 4 R. Sussex
WO169/5069	War Diary, 5 R. Sussex
WO169/5076	War Diary, 5 E. Yorks
WO169/5237	War Diary, 1 Fd Park Sqn RE
WO169/5232	War Diary, 1 Fd Sqn RE
WO169/5233	War Diary, 2 Fd Sqn RE
WO169/5234	War Diary, 3 Fd Sqn RE
WO169/5236	War Diary, 6 Fd Sqn RE
WO169/5237	War Diary, 7 Fd Sqn RE
WO169/5238	War Diary, 9 Fd Sqn RE
WO201/2813	War Diary, 9th Australian Division: Report on Lightfoot operations, Oct-Nov 42
WO201/425	War Diary, Battle for Egypt Oct-Nov 42
WO201/433	War Diary, Operation LIGHTFOOT: Memorandum No.2 by Army Commander
WO201/449	War Diary, Lessons on Operations. El Alamein to conclusion of Tunisian campaign
WO201/540	War Diary, Weekly desert reviews: Intelligence Reports Jun-Aug 42

WO201/542	War Diary, Short account of operations 8th Hussars 23 Oct-13 Nov 42
WO201/543	War Diary, Jun-Oct 42 Routes recce report
WO201/544	War Diary, 1st South African Division: Op Orders
WO201/545	War Diary, Notes on AFVs on Operations 23–29 Oct 42
WO201/547	War Diary, 2 RB Account of action at 'SNIPE'
WO201/548	War Diary, Protection of railways Western Desert, Mar-Oct 42
WO201/549	War Diary, XXX Corps' Report on Battle of Alamein
WO201/550	War Diary, Alamein: précis of study
WO201/551	War Diary, XIII Corps' operations report: Sep-Oct 42
WO201/552	War Diary, 1 Greek Bde: operations report
WO201/553	War Diary, El Alamein: notes for lecture
WO201/554	War Diary, Reports on Operations 9 Armd Bde
WO201/555	War Diary, HQ RA Eighth Army. Operations Report El Alamein
WO201/556	War Diary, XIII Corps: appreciation on operations, Aug–Nov 42
WO201/557	War Diary, El Alamein: notes with maps of final breakthrough
WO201/561	War Diary, 4th Indian Division, Orders, Instructions and Reports
WO201/564	War Diary, 8th Armoured Division: order of battle
WO201/566/7	War Diary, AFV state
WO201/571	War Diary, Locations Oct-Nov
WO201/573	War Diary, X Corps Training Instructions
WO201/574	War Diary, El Alamein: Army reserve positions Aug-Dec
WO201/575	War Diary, 3 K's O. Hussars report of operations at El Alamein
WO201/576	War Diary, Eighth Army Commander's conferences
WO201/577	War Diary, Notes on maintenance 1940–1943
WO201/580	War Diary, Ops summary: Oct 42–Mar 43
WO201/581	War Diary, Lessons from recent operations, 10th Armoured Division
WO201/583	War Diary, Lessons from battle of Egypt, 1st Armoured Division
WO201/593	War Diary, Eighth Army operations Nov 42–Apr 43: lectures
WO201/597	War Diary, 9th Australian Division Summary of artillery operations Oct 42–May 43
WO201/599	War Diary, Eighth Army Operations Nov 42–May 43
WO201/600	War Diary, Eighth Army locations Sep 42–May 43
WO201/601	War Diary, Eighth Army operations: North African campaign
WO201/602	War Diary, Eighth Army operations: El Alamein to Tunis Oct 42–May 43

WO201/603	War Diary, Conference on lessons from recent operations, Sep 42–May 43
WO201/605	War Diary, Battle of Egypt. Narrative by Lt Col Oswald
WO201/606	War Diary, 7th Armoured Division Operations Alamein to Tunis
WO201/609	War Diary, Eighth Army diary of events and intelligence summaries. Nov 41–Jun 43
WO201/2140	War Diary, Weekly desert reviews Aug-Sep 42
WO201/2141	War Diary, Enemy methods, organization and supply Jun–Oct 42
WO201/2154/5	War Diary, Eighth Army intelligence summaries
WO201/2259	War Diary, SUPERCHARGE orders and instructions Oct–Nov 42
WO201/2489	War Diary, Appreciations and reports on review of Eighth Army admin situation Apr-Jun 42; preparations for offensive operations
WO201/2494	War Diary, Tactical Recce reports: Egypt and Western Desert
WO201/2495	War Diary, 9th Australian Division Report on Operations El Alamein 23 Oct–5 Nov
WO201/2496	War Diary, Battle of Egypt publication Nov 42
WO201/2501	War Diary, Eighth Army daily diary Nov 42–Mar 43
WO201/2502	War Diary, Eighth Army weekly summary of operations
WO201/2588/91	War Diary, Training: misc.
WO201/2605	War Diary, AFV situation Jul 42–Jun 43
WO201/2699	War Diary, Commander in Chief's Despatch
WO201/2700	War Diary, Sep 42. Notes by Commander on battle of Alamein
WO201/2774	War Diary, Operation LIGHTFOOT: orders and instructions
WO201/2813	War Diary, 9th Australian Division Report on Lightfoot operations 23 Oct-5 Nov 42
WO201/2826	War Diary, Report on operations 9th Australian Division El Alamein 23 Oct-5 Nov 42
WO201/2825	War Diary, Lessons from Operations; Middle East Training Memorandum
WO201/2826	War Diary, Report on Operations: 9th Australian Division
WO201/2845/8	War Diary, Report on camouflage
WO201/2856	War Diary, Commander in Chief's Despatch: Western Desert
WO201/2877	War Diary, RA Notes on Eighth Army at El Alamein 23 Oct-4 Nov
WO212/430	War Diary, GHQ Middle East: Order of Battle
WO212/431	War Diary, Middle East, Nov 42: Operational Order of Battle

Index

Individuals